Hands-On Swift 5 Microservices Development

Build microservices for mobile and web applications using Swift 5 and Vapor 4

Ralph Kuepper

BIRMINGHAM - MUMBAI

Hands-On Swift 5 Microservices Development

Copyright © 2020 Packt Publishing

Commissioning Editor: Kunal Chaudhari
Acquisition Editor: Heramb Bhavsar
Content Development Editor: Aamir Ahmed
Senior Editor: Hayden Edwards
Technical Editor: Sachin Sunilkumar
Copy Editor: Safis Editing
Project Coordinator: Kinjal Bari
Proofreader: Safis Editing
Indexer: Tejal Daruwale Soni
Production Designer: Jyoti Chauhan

First published: February 2020

Production reference: 1280220

Published by Packt Publishing Ltd.
Livery Place
35 Livery Street
Birmingham
B3 2PB, UK.

ISBN 978-1-78953-088-9

www.packt.com

To my wife and our two sons, for living life with them is a joy.

– Ralph Kuepper

Packt.com

Subscribe to our online digital library for full access to over 7,000 books and videos, as well as industry leading tools to help you plan your personal development and advance your career. For more information, please visit our website.

Why subscribe?

- Spend less time learning and more time coding with practical eBooks and Videos from over 4,000 industry professionals

- Improve your learning with Skill Plans built especially for you

- Get a free eBook or video every month

- Fully searchable for easy access to vital information

- Copy and paste, print, and bookmark content

Did you know that Packt offers eBook versions of every book published, with PDF and ePub files available? You can upgrade to the eBook version at www.packt.com and as a print book customer, you are entitled to a discount on the eBook copy. Get in touch with us at customercare@packtpub.com for more details.

At www.packt.com, you can also read a collection of free technical articles, sign up for a range of free newsletters, and receive exclusive discounts and offers on Packt books and eBooks.

Foreword

I had the pleasure of meeting Ralph in person at the first Server-Side Swift conference in Berlin in 2018. We met again at the next conference in Copenhagen. Ralph is quite a friendly person and we spent a lot of time getting to know each other and sharing ideas.

Ralph's experience studying and practicing business spanning over a decade have given him unique insights into the problems facing web developers today. In addition to his business acumen, he also has a deep understanding of programming. A man after my own heart, he's always eager to try new things and share his knowledge with others.

A few months before we met in person, Ralph's company, Skelpo, became Vapor's second major sponsor. This early support for the framework has proven to be invaluable. Beyond mere sponsorship, Ralph has been actively involved with the development of the framework. He is quick to adopt changes and give feedback. This feedback is critical to Vapor's success and shows his mastery of the framework.

What's more, Ralph is now well-known throughout the Vapor community. He has created many opportunities for contributors to work on related projects and give back to the framework. His work bolsters the community and helps the ecosystem to thrive. People like Ralph make open-source special and push software engineering forward.

I hope you enjoy the knowledge he has worked to compile and share with you in this book. Let it inspire you to try new things and share your knowledge with others.

Tanner Nelson

Creator of Vapor

Contributors

About the author

Ralph Kuepper has worked in the web and software industry for over 15 years. He started his own company when he was 17 years old while still attending high school and college. Over the years, he has worked on projects for companies such as Adidas, KIA, and Honda. Coming from a traditional background of developing backends and websites using PHP and a monolithic approach, he has embraced and fine-tuned a Swift-based microservice approach for the last 4 years. His company, Skelpo Inc., has been actively involved in the development of the Vapor framework and has contributed a variety of open source microservices as well as related packages.

First, I would like to acknowledge my amazing best friend and wife, Elizabeth, for all the patience she had with me writing this book. Writing a book is a long and intense job and I appreciate all the support gave me in the process.

I would also like to acknowledge the great staff and editorial team at Packt Publishing. Especially, I would like to thank Aamir Ahmed for his continual encouragement, direction, and support during the writing process.

I'd also like to thank the technical reviewer, Caleb Kleveter, for providing invaluable insight and feedback from someone intimately familiar with Swift. Lastly, I want to thank Tanner Nelson, the founder of Vapor, for his dedicated support and, ultimately, writing the foreword of this book!

About the reviewer

Caleb Kleveter is a contract software developer for Skelpo Inc. He has been working with Swift for the past 5 years since its release at WWDC 2014 and has been building microservice applications in Vapor for the past 3 years. Caleb also holds a maintainer status on several of the core Vapor repositories, has published several articles on Medium covering how to build backend applications using Vapor and the Fluent ORM, and has spoken at the ServerSide.swift conference on how to build resilient microservice applications in Vapor. Besides Swift on the server, Caleb also enjoys dabbling in other technologies, such as Vue.js, RegEx, and X86 Assembler, and spends his spare time writing streaming text parsers.

Packt is searching for authors like you

If you're interested in becoming an author for Packt, please visit `authors.packtpub.com` and apply today. We have worked with thousands of developers and tech professionals, just like you, to help them share their insight with the global tech community. You can make a general application, apply for a specific hot topic that we are recruiting an author for, or submit your own idea.

Table of Contents

Preface

Vapor, written in Swift, is one of the best frameworks available for building scalable and maintainable web applications. Since Swift compiles to a native app, it provides excellent performance while keeping code clean, readable, and easy to learn. It is particularly suited for microservices as Vapor was written with microservices in mind.

Hands-On Swift 5 Microservices Development aims to teach you how to build a next-generation web application. We will work through the development of an e-commerce backend that is written in Swift using the Vapor framework. You will explore how microservices operate together best and what is important for them.

We'll start by introducing microservices first and explaining how they operate. Then we will look at Swift on the server and which options we have. After that, we will combine the two and start working on Swift microservices. Throughout the course of the rest of the book, we will cover everything from writing user management services all the way to deploying the services on cloud platforms. After reading this book, you should have everything you need to write your own applications.

Who this book is for

Hands-On Swift 5 Microservices Development has been written for any Swift developers, either iOS, macOS, tvOS, watchOS, or iPadOS, who want to use the same language they have learned to love for server backends as well. If you also already know some server-side Swift, you might find this book interesting as it introduces how to write microservices. Knowing a little bit of Swift is required to read this book but you don't need to know it all; we will go over everything you need as long as you know basic Swift.

What this book covers

Chapter 1, *Introduction of Microservices*, starts off the book by introducing the concept of microservices and how they are used. Besides the concept itself, some real-life examples are examined and used to illustrate the value of microservices.

Chapter 2, *Understanding Server-Side Swift*, deals with the current state of Swift on the server, taking a deep look into the internals of Swift and its appeal for server development. The unique features of Swift 5 are also addressed in light of server development.

Chapter 3, *Getting Started with the Vapor Framework*, introduces Vapor as the leading framework for server-side Swift, exploring how Vapor operates and what Vapor applications look like.

Chapter 4, *Planning an Online Store Application*, starts the process of writing our example backend for an e-commerce app. We will plan it to demonstrate how microservice applications should be planned.

Chapter 5, *Creating Your First Microservice*, guides you on how to develop your first microservice. We will write a template service that we can use to develop the services of our demo application.

Chapter 6, *Application Structure and Database Design*, walks you through setting your system up for microservices, taking a quick look at Docker environments. How to run microservices is also discussed to allow easy microservice development.

Chapter 7, *Writing the User Service*, begins to put everything together by writing the first service of our e-commerce backend. A user service serves as the central user authority to verify users and in this chapter, we go into a detailed discussion about what this looks like.

Chapter 8, *Testing Microservices*, deals with the concept of testing microservices and how that is best done. We will look into unit and functional testing and which is used when.

Chapter 9, *Product Management Service*, covers writing our second microservice for the backend. Products are a central element in e-commerce and this chapter discusses what a service for such objects looks like.

Chapter 10, *Understanding Microservices Communication*, explains that when our microservices need to communicate, we want to maintain some rules. In this chapter, we look at what, exactly, inner microservice communication should look like and what to avoid.

Chapter 11, *Order Management Service*, uses the knowledge from the previous chapters to write a service that actually communicates with other services. We also address how external services can be integrated.

Chapter 12, *Best Practices*, discusses some general best practices for Swift, but specifically for microservices.

Chapter 13, *Hosting Microservices*, deals with the fact that hosting microservice applications is not the most trivial task. In this chapter, we explore what hosting microservice applications look like and what we need to do so.

Chapter 14, *Docker and the Cloud*, follows on from learning about the general hosting of microservices by looking at which cloud providers enable us to do it and how.

Chapter 15, *Deploying Microservices in the Cloud*, covers bringing our example backend online. We will walk through the entire setup on AWS ECS and will then set up a Continuous Deployment (CD) to automatically deploy our code.

Chapter 16, *Scaling and Monitoring Microservices*, discusses how we can scale microservices in cloud setups. We will take a look at the most common cloud providers and their strategies.

To get the most out of this book

This book is for people who have worked with Swift before, on any platform. As long as you have a basic understanding of Swift, you should get along alright. I'm assuming you are operating on a macOS system that is running the newest version and that Xcode 11 or newer is installed. It will be beneficial if you have worked with servers before, even if not Swift servers. Also, if you have worked with any databases before and have a foundational understanding of how relational databases operate, that will be helpful.

 Important: This book was written while Vapor 4 was in alpha stage and later in beta. All of the code has been updated to work with the latest available version, however, as Vapor progresses into release stage, there might be small changes that cause compile errors. You can check out the corresponding GitHub code to get the up-to-date compile code for each chapter.

Download the example code files

You can download the example code files for this book from your account at www.packt.com. If you purchased this book elsewhere, you can visit www.packtpub.com/support and register to have the files emailed directly to you.

You can download the code files by following these steps:

1. Log in or register at www.packt.com.
2. Select the **Support** tab.
3. Click on **Code Downloads**.
4. Enter the name of the book in the **Search** box and follow the onscreen instructions.

Once the file is downloaded, please make sure that you unzip or extract the folder using the latest version of:

- WinRAR/7-Zip for Windows
- Zipeg/iZip/UnRarX for Mac
- 7-Zip/PeaZip for Linux

The code bundle for the book is also hosted on GitHub at https://github.com/PacktPublishing/Hands-On-Swift-5-Microservices-Development. In case there's an update to the code, it will be updated on the existing GitHub repository.

We also have other code bundles from our rich catalog of books and videos available at https://github.com/PacktPublishing/. Check them out!

Conventions used

There are a number of text conventions used throughout this book.

CodeInText: Indicates code words in text, database table names, folder names, filenames, file extensions, pathnames, dummy URLs, user input, and Twitter handles. Here is an example: "Create a new folder for the project and name it Shop Backend."

A block of code is set as follows:

```
import App
import Vapor

var env = try Environment.detect()
try LoggingSystem.bootstrap(from: &env)
let app = Application(env)
defer { app.shutdown() }
try configure(app)
try app.run()
```

When we wish to draw your attention to a particular part of a code block, the relevant lines or items are set in bold:

```
import App
import Vapor

var env = try Environment.detect()
try LoggingSystem.bootstrap(from: &env)
let app = Application(env)
defer { app.shutdown() }
try configure(app)
try app.run()
```

Any command-line input or output is written as follows:

```
$ git --version
```

Bold: Indicates a new term, an important word, or words that you see onscreen. For example, words in menus or dialog boxes appear in the text like this. Here is an example: "Now add the following code to the **Tests** tab in your **Auth** request."

 Warnings or important notes appear like this.

 Tips and tricks appear like this.

Get in touch

Feedback from our readers is always welcome.

General feedback: If you have questions about any aspect of this book, mention the book title in the subject of your message and email us at customercare@packtpub.com.

Errata: Although we have taken every care to ensure the accuracy of our content, mistakes do happen. If you have found a mistake in this book, we would be grateful if you would report this to us. Please visit www.packtpub.com/support/errata, selecting your book, clicking on the Errata Submission Form link, and entering the details.

Piracy: If you come across any illegal copies of our works in any form on the Internet, we would be grateful if you would provide us with the location address or website name. Please contact us at copyright@packt.com with a link to the material.

If you are interested in becoming an author: If there is a topic that you have expertise in and you are interested in either writing or contributing to a book, please visit authors.packtpub.com.

Reviews

Please leave a review. Once you have read and used this book, why not leave a review on the site that you purchased it from? Potential readers can then see and use your unbiased opinion to make purchase decisions, we at Packt can understand what you think about our products, and our authors can see your feedback on their book. Thank you!

For more information about Packt, please visit packt.com.

Introduction to Microservices 1

In this first chapter, you will get to know the basics of microservices. They have been an upcoming trend over the last few years and gained popularity particularly amongst start-ups and projects that are built to grow. Their appeal is that they are designed to be scalable but also offer great flexibility to the programmer. By the end of this book, you will be capable of writing your own microservices for apps and frontends using the Swift framework, Vapor. This chapter will give you an overview of what microservices are and how they are useful in web development.

Microservices are small, individual services that form an application by working together. In contrast to that, monoliths are applications that are operating out of one central service that does not depend on other services. Most traditional off-the-shelf systems such as WordPress and Drupal are monoliths.

Both microservices as well as their counterpart, monoliths, are central elements of modern web development and before you start developing your own, you should understand the essential theory for their usage. You will specifically explore the following topics in this chapter:

- What is a microservice?
- Understanding why to choose microservices
- Understanding why not to choose microservices
- Who is using microservices?
- Monolith versus microservices
- Upgrading from monolith to microservices

After reading this chapter, you will be prepared to start working on your microservices.

What is a microservice?

Let's quickly define what we mean when we use the term *microservice*.

As the word already gives away, *microservice* consists of *micro* and *service*. Micro is smaller than *small*. A microservice by definition should be as small as possible. The other word, *service*, refers to the function of a microservice: it should do something for us. In this book—and in general—we call them **microservices**, the plural form of microservice. We do that because a microservice usually operates together with other microservices. A microservice application consists of multiple microservices working together and alongside each other.

Almost all major players, such as Google, Amazon, and Facebook, started out as so-called *monolithic* applications. What does that mean? In essence, a monolith is an application that operates as one large code base. Popular examples include WordPress, Joomla!, Magento, and Drupal; they typically run on one server for the frontend, PHP oftentimes. If you need to scale such an application, you would add more frontend servers that all do the same thing; they are replicas of each other.

While that would solve the demand issue, another problem exists as well: every time the web page is updated, by changing the source code, a single error could bring down the entire web page. The dominant web technologies for so-called *monolith* web applications used to be primarily PHP and some used to be Java and Perl. Wikipedia, Yahoo!, Facebook, and many others rely on PHP to this very day. Over time, additional scripting languages such as Python and Ruby entered the race. However, the following problem prevailed: changing source files could introduce bugs and bring down the entire site because every PHP file is usually somehow connected to the others. As the companies grew, they adopted another approach, which has proven to be much more reliable for continuous growth and maintainability. The approach, *microservices,* includes the idea that a web application does not consist of one big monolith anymore but is divided up into *many independent* services that work together.

The approach itself is not all that new; logistic companies had implemented such a strategy for their structures as well. But growing internet tech companies used this method to solve two of their main problems:

- **Scalability:** Individual services are much easier to scale than scaling the entire system.
- **Maintainability:** When changing or adjusting one service, it will not affect the other services, which creates a more solid and stable system overall.

Now, not only the general approach has changed but also the field of programming languages. While in early 2000 just a couple of languages were used for developing web applications, we have a lot more options such as Swift, Go, Python, and JavaScript that are available now.

For all of the intents and purposes of this book, let's use the following definition of microservices: *a **microservice** is a small service that runs along with other services and builds the application together with the other services.*

Rules for using microservices

There is no actual official definition of what a microservice is and is not; however, the following rules generally apply to commonly used microservices:

- A small unit of a backend infrastructure
- Operating as independently as possible (meaning, no or little communication with other microservices)
- Performing a service (such as processing data or offering an API)
- Offering as little functionality as reasonable
- Operates with its own database

 The last point is critical as you might be tempted to leave all data in the same database or the same database server. Leaving all data on the same database server might be an okay choice for small projects in the beginning, but you should never use the same database across multiple microservices.
The same applies to common code or libraries; it should always be separate. You might develop a central library that is shared; however, that might become a problem later on. Zalando, for example, implemented a strict policy prohibiting this (`https://www.infoq.com/news/2016/02/Monolith-Microservices-Zalando`).

To conclude, a microservice is the smallest and most isolated unit possible of the business logic and is needed for the server application. Now, let's look at the cases when microservices are a great choice!

Understanding why to choose microservices

Let's look at some of the reasons why you might want to choose microservices for your applications. Not every application should utilize microservices, as you will see in the next section. Very distinct reasons warrant the use of microservices. Let's take an example to justify why we want to choose microservices.

Let's pretend you want to develop a simple e-commerce app. If we say that there are three different elements of microservices in an app, User, Product, and Order. The app should cover the following features:

- User: Log in
- User: Register
- User: Change addresses
- User: Change payment methods
- Products: Show the list of products in a category
- Products: Show details about an individual product
- Order: Submit an order of products
- Order: Submit payment for an order

You could develop the backend for such an app as a monolith, of course. It would, without a doubt, be a rather big application and require many models and controllers. But if you were to develop the same app with microservices, you could end up with three more flexible packages, such as the following:

- User Manager
- Products Manager
- Order Manager

You can now enjoy the following benefits from using microservices:

- Effective team management
- Reusable code base
- Flexible scope of functionality
- Maintainability
- Scalability
- Mixed stacks

Let's dive into each of these sections now.

Effective team management

If you have ever worked in a team on a bigger monolithic application, you know very well how chaotic and unorganized it can get. Various preferences, styles, and trains of thoughts are commonly joined together, resulting in a decently sized mess.

With microservices, you can assign different services to different team members. In the preceding example, if you happen to be a three-member team, each one of you could develop one service. The added efficiency will not just increase productivity in the beginning but carry through the entire project.

Spreading out the workload across multiple people working separately but still together is a significant benefit for all of the teams. Imagine you have to manage 500+ programmers for a big project (think Facebook or Google). It is close to impossible to function well over a longer period of time if everyone is using the same code base. If the application is split up into small microservices, you can have a lot of 10-people teams that are working on various services. While this comes with its own challenges, it will certainly reduce the potential for error in the code itself.

But even if you happen to be in a small team, few developers can experience a noticeable increase in productivity when developing microservices.

In essence, microservices allow you to spread work out effectively in a team.

Reusable code base

For the sake of this discussion, let's assume that you have already written a user manager once before and now you can use it again. With microservices, you can use and reuse any given service that you have developed previously. If a service does not quite fit your case, you could just modify it instead of writing it from scratch.

Reusing the same code across multiple projects saves you valuable time and resources. You may even start thinking about microservices abstractly so that you purposefully can reuse the services. You can try to define a set of functions that fit more than one project for you to reuse with other projects.

Let's take a look at the aforementioned user manager service. Almost all applications that interact with users have a login. In most cases, the functionality is pretty much identical, as shown here:

- Log in via email and password
- Registration with email verification

- Forgot password; send recovery email
- Log out
- Delete account

Once you have written this service you can easily implement it with other projects.

Another similar case is when you are choosing a SaaS solution for user management. Examples include AWS Cognito, Auth0.com, Okta, and Backendless. Microservices allow you to easily incorporate such services to save yourself the time and effort of writing a user management solution at all in this case. Naturally, the same principle applies to other types of services as well.

To summarize, microservices allow you to reuse existing code for new projects and save time and effort. Next, let's explore the scope of functionality.

Flexible scope of functionality

We know that this app will grow and that users will need more features. Microservices are ideal for such cases because you can simply add more services for functionality or modify the ones that you already have. Take the earlier example; you start out with a very manageable and small set of features. If you know these are all of the features you will ever need, there would be no reason for not using a simple monolithic approach for this. The reality, however, is that many projects grow, both in terms of users and mostly in terms of what they offer. You may decide to add functionality to your offering or to significantly change it.

Imagine you need to add a new payment method to your online shop. In a monolith, you need to work on and deploy the entire application, which comes with risks. However, in microservices, if you have the order manager, you can simply add the payment method to that service and deploy it and you are good to go. The user manager and product manager do not need to be touched.

Microservices allow you to grow your functionality as you need and without needing to touch other parts of the software.

Maintainability

It makes a lot of sense to use microservices not only when your specifications may change, but also in cases where your requirements are highly defined. Microservices are easily maintained; each service can be updated, upgraded, and serviced individually without influencing the other services. This is particularly important with bigger applications as it reduces the risk and impact of potential downtime.

If you are serving a lot of users, you want to avoid downtime as much as possible. Because microservices are independent, you can replace them in time without going offline. You will explore deployments later on in more detail, but most cloud service providers have procedures in place that will keep your application up 100% of the time while switching out the services.

Additionally, you and your team can focus your efforts on the services that need it most. While one service is being heavily updated, the other services can stay the way they were. I have been in a project that had legacy microservices running for over two years because it worked reliably and effort was put into developing new features instead of updating the old ones. You should not neglect updating all parts of your system though, but microservices allow you to keep old infrastructure longer than with a monolith.

In conclusion, microservices allow you to work on them while other services stay as they are and therefore give you the ability to focus on what matters most.

Scalability

Another element to consider is that you want to be able to grow and scale your application easily. Microservices are arguably the easiest form of application for a server application to grow. Remember, we have individual and independent services running. It means, in principle, that no problem should have the same service run in many instances, for example, you could have 100 servers running the same service. Alternatively, it could also run as only one service, based on your needs.

Let's look into the following three distinct advantages microservices have when it comes to scalability:

- Auto-scaling
- Flexible cost
- Service-oriented availability

Auto-scaling

You can have your hosting provider automatically scale (up and down) according to your needs. Predefined and customizable rules allow you to define and to scale up and down. If you have an upcoming marketing gig (such as a TV promotion), your backend will automatically scale according to your demand without you having to adjust anything manually.

Flexible cost

This goes hand-in-hand with auto-scaling. You may pay for the infrastructure depending on your needs. In an ideal world, you would pay nothing for no users and increasingly more as you have more users. In reality, this rarely happens just like that, however, you do end up saving money as you don't need to buy more hardware than you need in most cases.

Service-oriented availability

Often, not every service is used equally. In the preceding example, the user service only performs authentication and registration. Once the user is authorized, this service is mostly irrelevant to the app. You may decide to have the email processing service to be a lot more available than your user service.

Concretely, this may look like five servers are running the product manager application while only one server runs the user and the order manager. As your app grows and changes, you can adjust this setup precisely to what you need.

So, we can conclude that microservices allow your application to grow effortlessly and you have many options for how you want your entire backend application to run.

Mixed stacks

Sometimes, you may find yourself in a situation where a part of your tech stack is using other technologies. You may want to write your microservices with Vapor and Swift but have a good bit of infrastructure in PHP. You can utilize microservices to keep some of the old parts while already developing new services. Your setup will then look like the following diagram:

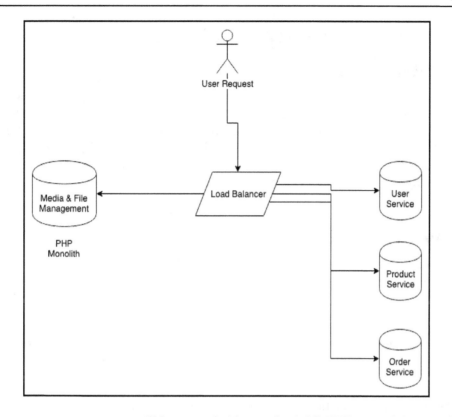

In this case, your user request will be routed *either* to the (old) PHP monolithic **Media &**
File Management service or to your new Vapor services. Your old monolith is actually
turned into a microservice itself, though it most likely covers more functionality than you
want it to have. But, deciding to go with microservices allows you to incorporate software
that you may depend on even if it is written in an entirely different language.

If you are wondering how the preceding example would look like in real life, most
microservices are operating out of *containers* (for example, Docker containers). These
containers operate as mini-servers and are completely isolated. So, even with just one actual
hardware server, you can implement the preceding scenario with a local load balancer such
as nginx.

Hence, microservices allow you to integrate older parts of your infrastructure while already
using your newer parts.

Understanding why not to choose microservices

You have seen several reasons to choose microservices. Now, let's look at reasons why not to choose microservices. As with everything, the strengths of microservices are also their weakness. While this book is about writing microservices, you should not think that microservices are the answer to every problem. There are many examples of why microservices are actually the wrong choice for certain problems. Here is a list of some of the reasons why not to choose microservices.

Initially more work

The first and most obvious reason why you would not want to choose microservices is that it is usually a bit more work initially. To set up the entire system and connect the services and get them all up and running the way you need to often requires more work than with a monolithic application.

It starts by setting everything up and building a working environment. A monolithic application will require you to run the application only. So, once you start your main application, you are good to go.

A microservices application, however, requires a setup in which multiple applications are running at the same time. Alternatively, you could design your application to receive test data from static files; this, however, does not replace testing with the actual services. You can archive such a setup easily in a deployment situation; cloud providers are doing an excellent job in helping us here. However, when you start developing, it can be a good amount of work to set everything up. In the next chapter, you will set up your own workspace.

Additionally, microservices demand planning. You cannot perform some changes as quickly as you would in a monolithic application. If you are only building a simple proof-of-concept for your backend, you might be better off starting as a monolith. If you need something implemented that is critical in timing, microservices might not be your best option.

So, a good thing to keep in mind when working with microservices is that microservices demand some planning and often take longer to start.

Increased complexity

When developing monolithic applications, you usually have everything in the same code base. As long as a project is small, the lack of complexity makes it easier for you to maintain it. Additional features and changes can be implemented with the same stack, language, and frameworks you have been using so far.

Microservices, on the other hand, can be a bit more complex (or messy even). Adding a new feature is not always trivial and may require changes in numerous services. The services themselves may also have different stacks. You may have a legacy service running PHP combined with a Swift Vapor service for another part of the app. Adding a feature requires you to work in PHP as well as Swift.

If you know your exact scope for a project and don't expect any changes, there is no reason not to implement it like a monolithic application.

Microservices can increase the complexity of a project, compared to traditional technologies such as PHP, which you should keep in mind. The same can be said about most microservice technologies though, regardless of programming language. Let's take a look at troubleshooting and debugging now.

Debugging and troubleshooting

Debugging and troubleshooting is yet another issue you will need to consider. It can be quicker and easier to debug one application as opposed to two or more microservices. **Debugging** goes hand in hand with complexity; bugs will not be found as quickly as they can be in a monolithic application. As a matter of fact, this topic is important enough for this book to have an entire chapter on it.

If you are dealing with an application that is limited in scope and functionality is not expected to grow, a monolithic approach might be better than a microservice approach. That said, I have personally seen many projects start as "small and manageable" pretty suitable for monolithic applications. But then they grow, and the benefits quickly turn into serious problems. If you think all of your applications should be suitable for growth, take a microservice approach.

It can take more time to find bugs. Because services are often somehow connected, it can be pretty hard to boil a symptom down to a bug. I have seen a small symptom come out of many unrelated errors.

To conclude, debugging a microservice backend is more complex and time-consuming than for monolithic applications, however, there are also great benefits with using them. This is why we will look at a list of companies that are using microservices and have switched away from monoliths.

Who is using microservices?

After learning about the pros and cons of microservices, let's take a look at who is using them. The following examples are not exclusive and were selected with modern web applications in mind. If you want to develop an app that has the potential to become as big as Netflix, why not check out how things work well for them?

Amazon

It will probably be no surprise to learn that Amazon is one of the first big companies that utilized the internet and implemented microservices. Amazon, like many others, started out by being a big monolithic application. As it grew, additional programmers were hired and started working on the application. As you can imagine, over a hundred developers all working on the same code base will ultimately result in chaos and conflicts. This also happened in the years around 2000; so many modern tools (such as Git) were not nearly as advanced as they are today. Back then, Amazon began to break the big application up into more manageable and usable sub-units, called microservices.

Amazon is now deploying every 11.7 seconds (`https://blog.newrelic.com/technology/data-culture-survey-results-faster-deployment/`). Despite the challenge of having to enable hundreds of developers to work on the platform, Amazon also solved another problem: growth. Because `amazon.com` runs as a microservice application, it has no downtime. Amazon can take as many visitors as it gets because the system is managing itself.

By the way, Netflix, Uber, and many others are using **Amazon Web Services** (**AWS**). Amazon not only developed the concept and infrastructure for itself but is selling it to others who can use it for the same benefits.

Another noteworthy point is that Jeff Bezos has always advocated for small teams regardless of the size of the company. He claims that a team should not be larger than what two pizzas can feed (`http://blog.idonethis.com/two-pizza-team/`). As stated earlier, spreading the work out over to multiple people also applies to big corporations: keeping teams small increases efficiency.

Netflix

Netflix, similar to Amazon, used to be a gigantic monolithic application. And just like Amazon, Netflix split it up into many microservices to accommodate its growth. Now, Netflix is deploying thousands of times a day.

A graphical representation of its API can be found at `https://www.slideshare.net/adrianco/netflix-velocity-conference-2011/43-API_AWS_EC2_Front_End`

You can see how various components are working together to provide speedy delivery of content. Similar to Amazon, Netflix also had to face challenges in terms of development and growth. Using microservices allows it to address both.

Now, Netflix is serving more than 130 million accounts daily with possibly up to 400 million viewers (`https://www.cheatsheet.com/entertainment/how-many-people-use-netflix.html/`). These numbers should tell you how powerful a well-designed microservice architecture can be.

The bottom line is Netflix is one of the most frequently visited websites worldwide, and its approaches can teach you how to serve that many people.

Uber

Flask with Python was the basis for Uber's monolithic application. Over time, it rewrote its entire logic in smaller Python and Go services. This did not only allow Uber to optimize services according to need but also leverage the ability to use another technology for certain parts of its service. Using Go, Uber was able to increase the performance of its discovery layer.

The process of utilizing microservices well took years for Uber, and Matthew Mengerink said about fully integrating with the cloud:

> *"We predict it will take two years to both integrate fully with the cloud and get the platform operating thoughtfully with great tools."* (`https://eng.uber.com/core-infra-2018/`)

Note that Uber has many thousands of employees and thousands of developers working on its infrastructure. This example should show you that it can take a long time to incorporate microservices meaningfully, even if you have a lot of engineers.

To conclude, even big companies like Uber need their due time to transition to microservices properly.

A lot of other companies

Microservices are not limited to big corporations with massive users. As you read in the list of reasons for microservices you can choose microservices even as you are just starting an application. It is often easier to start with the end in mind, rather than settling for the quicker or more expensive option in the long run.

Besides the companies listed previously, the following companies have been known to use microservices as well:

- **Comcast Cable:** `https://qconnewyork.com/ny2015/ny2015/presentation/partial-failures-microservices-jungle-survival-tips-comcast.html`
- **eBay:** `http://www.addsimplicity.com/downloads/eBaySDForum2006-11-29.pdf`
- **SoundCloud:** `https://developers.soundcloud.com/blog/building-products-at-soundcloud-part-2-breaking-the-monolith`
- **Karma:** `https://blog.yourkarma.com/building-microservices-at-karma`
- **Groupon:** `https://engineering.groupon.com/2013/misc/i-tier-dismantling-the-monoliths/`
- **Hailo:** `https://sudo.hailoapp.com/services/2015/03/09/journey-into-a-microservice-world-part-1/`
- **Gilt:** `https://qconnewyork.com/ny2015/presentation/microservices-and-art-taming-dependency-hell-monster`

- Zalando: `http://www.infoq.com/news/2016/02/Monolith-Microservices-Zalando`
- Capital One: `http://www.capitalone.io/blog/why-capital-one-is-at-aws-re-invent-2015/`
- Lending Club: `http://neo4j.com/blog/managing-microservices-neo4j/`
- AutoScout24: `http://www.infoq.com/news/2016/02/autoscout-microservices`

There is no clear statistic as to how many small companies are using microservices. The following list contains a few projects where I personally know the people operating them and know they are using microservices:

- Fuelish (`www.fuelish.de`)
- ReviewSender (`www.reviewsender.com`)
- MyParkplatz24 (`www.myparkplatz24.de`)
- Vapor Cloud (`https://vapor.cloud/`)

Most companies mentioned here are very big and serve a lot of users. Likely, you are not in a position where you face the same problems; however, you can already learn from these companies to avoid making the same mistakes. Here are the key takeaways:

- Microservices are used across the board for companies with many users.
- Microservices were built not only for scalability but also for internal management.
- Microservices make a system complex.
- Many big companies started out with a monolith but turned it into microservices.

In this section, you have seen some of the big players who use microservices and their reasons for their decisions. Don't forget that almost all of them started out as a 1-3 people company and a monolithic system. If you want your app to grow quickly and efficiently, microservices will not disappoint you. Now, let's directly compare monoliths and microservices.

Comparing monolith and microservices

Let's take a moment and compare a monolithic application with a microservice application. The following diagram shows the most obvious difference between microservices and a monolith; monoliths are everything in one piece as opposed to microservices, which are split up in to different parts:

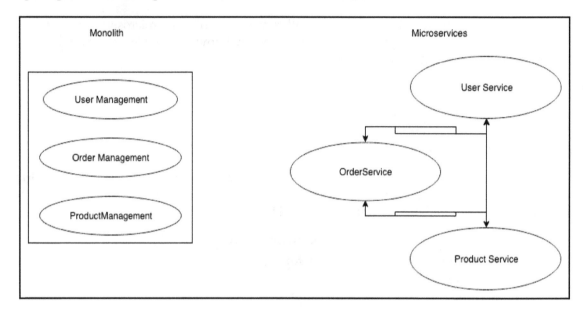

As you can see, the most obvious difference is that a monolith is *one* code base. Every code is within the same project and connected. In contrast to that, microservices are loose and independent but are often working together.

In the following subsections, we will compare concepts that highlight the difference between microservices and monoliths:

- Reusable code base
- Multiple versions online
- No downtime
- Updates are as slow or fast as required
- Common microservice use cases

Let's start by looking at the reusable code base.

Reusable code base

This concept exists with monolithic applications as well as microservices. For monoliths, it's most commonly called *plugins* or *modules*. A lot of commonly used platforms are heavily utilizing this concept. Examples include WordPress, Magento, Drupal, Redmine, and Wikimedia. Many websites utilize plugins to extend the core functionality of the underlying monolithic system.

The underlying principle is to use the same code base across multiple use cases and projects. For monolith applications, however, all elements of that system will need to use the same programming language. For example, a WordPress plugin will need to be in PHP, just like WordPress. In opposition to that, microservices can be in various programming languages. You can have one service written in PHP but another one in Swift—they will work together just fine.

In a monolithic application, all parts are co-dependent on each other. If one part fails, all other parts are potentially affected. For example, one faulty plugin may cause the entire site to not load on certain or all parts. Microservices can be at various stages and not be impacted by others. Also, a non-operational service will not bring down the entire system. At the same time, it can be much harder for someone very familiar with one programming language and framework to work another piece in the same system. A monolithic application can be easier to maintain.

Both approaches allow you to reuse code; microservices, however, are a lot more flexible by allowing you to use various languages and versions together, whereas monoliths do not. Next, we will look at multiple versions online, another feature of microservices.

Multiple versions online

You can run two versions of the same microservice at the same time. If you have a user base that is using an old version of your API, for example, you can keep the old service available for them. Especially when updating apps, it often happens that not all users update to the newest version as soon as they can.

For the clients/users to differentiate between different versions of your service, you often use URL-identifiers such as `https://api.domain.com/v1/users` versus `https://api.domain.com/v2/users`

Notice that it contains a versioning string in the URL. The little `v1` indicates that we want a specific version of this API service. We could run a second version of this service that is using `v2` as an indicator and would return a different return-code.

You could, of course, deliver the same result using a monolithic application; however, in this case, you don't need to deploy two versions of the entire application but only this particular service.

Microservices allow you to keep legacy versions available without having to keep the entire old infrastructure alive. Let's take a look at how microservices allow you zero downtime.

No downtime

As mentioned before, most hosting providers offer some **Continuous Integration** (**CI**) tools to keep downtime to a minimum. The principle is that you start the new version of the service first and then deploy it. Once it is up and running, the load balancer will lead traffic to the new service. Once the new service is fully functional, the old service will be turned off. The effect is that the user experiences no downtime.

A monolithic application can do the same; however, it takes a lot more work, energy, and server power to run a whole second instance of the entire application. If you need 100 servers for average traffic, you would need twice that many servers to complete deployment with this method. With microservices, you can only deploy the service in question while having minimal server overhead. Don't forget that most bigger updates usually require some database adjustments as well.

A monolith almost always uses one and the same database for the entire project. Even if you deploy your monolith in a way that two versions exist at the same time, it is a lot more complicated to do it with databases, especially when data is constantly being added or modified. On the other hand, each microservice is using its own database and you only need to work on the one you are updating.

Microservices are most efficiently used when they allow you to update with no downtime, which leads us to the next topic: updates are as slow or fast as required.

Updates are as slow or fast as required

You can update only the services you want/need, allowing you to spread an update out. Especially for young companies and start-ups, it is widespread to have unclear and changing specifications. As changes and new features come in, you can gradually update your backend. For a lot of cases, adding features is equivalent to adding new services.

For example, if you have a social media app and you want to offer the functionality to comment on posts, it would only take you to add a Comment Service. This service would do nothing else but record comments on content.

If you are then tasked later on to add an "Answer" feature to your app, it could be an extension of the Comment Service. This feature could also alternatively be its own new service. Either way, adding these features can be done without touching the other parts of your backend at all!

To conclude, microservices allow for gradual functional extensions. Finally, let's explore common microservice use cases.

Common microservice use cases

Here is a short, non-exhaustive list of the common use cases for microservices:

- Authentication
- Profile management
- Address verification
- Email handling
- Payment processing
- Social media streaming
- Order management
- Content management

This list can be extended by adding many more use cases to it. You might wonder how these small pieces of functionality can even function like an app. The next section will go into how to upgrade a monolith to microservices and explain how to draw the lines.

 Microservices are services that perform just one or two functions.

Upgrading from monolith to microservices

Upgrading from a monolithic architecture to microservices is essentially to continually replace parts of the old application with new microservices. While this section talks about upgrading a monolith, it can also be taken as a planning step for an entirely new application. You will see how to conceptually upgrade a monolith to microservices; there is no code mentioned at this point because you will see this in much more depth later in this book. You should, however, see the concept underneath after reading this section.

They may not fit your specific application but are generally widespread among monolithic applications. This approach is referred to as **Model-View-Controller** (**MVC**). The components of this approach are defined as follows:

- A Model represents an instance of a data type, for example, User, Product, and Order.
- A Controller represents a logic executor that typically takes input in and returns the output in the form of serialized models, for example, UserController, OrderController, and ProductController.
- A View represents an output from the controllers, often either HTML, XML, or JSON.

Many current web technologies are built on top of the MVC concept, such as the following:

- PHP (Laravel, Symfony, and Zend Framework)
- Ruby (Ruby on Rails)
- Java (Spring MVC and Vaadin)
- Go (Revel and Iris)
- Python (Django)
- Swift (Vapor, Kitura, and Perfect)

 Note: Most of the frameworks mentioned here also allow you to abandon the MVC pattern.

The goal is now to convert an MVC application into a microservice application.

Let's go through the following sections:

- Decoupling business logic
- Reorganizing your monolith
- Integrating microservices

We start by decoupling business logic.

Decoupling business logic

We start by separating business logic. What is your application doing? Answer this question in terms of which aspects are involved. For an online shop application, the answer would look like the following.

What does the application do?

The application does the following things:

- Takes orders
- Processes orders
- Returns products
- Creates products
- Updates products
- Deletes products
- Accepts credit card for an order
- Accepts PayPal for an order

You can be as detailed as you like with this list; it is not a final list of microservices. You will then use this list to identify common components.

What are the common components?

By looking at the preceding list, we can easily tell that we are dealing with the following components:

- Orders
- Products
- Payments

This list is now a lot closer to what we want the microservices to define for us. You may still decide to combine one or two entries in this list but you can now see which microservices make the most sense for you.

You want to reorganize your monolith in a way that makes it easy to remove parts of its functionality to be replaced with microservices.

Reorganizing your monolith

Chances are you will not be able (or want to) update the entire application in one big swap. Depending on the size of the project, it can take weeks, months, and even years for this process to be completed. If you plan on swapping your entire monolith with microservices in one go, you can skip this step. Companies such as Facebook have done this over many years while keeping parts of their old stack. However, even when you intend to keep some of your old monoliths, it still needs to be adjusted to work with microservices. The two main areas to adjust are authentication and business logic.

Using authentication

Microservices typically do not use a shared session model for authentication, which is a prevalent model for monoliths. Whichever model you are currently using, your microservices, as well as your monolith, need to interact with it. A very common and often used standard is called **JSON Web Token** (**JWT**); it allows microservices to authenticate requests.

You will need to modify your monolith to be able to communicate with microservices. There are more ways than just JWTs but because of their benefits and their popularity, I would recommend you use them. In essence, the following are the characteristics of JWTs:

- Self-contained (no central verification)
- Broadly adopted (every framework has a library for them)
- Easy to debug and troubleshoot
- A concept that allows easy security

 JWTs themselves are neither safe nor the best choice. They do, however, provide a good starting point and are often good enough. If you are developing for a high-security application like in banking, you should not use JWTs.

You could also use a "shared session" token instead of JWTs; the principle remains the same: your monolith, as well as your microservices, need to be able to verify the requests.

Adjusting business logic

Once your monolith can communicate with microservices, you can start to separate the business logic. A well-organized monolith application may have done this already. For example, if you are using controllers, you want to end up with the following for our previous example:

```
OrdersController
ProductsController
PaymentsController
```

The reason you want to end up with a structure that separates the business logic is that you can then replace each individual component piece by piece.

So, adjust your monolith to communicate with your microservices and split it up to be easily replaced by them.

Integrating microservices

Now you are at a place where you can introduce your microservices. Each microservice should represent a piece of the business logic and should remain as independent as possible. Given that you have organized your controllers in a way outlined in the previous step, you will now be able to create the following microservices:

```
Orders Manager
Products Manager
Payment Manager
```

You can replace the services as you see fit and as your speed allows. Having your monolith optimized in a way that allows you to replace controllers by services will make this a painless process.

In this section, we learned how to approach integrating a monolith into microservices by decoupling the business logic, reorganizing the monolith, and then lastly, integrating microservices. Let's summarize this chapter!

Summary

In this chapter, you learned the basics of microservices. After defining them, you explored what a microservice is and how it functions. You looked at the reasons when to use microservices and when to not use microservices. After looking at current players using microservices, you saw a detailed comparison of a monolithic application and a microservice application. Finally, you learned how to conceptually upgrade a monolithic application to a microservice application. This chapter served as the basis for the rest of this book.

For you to make sure you understand the concepts so far, go through the following questions and answer them as best as you can. It is essential to be able to answer all of them or the rest of this book will make little sense to you.

In the next chapter, you will learn more about the current status of server-side Swift and why it is an excellent choice for backend applications.

Questions

To check your understanding of microservices, go through the following questions and answer them accordingly. You can see the example answers in the appendix of this book:

1. What is a microservice and what is the definition?
2. List three reasons why microservices can be helpful.
3. List three reasons not to choose microservices.
4. List four differences between a monolith and microservices.
5. Draw a diagram of the infrastructure of the example online app in this chapter.

Understanding Server-Side Swift

2

Swift is a very young language as it was just released in 2014. It was designed to be a language with an easy syntax but that is as powerful as C. In this chapter, you are going to learn why Swift is an excellent choice when it comes to developing server applications. Swift arrives as a fresh alternative to all current and established solutions.

This chapter will introduce you to the *server side* of Swift; the basic understanding of Swift itself is something you should be familiar with already. At first, you are going to look at Swift as a generic language and why it fits well into the server world. Afterward, we look at the performance Swift delivers compared to other web technologies. A review of the current state of Swift for servers and an introduction to the new features of Swift 5 will sum this chapter up.

The following topics will be covered in this chapter:

- A quick review of Swift
- Swift performance
- Swift on the server
- The features of Swift 5

Once you have read this chapter, you will be well prepared to start using Swift for your application.

Technical Requirements

You will need the following software components up and running:

- Vapor Toolbox
- Swift 5
- XCode (11+)
- macOS or Linux

We will assume you are using macOS but all this should work the same under Linux.

You can find all the code for this chapter in the following Git repository: `https://github.com/PacktPublishing/Hands-On-Swift-5-Microservices-Development/tree/master/Chapter 2`

A quick review of Swift

To write server apps in Swift, we require an understanding of where Swift comes from and how it fits into the world of server languages. Swift was invented by Apple engineers as an alternative to C-derivatives, for example, C++, and, Objective-C, Objective-C++. After initially keeping Swift proprietary Apple then released Swift as open source for macOS and Linux. You might have wondered why Apple would bother to make Swift available on Linux, as Apple doesn't usually release any Linux products (not even iTunes).

Swift was designed to be a native language from the very beginning. It means an application gets compiled into binary code that runs directly on the processor, making it the fastest way for an application to run.

When Apple released Swift for Linux, there was little application. The UI was still functioning only on Apple devices, but a good bit of the essential frameworks, Foundation, in particular, was functional on Linux. These frameworks opened the door for some early web frameworks that took Swift and connected it to C libraries that would allow Swift code to run as a web server.

The Perfect framework was the first framework that did this. In September 2016, Tanner Nelson wrote the first version of the Vapor framework, which was loosely based on the Laravel framework (PHP). In May 2017, Vapor 2 was released, which was the first Swift framework that didn't rely on a C library to provide web server functionality. In the meanwhile, IBM started to work on Kitura, yet another framework allowing Swift to be used for web applications.

In early 2018, Apple released SwiftNIO, which is a network library for Swift. You can think of it as "Netty for Swift" if you are familiar with Netty (Java). To put it simply: SwiftNIO provides a very foundational framework to operate in a network and in files, such as opening connections, sending data, receiving data, sending streams, reading streams, and similar operations.

By releasing SwiftNIO, Apple now gave developers an essential set of features to work on server applications. SwiftNIO, like Swift, was also released for Linux.

 While Swift has so far been released for macOS and Linux only, work-in-progress versions of Swift and SwiftNIO for Android, Windows, and other platforms exist. While Apple has not announced any plans for support, as an open source project, Swift and NIO can undoubtedly grow in maturity on other platforms. Swift on Linux runs on all available Linux flavors, though only Ubuntu is officially supported.

Let's take a brief look at the history of Swift in the context of other programming languages.

From Fortran to Swift

In this section, we want to take a look at the development of Swift, from Fortran, a very old programming language, up until Swift.

The following diagram and the timeline next to it highlights well how Swift combines the best of numerous worlds:

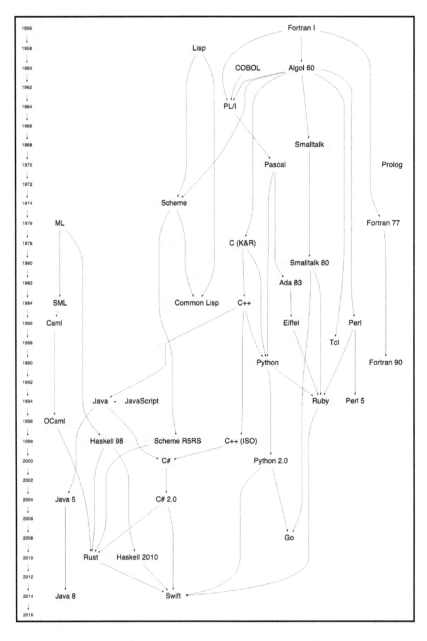

(Source: http://rigaux.org/language-study/diagram.html)

It stands out that Swift was influenced by Rust, Ruby, Python, Haskel, and C#, making it a very modern language that copied some of the most loved features of the other languages.

Now, we have learned about the history of Swift and where its place is in the world of programming languages. Let's look at Swift's performance compared to other popular web technologies next.

Swift performance

Swift is competing with a good number of frameworks and languages. Some might argue that performance is only one out of many factors that should be considered when choosing a technology. While that is undoubtedly true, think of this: you want to build a project in a way where technology will not hold you back much. Facebook, as well as Uber, has spent years rebuilding and reworking their infrastructure. No matter what technology you choose, you will most likely refactor your application as well. However, having selected a stack that allows you to do so gracefully is crucial.

You could be looking at some raw benchmarks in this section, but I think it makes more sense to analyze with a bit more depth what performance holistically looks like for a project. When comparing Swift to its competition, you want to stay as clean and objective as possible; the following comparisons attempt to assess the situations objectively and as close to the real world as possible.

Almost any website can run with any of the languages available. The question is often not *"Is it possible?"* but rather *"Does it make sense for us?"*. In some cases, speed and performance are more important than convenience. In other cases, it's the exact opposite.

Let's briefly dig into the following types of languages:

- Scripting languages: PHP, Python, Ruby, JavaScript, and so on
- Virtual machine languages: Java, .NET, and Scala
- Native languages: Go, C, Rust, and Swift

Afterward, you will see some metrics of Vapor, the most popular Swift framework.

Scripting languages

Script languages are not being compiled into a native binary but interpreted on-the-fly. So, every request to the server is treated individually and mostly isolated. The server then calls the language interpreter to work through the requested file (`index.php`, for example). Every time a script is called the server program needs to be started again. Naturally, this is not the fastest way to respond to a request.

A lot of mechanisms to speed up this process were invented over the years. All of them are essentially trying to do the following:

- Cache interpreted code.
- Cache various outputs and inputs as a whole.
- Reduce the amount of overhead.

A lot of optimization for these languages is solely the idea of caching what they have compiled already and then returning it from caches when appropriate. There is principally nothing wrong with this approach, but it makes it difficult to compare performance. You want to assume the worst scenario, which is an empty cache when evaluating the pure speed of an application. Caching can be added later—even to an already speedy application.

The most popular scripting languages include Ruby, Python, PHP, JavaScript, and Typescript. All of them have various environments and interpreters, some of which are faster than others. They all share that they are naturally not compiled into binary code and will consequently always fall behind native languages. On the other hand, they enjoy a rich community and have gained many fans due to their simplicity.

Let's look at some real-life examples of websites dealing with scripting languages.

Facebook

Facebook started all in plain PHP and over a decade came up with its own PHP-flavored server called Hack. Hack started out as an initial attempt to compile PHP to a native binary file. It failed, however, due to the unforeseeable internal structure of a PHP program (dynamic variables, inconsistencies, and so on). Hack ended up being a PHP version that was modified to fit Facebook's internal needs. However, Hack is now running as a Virtual Machine (VM), not as a native application.

The reasons for Facebook were that it wanted to keep its dependencies and existing libraries operational while also increasing performance. While Facebook shows that scripting languages can certainly get very performant, it also shows how discontented Facebook became over time with PHP.

Twitter

Twitter started, like Facebook, as a monolithic application. It was written as a Ruby-on-Rails application. However, the increase in traffic caused Twitter to rewrite its backend entirely using the **Java Virtual Machine** (**JVM**), which means programming languages such as Java, Scala, and Clojure were used. Twitter also specifically attributes the microservice architecture as part of its path forward with regards to meeting traffic needs.

 Read https://www.slideshare.net/caniszczyk/twitter-opensourcestacklinuxcon2013 for more detailed information on Twitter's stack.

Uber

Uber has transitioned critical services from Python to Go by now. In this case, it was partially for performance, but not in the same way Facebook was affected. Uber needed *some* of its services to be fast, concretely, live position updates. Uber chose Go because it was able to get better performance.

It is interesting to see how big players have started to transition some of their services from scripting languages to native ones.

Let's explore VM languages next.

VM languages

The most commonly used language in this category is Java. JVM has a long track record for being an enterprise-class web technology. On the other hand, .NET by Microsoft allows you to write in a variety of languages; often, C# stands out as the most common one for server applications.

Right between JVM and .NET is Scala—which is a new language that can compile into either .NET or JVM.

VM languages have the advantage that they are pre-compiled. They are not interpreted on-the-fly like scripting languages but pre-compiled into VM-specific byte code, which is then run on the VM. It comes with a good performance boost.

Apple, IBM, and LinkedIn are three examples that are using Java in a lot of their infrastructure.

Because VM code runs on the actual VM, and the engine is an extra layer on top of the operating system, VMs typically need a lot of RAM to operate smoothly. It is very common for the JVM to run on multiple GBs of RAM even for relatively simple applications.

 Read `https://people.cs.umass.edu/~emery/pubs/gcvsmalloc.pdf` for more information on JVM RAM usage.

Native languages

Swift is a native language that compiles into native apps! So are C and C++. C (and C++) is inevitably the fastest language because it is so close to machine code (leaving Assembler aside). Many scripting languages directly plug into C for this reason. Node.js, PHP, and Python often directly utilize C functions, and those will always be very fast. Naturally, a pure C server will be the fastest server you could develop.

So, why not write our servers in C, you might ask? The reason you don't necessarily want to do that is that C is not convenient or safe in terms of memory leaks. It is complicated (some say impossible) to write good memory-safe programs in C. For web projects, this problem leads to the creation of Go (sometimes referred to as Golang), Rust, and Swift. All three were invented with the thought in mind to keep the performance of C/C++ but get better memory safety.

Go and Rust kept a mostly C-like functional style whereas Swift got inspirations from other object-oriented languages such as Java and scripting languages such as Ruby and Python. All three languages compile into native code, which means they run faster by default than the other two types of languages. No clear metric would show if any of the three is faster than the others. A good programmer could probably create equally performant programs in either language.

All three languages have been picked up by major players for critical performance tasks. For Swift, big players using it for web services include the following:

- Apple
- IBM
- Mercedes
- Audi

The main reason Swift is exciting to big corporations is that a native application leaves a much smaller RAM footprint. Imagine what difference it can make if you can achieve the same results but only need 25% of your hardware.

Comparing frameworks

As said before, it is not easy to compare languages, let alone frameworks, to each other. One framework might be extremely fast in doing one job whereas completely slow in another position. The following metrics have been recorded with Vapor 3 and a few other frameworks. Take them with a grain of salt, and as technologies continually develop, don't use them as hard numbers because any software update can change the balance:

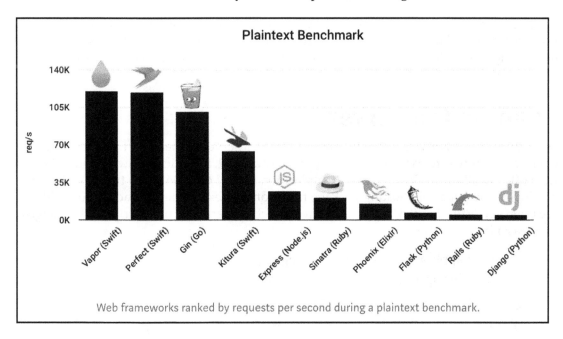

Web frameworks ranked by requests per second during a plaintext benchmark.

(Source: https://medium.com/@codevapor/vapor-3-0-0-released-8356fa619a5d)

It shows how all three Swift frameworks perform well compared to other well-known frameworks. You can see that the Swift frameworks outperform the other frameworks, except for Go, quite significantly. The scripting languages do not perform well as they are not natively compiled. The key to performance is that Swift compiles natively and can run directly on the processor.

We have looked at the frameworks and Swift's performance overall, so let's look at some specific Swift features now.

Swift's features

Here is a summary of all of the things that make Swift an attractive choice for server development:

- A modern language built with the modern paradigm
- A native language with native performance
- Very low RAM usage
- Linux-friendly
- Universal usage can create apps for other OSes as well

There are certain situations and ways in which other languages are faster than Swift; however, overall, Swift offers the most significant performance benefits through its native design and low RAM footprint. Let's now explore what Swift looks like on a server.

Swift on the server

What does it look like to run a Swift application on a server? When Swift was released as open source, it was released for Linux right away as well. Specifically, Swift favors the Linux flavor, Ubuntu. Hosting a Swift application is very different from traditional web hosting. If you get a web hosting package from companies such as GoDaddy, you will not see them say "Runs Swift 5". Most mainstream web hosters only offer scripting languages. The reasoning is simple:

- Most applications use scripting languages.
- Scripting applications can share the same server.

Swift, on the other hand, as a native language, *is* the actual web server itself. What that means is that your Swift application is directly responding to incoming requests. Let's look at the following aspects of server-side Swift:

- A self-contained server
- Linux/Ubuntu
- SwiftNIO
- Docker

Let's dive into it.

Self-contained server

A self-contained server is a program that does not need another program to run. A PHP script, for example, will run through at least two other programs: PHP (the compiler) and Nginx, Apache, or another HTTP(S) server. A self-contained server such as a Swift application, however, is the only application that needs to run; it answers HTTP(S) requests directly.

Let's look at a small Swift web server:

```
import Vapor
let app = try Application()

app.get("hello") { req in
    return "Hello, world."
}
try app.run()
```

Without going into much detail, the crucial part is the last line:

```
try app.run()
```

The application does not close; it keeps running. What the framework (Vapor) and the network library (SwiftNIO) are hiding here is that the application is actively listening to incoming connections over TCP on a given port (8080 by default). So, incoming requests are answered directly by the application and, by extension, the return statement.

If you have a background in dealing with scripting web applications, you may find a lot of perks in self-contained servers. In scripting languages, every request is usually isolated. Every request is treated individually, and you have no access to the other requests that are coming in. Technologies such as Memcached are designed to bridge this for you to share information between requests.

In Swift servers, however, the process, the running application, is the same for all requests. You can share memory, objects, and instances across requests. It not only allows you to centralize some of your logic (such as the database), it also saves you a lot of memory and CPU power.

Now that you have learned how a self-contained server operates, let's take a look at the hosting operating system: Linux/Ubuntu.

Linux/Ubuntu

When Swift was open-sourced, it was delivered Linux-compatible. Ubuntu is the official flavor of Linux that Swift currently supports. Numerous other platforms that are Linux-based are being developed currently; for servers, the best option was and remains Ubuntu.

Ubuntu has been and still is a favored Linux-distribution for server applications way before Swift. A lot of other technologies are running reliably and well on Ubuntu, and so it is not surprising Apple decided to support Ubuntu primarily. Since Ubuntu is also open source and has a large user base, it is unlikely that using Ubuntu for Swift applications will disappoint. Initially, Swift on Linux had some compatibility issues; however, with every Swift version, those have been eliminated.

In the distant future, it is thinkable that Swift applications might run on other platforms, including Windows and it might be another hosting option, but you might ask why you would want that since Linux has been reliable and stable. According to one of Swift's authors, Chris Lattner, *"the ultimate goal for Swift has always been and still is total world domination. It's a modest goal."*(https://oleb.net/blog/2017/06/chris-lattner-wwdc-swift-panel/#in-which-fields-would-you-like-to-see-swift-in-the-future)

So, for a Swift app to run on a Linux server requires a few libraries and tools to be installed—most of which can be done with package managers. As the Swift ABI is still maturing, you will almost always deliver the source code with your app. The server will then compile it into the executable you need for the respective OS version. As time goes on, this might soon change into a more library-oriented approach in which you can compile locally and simply move the compiled file.

 You can already compiling the executable and move it by itself. The problem is that the target OS might not have the correct Swift libraries installed, or you might not have the right OS handy (for example, compile on macOS while wanting it to run on Linux).

To conclude, right now Ubuntu is the most promising and reliable way to launch a Swift application on a server. In this next section, we will explore how to achieve that without necessarily having Ubuntu running.

After looking at the actual OS that will run Swift, let's explore an alternative that allows Swift to run on other hosts as well: Docker.

Docker

When deploying your application, you can run it on macOS or Ubuntu. In the world of servers, it is a lot more economical to use Ubuntu than macOS (as macOS is only supposed to run on Apple hardware, whereas Ubuntu can run on any hardware). So, you want an Ubuntu server running for Swift. Let's talk about a popular and essential way to make things easier. Docker has been an upcoming trend over the last years. It is a container system that allows for operation-system-level virtualization. What that means is that you can run applications on your machine as if you have another operating system installed.

Docker containers are packages that include everything to run certain software. For example, the Swift container has everything you need to run Swift applications in Docker. Instead of using separate kernels during virtualization (like many VMs do), Docker uses the same kernel and isolates the resources and RAM for each container.

The implications of Docker are huge, especially for microservices: instead of having to deal with many different servers for an application, it is now possible to only deal with Docker containers. So, particularly when developing a microservices application, it is beneficial to run multiple services in separate Docker containers as they all run on the same hardware. It also allows for an interesting scaling opportunity since the applications operate without needing to worry about the underlying OS. For example, if you need to run 100 instances of one service, you could run it on one big server or 20 smaller services—your application won't know nor notice the difference.

The relevant elements of Docker are the following:

- Images: These contain everything to run.
- Containers: These have image instances that are running.
- Repositories: Like GitHub, these are just for Docker images.

Furthermore, a Docker container can specify how much CPU and RAM it needs. This prevents applications from stealing resources from each other.

Let's now look at the last central piece of server-side Swift: SwiftNIO.

SwiftNIO

What is SwiftNIO? It is the official library Apple offers for managing and dealing with network connections and data streams, including filesystems. SwiftNIO provides all of the tools, protocols, and features you would need to operate in a network.

 Before SwiftNIO, Swift server applications had to rely mostly on external C libraries. While this is not a problem in principle, having a pure Swift network library allows for better debugging and cleaner code.

SwiftNIO is a big step forward to the server-side Swift world since it standardizes network communication and delivers the tools—in Swift—you need to build performant and reliable network applications. Apple has invested a lot of time and energy into SwiftNIO for it to be the main go-to tool when it comes to the network.

At this point, SwiftNIO is used in all major network libraries and frameworks that are developed for server applications in Swift. The convenient part of it is that framework developers—and by extension, you—don't need to worry about debugging hardly any network issues anymore because Apple has taken that part over.

For all the intents and purposes of this book, SwiftNIO is something essential to be aware of, but it will mainly stay in the background. Vapor—along with other frameworks—build around NIO in a developer-friendly way.

SwiftNIO allows us to operate asynchronously, we can send and receive data without having to worry about the exact timing or the network connection. This leads us to look at asynchronous events in general.

Asynchronous events

If you have dealt with network connections in the past, you will be familiar with the concept. There are two ways of looking at requests: synchronously and asynchronously.

Synchronously means you send a request (for example, to a server) and your code will wait for a response before it continues. An example would look like this. This is the actual code from a Vapor 2 project:

```
let user = User()      // User is a model that is connected to a database
user.id = 2            // set some attribute
try user.save()        // saves this model to the database
print("saved")         // this line is called after we saved
```

The last line is only called after the user is saved; the whole program waits for the saving process to be finished. In contrast to the synchronous approach is the asynchronous method. The following is the same code, now written for Vapor 4:

```
let user = User()
user.id = 2
return try user.save(on: request.db) { _ in
    print("saved")
}
```

You can see here that we are returning an `EventLoopFuture<User>` (line 3), but we are also not printing the `"saved"` string right after the return statement (because it would never be called), but we put it in a callback function. The fundamental difference here is that deal with the fact that we **do not know** when the user is saved. The database might be busy or slow; it might take 1 or 10 seconds. But when it is saved, we know that the callback function is called and then we print the `"saved"` string.

SwiftNIO is all based on the concept of asynchronous events; it handles all of the magic in the background for us, and we do not have to worry about it.

 The reason we are not using synchronous calls (anymore) is that it can and most certainly will create problems for us down the line. Synchronous events in an asynchronous environment (which networks are) create issues that can look like deadlocks or threading complications. Using synchronous code causes threads to "wait" until they have finished; using asynchronous frameworks allows us to use the CPU resources in the meantime for different activities.

Now, let's look at some of the new features Swift 5 has brought to the table.

Features of Swift 5

You already have an understanding of how Swift works. In this section, we are looking at some of the newest features that Apple has released at the time of writing this book. There are a lot of bug fixes and changes in every Swift update, but the following features are particularly noteworthy for us in Swift version 5:

- ABI stability
- Raw strings and UTF8 strings
- Result type
- Future enum cases
- Flattening nested optionals

There are a couple more interesting new features of Swift 5. However, this section only contains the ones that will be most relevant for server development. Take a look.

ABI stability

One particularly interesting new feature is that Swift is now ABI-compatible with version 5.0 and later ones. It means that libraries, frameworks, and applications could have different Swift versions but remain compatible with each other. As the number of libraries and frameworks for server-side Swift keeps growing, this will be a significant improvement to prevent version locks.

For example, you write your application with Vapor 4.0 and Swift 5, but then a little later Swift 6 is released. Let's pretend Swift 6 is somewhat incompatible with Swift 5. You can then rely on the fact that Vapor 4.0 can be compiled with Swift 5 and your app with Swift 6 while they can still run together without any conflicts.

It also opens the door to deliver applications, libraries, and executables without having to deliver the code. While this is possible already, every compiled Swift application is self-contained and specific to a platform at this point. As ABI stability will be increasingly adopted, it could be possible to not have to compile frameworks and libraries anymore, but just use the delivered libraries.

ABI stability is by far the most important improvement. Next to it are raw strings and UTF8 strings.

Raw strings and UTF8 strings

Swift 5 has rewritten how it deals with strings internally. Most of it is under the hood and not of practical relevance, but this one has some actual usage: raw strings.

They allow you to write a string that is not interpreted in any way, as in this example:

```
let rawString = #"This is a raw string with some "quotations marks" that
are not being interpreted."#
```

Earlier versions of Swift would understand the quotation marks as the end of the string, but Swift 5 accepts them now. If you needed to use a variable within a raw string, you could still do that like this:

```
let age = 27
let rawString = #"My age is \#(age)." // string interpolation happens
                                      // almost like before in raw strings
```

Raw strings will be useful whenever you have a lot of special characters within a string—like in regular expressions, for example. On the subject of strings, Swift 5 switched from UTF16 to UFT8 strings, which caused a massive increase in performance.

Strings are important in almost every application, and seeing this improve is extremely helpful for us. Next, we want to look at the result type in Swift 5.

Result type

Swift 5 introduces a result type for common functions in which the result is either of the expected type or a failure. It is implemented as an enum with only two cases: success and failure.

Let's assume we build a user login and the result might either be the user itself or an error. For purposes of simplicity, let's consider the error in our case would be `WrongPasswordError`. In a real-world example, there would probably be more errors (timeout, connection, and so on):

```
func userLogin() -> Result<User, Error> {
    if (...) {
        return .success(user) // assume we got the `user` from somewhere
    }
    return .failure(WrongPasswordError)
}
```

When we are now trying to deal with a login attempt, we can nicely filter out the result:

```
switch userLogin() {
    case .failure(let error):
        // ...
        break
    case .success(let user):
        // ...
        break
}
```

The nice additional benefit to this type is that it can be used in asynchronous and complex code and allows for standard ways of dealing with errors. As frameworks and libraries adapt to this type, it will allow for predictable error handling.

Future enum cases

Imagine you have an enum :

```
enum ConnectionError: Error {
    case timeout
    case badRequest
}
```

If you are checking an error from a result, you will do it like this:

```
switch (error) {
    case .timeout:
        print("timeout")
    case .badRequest:
        print("bad request")
    default:
        print("another request")
```

As frameworks and libraries develop, the ConnectionError enum could be extended by a future version of a framework or library. Adding another case to the enum could look like this:

```
enum ConnectionError: Error {
    case timeout
    case badRequest
    case denied
}
```

If a newer version of a framework updates this, it will cause your old code to select the default case, and you would not even notice that there is a new case. By adding a little attribute, @unkown, to the default case, you tell the compiler to warn you if the switch block is no longer exhaustive. This is a huge benefit to making sure enum cases are exhaustive even when new cases come along later on. Our switch statement now looks like this:

```
switch (error) {
    case .timeout:
        print("timeout")
    case .badRequest:
        print("bad request")
    @unkown default:
        print("an unkown request request")
```

The added case for the enum will now cause a compiler warning—but it won't break our code. This is important as this might happen in other external libraries as well. So, you don't need to worry about it in terms of compiling your software, but it is beneficial to be informed about this change. Swift 4.2 would not notify you nor would it break the code.

Flattening nested optionals

This addresses a problem where you are trying to get the return value of a function from an object that might be null. For example, we have a `Product` class that has a `getPrice()` function that returns an `Int` instance:

```
class Product {
    func getPrice() throws -> Int {
        return 10
    }
}
var product:Product? = nil
var price = try? product?.getPrice()
```

In Swift 4.2, `price` would be an "optional optional Int" (`Int??`); however, in Swift 5, we can change the last line to this:

```
var price = try? product?.getPrice()
```

And now we only have one level of optionals as opposed to two. While this example is elementary, it is a powerful feature as you might be chaining a lot of optional functions together in a server application.

We have now seen what new features Swift 5 brings; a lot of them are very useful for backend development. In the next chapter, we will look at Vapor, the most popular server-side Swift framework.

Summary

In this chapter, you looked at the history of Swift and why it stands out from other languages. You then learned why Swift has been leaning toward server development from the beginning. After looking at Swift's performance compared to other languages and frameworks, you learned about Swift on the server and what is currently supported. Docker and SwiftNIO should be terms you can explain by now. Finally, you explored the features of Swift 5 and have seen examples of what the changes could look like in practice.

Go through the *Questions* section to validate your understanding of Swift on the server.

In the next chapter, you are going to explore the Vapor framework and you will be set up to create web applications with Vapor and Swift.

Questions

To see whether you understood the gist of server-side Swift, try answering the following questions:

1. Why is Swift being a native language helpful?
2. What is the preferred OS for server-side Swift applications at the moment?
3. What is SwiftNIO?
4. How does Docker help?
5. Name three of the added benefits of Swift 5.

Getting Started with the Vapor Framework

3

After learning about microservices and Swift, it is now time to focus on the framework you will use. Choosing the right framework is an integral part of our stack. After Swift was open-sourced, a couple of frameworks emerged as solid choices for web development. In this chapter, you will explore the Vapor framework and why it was chosen for this book over other frameworks.

At first, we will look at the Vapor framework and why it stands out. We will explore the features Vapor offers and look at some code examples. Afterward, we will learn how other frameworks compare to Vapor.

The chapter is structured as follows:

- The Vapor framework
- Comparing Vapor to Kitura, Perfect, and Smoke
- Installing Vapor
- Vapor in action

Let's get started!

The Vapor framework

Vapor is the most popular and loved Swift framework that currently exists. It has over 18,000 stars on GitHub along with an active community that is building the framework. In this section, we will dive into how the framework is designed and how it operates.

Let's take a look at the following:

- History of Vapor: Where did it all start?
- Hello World: A short and easy Vapor application
- General structure: Learning about the internal workings of Vapor
- SwiftNIO – futures and promises: How does SwiftNIO integrate with Vapor?
- Controllers: Logical buildings blocks
- Databases and models: Storing data
- Views: Serving HTML

History of Vapor

Vapor was invented by Tanner Nelson in 2016, soon after Swift become open source. The initial version relied on some external C libraries for sockets (answering HTTP requests) and was rewritten to become Vapor 2, which was only using one C library for the MySQL extension. Tanner wrote Vapor loosely based on the Laravel (PHP) framework, which he liked from a structural perspective.

Vapor 2 went through a strong growth period in which some corporate sponsors joined to support the framework. Similar to scripting frameworks, Vapor 2 uses a synchronous approach when dealing with connections. This becomes a pain point for users as it can cause apps to freeze or experience other network issues. The reason this happens is that the app is not using its CPU time wisely and race conditions can exist. Therefore, Vapor 3 was designed to be asynchronous from the beginning. It even featured its own asynchronous layer before SwiftNIO. After Apple released SwiftNIO in early 2018, it was incorporated into Vapor within a week. Vapor 3 was fully released in May 2018.

Vapor 3 brought many changes to the framework – the primary one being that almost every transaction was now handled asynchronously by SwiftNIO. After a few months of bug fixes, the first ideas for Vapor 4 started to form.

At the time of this writing, Vapor 4 is currently in beta and is an updated and improved version of Vapor 3. The feedback from Vapor 3 along with the learnings was compiled into a new release, with some breaking changes, resulting in Vapor version 4. In practical terms, it does not take much work to get a Vapor 3 application functional under Vapor 4.

Hello World

Vapor is opinionated in regard to its structure and internal setup. An opinionated framework provides you with a lot of guidance for your structure, such as file formatting, folder hierarchy, and naming conventions.

The official "Hello World," however, can comprise seven lines:

```
import Vapor
let app = try Application()

app.get("hello") { req in
    return "Hello, world."
}

try app.run()
```

As you can see, a Vapor application requires only one element to operate as a server: the application object. The application operates as the router and manages all the URL access points and forwards them to the controller functions or classes.

Vapor is an opinionated framework, which means it encourages certain standards for how to structure your files and the content of your files.

General structure

Vapor recommends a structure for its apps, though it is not enforced. You can read more details about the structure at `https://docs.vapor.codes/4.0/folder-structure/`.

A simplified Vapor application structure looks like this:

```
Public/
Sources/
Sources/Run/main.swift
Sources/App/Controllers/SomeController.swift
Sources/App/Models/AModel.swift
Sources/configure.swift
Sources/routes.swift
Tests/
Tests/LinuxMain.swift
Tests/AppTests/AppTests.swift
Package.swift
```

`Package.swift` is the **Swift Package Manager** (**SPM**) file that contains all the targets and dependencies. Take a look at it here:

```
// swift-tools-version:5.1
import PackageDescription

let package = Package(
    name: "app",
    platforms: [
        .macOS(.v10_14)
    ],
    products: [
        .executable(name: "Run", targets: ["Run"]),
        .library(name: "App", targets: ["App"]),
    ],
    dependencies: [
        // A server-side Swift web framework.
        .package(url: "https://github.com/vapor/vapor.git", from: "4.0.0-
          beta.2"),
        .package(url: "https://github.com/vapor/fluent.git", from: "4.0.0-
          beta.2"),
        .package(url: "https://github.com/vapor/fluent-sqlite-driver.git",
          from: "4.0.0-beta.2"),
    ],
    targets: [
        .target(name: "App", dependencies: ["Fluent", "FluentSQLiteDriver",
          "Vapor"]),
        .target(name: "Run", dependencies: ["App"]),
        .testTarget(name: "AppTests", dependencies: ["App", "XCTVapor"])
    ]
)
```

A Vapor app technically needs only one dependency: `Vapor`. This package includes all the general things that a server application would need; for example, the application, router, services, JSON, helpers, and more.

You will often find yourself needing additional packages, though. In the preceding case, the app is using SQLite and, therefore, is including it alongside Vapor.

You have two targets in a Vapor application, as follows:

1. `Run` is the application containing the main function for Swift.
2. `App` is the actual application that is used as a dependency.

You might ask why Vapor would split this up in such a way. The reason is that you cannot have a test target with an executable target. So, in order for you to run unit tests on your application, it has to be a dependency.

In the folder *Controllers,* you put all your controllers for the application. For microservices, you should not need a lot of controllers as you try to reduce complexity. *Models* contain all the database models you are interacting with. The other files in *sources* are generic and configuration files for the app to know what to do.

 Note that Swift does not dictate the file structure, and neither does Vapor. You could have everything in one single file. It makes sense, however, to split classes, structs, and enums up by their logical function in order to find the code easily later on. Vapor encourages this as well.

Configuration

Vapor applications used to have config files. However, they were abandoned in Vapor 3 for two reasons – the first one being the primary one:

1. They are slow to parse and add extra layers (such as YAML or JSON).
2. They are potentially exposed and are a risk factor; environment variables can be passed on to the application at runtime and without inducing any files.

   The way to pass configuration settings to a Vapor application is by setting the system environment variables. In macOS, that is done by calling the following:

   ```
   $ export VARIABLE='value'
   ```

   All your required configuration settings should be in environment variables. These can then be passed on to the app either through the OS or through Docker. Later in this book, we will explore more complex examples of how configuration can work.

   Another way in which you can pass environment variables to Vapor is by creating a .env file that contains config variables like this:

   ```
   VARIABLE1=value
   VARIABLE2=value
   ```

This file will be loaded during the start of the application.

Middleware

A middleware is a very specific service that interacts with ingoing and outgoing connections before and after the controller functions have processed a request. They can be extremely useful to perform common tasks, such as the following:

- Convert every output to JSON, including errors
- Authenticate requests based on headers, cookies, and others
- Return static files that you might need

We will set up some of these middlewares to assist us as well.

Services

You might be familiar with services from other projects. They are single instance classes that perform common tasks for multiple controllers. In Vapor, services play a special role because of their asynchronous nature. Most database drivers are services, for example. Vapor 4 makes service objects on either the `application` instance or the `request` instance.

For example, for you to access the database, you can simply refer to `request.db` and it will return the correct database instance object. Vapor uses extensions to provide these variables and can save a lot of time that way. You could say that Vapor does not have services in the traditional sense, meaning through dependency injection or static linking, but through Swift's language design.

For example, let's look at how Vapor 3 operated:

```
let mailService = container.make(MailService.self)
```

In this traditional approach, services are initiated by request and we get them with a function, `make()` in this case.

Now, in Vapor 4 we can simply assume that the service exists on either application or request, we do not need to call a function but simply assume it is there:

```
let mailService = request.mailService
```

In the background and through Swift's language design the object is there and available.

RoutesBuilder

A router is the logic in an application that decides who, that is, which controller, gets to respond to a request. Vapor's approach is to have the RoutesBuilder protocol, which makes every conforming class a routing class. This is very powerful and – more importantly – very performant. HTTP supports nine different kinds of requests: GET, POST, OPTIONS, DELETE, PUT, HEAD, PATCH, COPY, and SEARCH. For us, the following four will be the most relevant: GET, POST, DELETE, and PUT.

Take a look at this code example:

```
public func routes(_ app: Application) throws {
    // Example 1
    app.get("hello") { req in
        return "Hello, world!"
    }
    // Example 2
    let someController = SomeController()
    app.get("models", use: comeController.index)
    app.post("models", use: someController.create)
    app.delete("models", AModel.parameter, use: someController.delete)

    // Example 3
    let group = app.grouped("v1")
    v1.get("user", use: someController.user)
}
```

The routes function is called by the configure function in configure.swift and is giving you an Application instance. You can now call functions of RoutesBuilder and assign callback functions for what you want the Application to do for specific paths.

Here, Example 1 is the most basic way of dealing with the router. For a specific URL ("/hello") we are returning "Hello, world!" to the screen.

Example 2 is now adding controllers. Paths (for example, "/models") are now redirected to the function of a controller (index). This gives us the ability to spread out logic out over multiple controllers.

Example 3 is adding a grouping function. Now everything that is using the group will need to match the group identifier. In this case, the URL would be /v1/user and it would call the "user" function in the controller.

SwiftNIO – futures and promises

SwiftNIO is a library that provides event-based data flow through networks and data streams, including files. An important part of that is to know and understand the event loop and what futures and promises are and the roles that they play.

Let's analyze the elements of NIO:

- EventLoop
- EventLoopFutures
- EventLoopPromises

EventLoop

An event loop is an ongoing `while` loop that is processing events. It provides thread-safety and allows the server to respond to multiple requests simultaneously, even when they share the same resources. Luckily, you don't need to worry about it too much. All you need to know is that Vapor and NIO are managing that part for you. It does mean, however, that you need to be aware of the following:

- You never know when you will be processed in the loop.
- Every input/output has to go through the event loop.

The way inputs and outputs are processed is through `EventLoopFutures` and `EventLoopPromises`. Let's see how:

EventLoopFutures

A future is an instance of a class that will have a value at some point in the future. So, when you receive a future instance, the future does not have a value yet. It will, however, have a value once it is processed by the event loop. So, in reality, you will rarely ever deal with futures outside of the event loop, which is why NIO refers to them solely as EventLoopFutures instead of just Futures. Futures are created through the event loop, like this:

```
let intFuture: EventLoopFuture<Int> = eventLoop.newSucceededFuture(result:
10)
```

You can see that our `EventLoopFuture intFuture` will contain the `Int` type. In this case, the future is already successful. Often, the futures you receive are waiting for an external event, such as a database responding.

In order to work with the value, you will have to attach a callback function that can access the final value using one of the provided methods for the EventLoopFuture type:

```
intFuture.whenSuccess { i in
    print("our value: ", i) // output: "our value: 10"
}
```

Now we have attached an observer to this future, which is called when the future has a value.

In reality, you will often want to receive the result of a future and convert it into something else. NIO gives two functions for that, which we will examine next.

map

If we want to return a future with a different type and value than before, we can use map:

```
let stringFuture: EventLoopFuture<String> = intFuture.map { i in
    return String(i)
}
```

You will notice that you need to do these conversions a lot, especially when dealing with a database. For example, you will receive a future of the DatabaseResult type but want to return a user. map is the function that allows you to perform those kinds of conversions.

flatMap

Another important function is flatMap. It is like a map but it returns another future that allows you to chain different operations. For example, you could receive a user from the database, change the name, and save it right after:

```
return User.query(on: request.db).filter(\.$id == 1).first().flatMap {
(user:User?) in
    if let user = user {
        user.name = "Steve Jobs"
        return user.save(on: request.db)
    }
    else {
        return request.eventLoop.makeFailedFuture(Abort(.badRequest,
          reason: "No user found."))
    }
}
```

What we are doing here now is that we are creating a future through the database object on the `request` instance. This future will contain a user from the database where the ID is 1, or `nil` if none exists. So, after the first line, we receive an optional class `User` in the callback. We change the name of `user` and return a new future that is saving the user. The second future is returned when the user is saved and is of the `Void` type. A lot of functions that operate but are not returning anything are of type `Void`.

 If we encounter an error, for example, the user does not exist, we can return a failed future. This way the listener of the future can react appropriately.

You can see that we are using `query(on: request.db)` for the first `EventLoopFuture` type. As stated earlier, all futures are running on the event loop. So, we are passing along the request (which references the event loop), and Vapor will return the correct `EventLoopFuture` type to us. The `flatMap` function is now using the result of that first future and maps it to another `EventLoopFuture` with another type (`Void`).

EventLoopPromises

`EventLoopPromises` are very similar to `EventLoopFutures`: that is, they either succeed or fail. This predictability is crucial because not all operations are always successful. If you lose the connection to a database, the process will fail – with a promise, you have the option of picking up the pieces after it fails.

Creating a promise goes hand in hand with futures:

```
let testPromise:EventLoopPromise<String> =
  eventLoop.newPromise(String.self)
print(promiseString.futureResult)        // Future<String>
promiseString.succeed(result: "Hello")   // completes the promise
                                          // successfully
promiseString.fail(error: ...)           // fails the promise
```

Promises can be helpful if you are not sure that the return will exist. For example, a promise is made that we will have a `String` here. This promise will either be fulfilled or denied. The difference to EventLoopFuture is that a Future is what is the result of a Promise. We are promising a result and a Future will be used to fulfill this promise.

Controllers

Controllers are the central decision-making element in Vapor. They are classes or structs that take an **input** from the router and convert it into an **output**. Input consists of data from the request. Most of the time, the data you are going to interact with is POST data, which is sent in the body of the request, the parameters of the requested URL or headers.

Technically, controllers are not necessarily needed. If you are going to render templates only, or if you only need a function or so, the callback for the router could be a function – not attached to a controller. It is, however, poor design to have an application more complex than a Hello World without controllers; the lack of structure would confuse readers.

Content

Data that is passed around in Vapor is often derived from the `Content` type. It's a class that conforms to `Codable`, which means that it can convert from and into JSON, XML, or any other data structure without any issues. Take a look at the following struct:

```
struct SomeData: Content {
    var stringValue: String
    var optionalValue: String?
    var anotherValue: Int
    var anotherContent: ClassThatIsContent
}
```

In JSON, the data could look like this:

```
{
    "stringValue": "a random string",
    "anotherValue": 10,
    "anotherContent": { ... }
}
```

We can use any object or class that is implementing the `Codable` protocol. All the standard types (`String`, `Int`, and `Bool`) are conformed by default. But we can also implement our own types. This allows us to represent even complex JSON structures easily by building all the needed structs (or classes).

 Note that Swift is a statically typed language. If you have dealt with dynamically typed languages before, be aware that Swift is not tolerating implicit conversions from `String` to `Int` and vice versa. To convert them, you need to use a function that is provided.

Content is a helpful protocol that allows you to write structs or classes for your inputs and outputs.

Requests

In most cases, you want to work with the incoming request. The protocol RoutesBuilder is passing this along into our function. An example controller class could look like this:

```
final class TestController {
    func doSomething(_ req: Request) throws -> String {
        return "we did something"
    }
}
```

As you can see, we are getting the Request object as a parameter of the function. Now we can interact with the data from the request. For example, if you want to parse the incoming body to become a model, you could do it like this:

```
struct InputData: Content {
    var someVariable: String
    var anotherVariable: Int?
}
func parseMe(_ req: Request) throws -> EventLoopFuture<HTTPStatus> {
    let inputData = try req.content.decode(InputData.self)
    print("our input data:", inputData)
    return req.eventLoop.makeSucceededFuture(.ok)
}
```

Our function is taking the request object and accessing the content variable to ask it to decode itself into an InputData instance. This is happening asynchronously which is why we return the EventLoopFuture type here.

Databases and models

Models represent data that is either stored or passed around. Generally speaking, models do not need to be connected to a database. In some cases, you may need a model just as another representation of data you have in another model already.

On the other hand, models are also a great tool to load data in and out of the database. One of the most desired and even most powerful features of Vapor is its **Object-Relational Mapping (ORM)**: Fluent.

In the next two sections, you will explore Fluent as well as its supported databases.

Fluent and FluentKit

FluentKit is an ORM for Swift; Fluent is the Vapor-specific adaption of it. Fluent connects your models to a database and manages to store, delete and query them for you. FluentKit is designed to be framework agnostic, so it can also be used in other server-side frameworks, or in clients as well.

A Fluent model

Let's take a look at the following example model:

```
final class User: Model {
    static let schema = "users"

    @ID(key: "id")
    var id: Int?

    @Field(key: "name")
    var name: String

    init() {
        self.name = ""
    }

    init(id: Int? = nil, name: String) {
        self.id = id
        self.name = name
    }
}
```

The `Model` class is a protocol that ensures our class is conformed to what Fluent needs so that it can work with the data.

Insert

Inserting a new model into the database is as simple as this:

```
// .. this must be happening somewhere were we have a Worker
let user = User()
user.name = "Steve Jobs"
return user.create(on: request.db) // returns a EventLoopFuture<User>
```

Saving models with Fluent means that the operation must run in the event loop and this must happen asynchronously.

Update

Updating an existing model is just as simple as saving it as follows:

```
// .. "user" is an instance of User
user.name = "Tim Cook"
return user.update(on: request.db) // returns a EventLoopFuture<User>
```

 If you aren't sure whether to create or update a model, you can also use "`save(on:)`"; it will determine, based on the primary ID, whether or not to update or create.

Delete

Deleting a model works – very similar to update and create – like this:

```
user.delete(on: request.db) // returns EventLoopFuture<Void>
```

Vapor differentiates between a hard and a soft delete. A hard delete means the entry is deleted from the database. A soft delete only marks an entry as deleted – which says it can be restored.

To enable soft deletes, you have to specify the key to the variable/column in the model like this:

```
final class MyModel: Model {
    // ...
    @Field(key: "deletedAt")
    var deletedAt: Date?
}
```

 It is usually best to use a soft delete, at least for a while. You can always delete them later; however, in practical terms, it has proven beneficial to keep entries for at least a few days after they are deleted.

Querying

One of the most frequently required functions is to find entries in the database. Fluent offers a variety of ways for how to do that. You will not learn all of them in this section, but you will gain a general idea instead.

All queries start with the model and then `query(on:)`, which initializes the `QueryBuilder`. After you have the `QueryBuilder`, you can apply as many filters as needed, determine the order and offsets, and get your results.

If you wanted to find a single model, the following function would do that for you:

```
Model.find(1337, on: request.db) // returns EventLoopFuture<Model> and
looks for the model with ID 1337
```

In case you are looking to build a more complex query, take a look at the following examples:

```
// The next query is equivalent to the first example above.
Model.query(on: request.db).filter(\.$id == 1337).all()
// returns a Future<[Model]>
// This is how you can an "or" or and "and"
Model.query(on: request.db).or { or in
    or.filter(\.$id == 1337)
        .filter(\.$id == 1338)
}
```

The `\.$id` notation refers to Swift's reflection features and is short for `\Model.$id`. It returns a reference to the variable within that class. Fluent then converts it into a valid SQL statement.

The following operators are available by default:

Operator	Type
==	Equal
!=	Not equal
>	Greater than
<	Less than
>=	Greater than or equal
<=	Less than or equal
~~	Contains; for `String`, this is LIKE `%foo%` and, for `Array`, this is IN `(...)`
!~	Does not contain; for `String`, this is NOT LIKE `%foo%` and, for `Array`, this is NOT IN `(...)`

Now, let's take a look at the supported databases.

Supported databases

Fluent is currently supporting the following databases:

- MySQL
- PostgreSQL
- Redis
- SQLite

Vapor does not have a native NoSQL driver. However, a community-provided package uses the MongoKitten driver. In this book, you will be using MySQL, but it is relatively easy to change that to PostgreSQL if you wanted to. NoSQL is an approach good for certain cases; in my experience, it is better to start with a relational database, though. Relation databases force you to plan your structure ahead of time, which pays off in the end when you have a lot of data. On the other hand, NoSQL can lead to data inconsistencies.

Views

Vapor provides a template system called Leaf. Leaf allows you to write templates with some logic in them and interact with controllers. Leaf templates end with `*.leaf` and are usually stored in the `/Resources/Views` folder.

Conveniently, you can return the rendering of a view as an `EventLoopFuture` type directly:

```
app.get("myTemplate") { req -> EventLoopFuture<View> in
    return req.view.render("example", ["name": "Vapor"])
}
```

In this case, `/myTemplate` is returning the content of `example.leaf` in the `/Resources/Views` folder and is passing forward a `"name"` variable that is set to `"Vapor"`. The template should look like this:

```
Hi #(name)!
```

If you need to show HTML pages with Vapor, you should check out the extensive documentation that is available for Leaf under `docs.vapor.codes`. Microservices might serve HTML directly, but their real intent is more geared toward providing an API. You will not need to write templates in this book, as most microservices do not serve HTML directly.

Comparing Vapor to Kitura, Perfect, and Smoke

In this section, you are going to learn a few key differences between Vapor and the other Swift frameworks. All frameworks are being used by various industries and players. Vapor does stand out as it emerged as a favorite on GitHub with having significantly more stars and active contributors than the other frameworks.

The three alternative Swift frameworks are as follows:

- Kitura
- Perfect
- Smoke

Let's explore each one of them.

Vapor and Kitura

Kitura started at around the same time as Vapor did, but it was, in fact, started by IBM. The most obvious and noteworthy difference between Vapor and Kitura is that Kitura is loosely modeled after the Express Javascript framework. Other APIs and libraries within the framework are similarly modeled after existing popular frameworks. For example, the templating system, Stencil, is modeled after Django and Mustache. In contrast, Vapor's overall design was originally somewhat modeled after Laravel (PHP); in this way, every aspect of Vapor has been developed to be as native to Swift as possible.

Kitura is released as fully open source under the Apache 2.0 license, whereas Vapor is released under MIT.

Both Kitura and Vapor use SwiftNIO, so they offer similar features. The reason Kitura was not chosen for this book is that Vapor provides a more Swift-native experience and has a significantly more active community.

Vapor and Perfect

Perfect was the first framework to allow Swift to run on the server. It was released even before Apple released Swift as open source. In contrast to Kitura and Vapor, Perfect is not very opinionated when it comes to styles and guidelines.

Similar to Kitura, Perfect was modeled after Express.

The most significant difference between Perfect and Vapor is that Perfect has not incorporated SwiftNIO yet. To this day, Perfect utilizes existing C libraries for its network activity. This can make debugging difficult and can create inconsistent APIs, which is why Perfect was not chosen for this book.

Vapor and Smoke

The Smoke framework is the most recent addition to the Swift server frameworks, as it only came out in 2019. It is developed by Amazon and is designed to address microservices behind existing cloud provider structures, such as AWS API Gateway. Smoke is not actively trying to be a contender like Vapor or Kitura. It is mostly geared toward AWS integrations. It was not chosen for this book because not every microservice application should and will run on AWS – so, you should select a cloud provider agnostic framework, which Smoke is not.

 While Smoke is – generally speaking – limited in its use, if you need specific small functions in AWS (such as in Lambda), you might find it very useful to have a Swift framework that can help you out (instead of having to switch to Java, Python, or another language).

Installing Vapor

Now it is time to install Vapor onto your machine. Let's make sure that you have all you need. It is essential that you use an up-to-date system in order for Swift and Vapor to function correctly. I am assuming that you are working on a macOS computer for this book. Everything server-related should also work fine on a Linux machine, though.

Prerequisites

Make sure that you have the following setup already in place:

- macOS Mojave or newer
- Xcode 10.2 or newer
- Homebrew: If you have not installed Homebrew, then go ahead and install it as described here: `https://brew.sh/`

 You could use Linux (Ubuntu) as well; this book assumes you are using macOS, though. The only difference is that Xcode does not exist for Linux but everything else should work the same.

Follow the given steps:

1. With Xcode, you have installed the Swift runtime and compiler already. Check the version by running the following:

   ```
   $ swift --version
   ```

2. It should display a version of 5.2 or newer.
3. Now it is time to install Vapor; we do that by adding the correct tab to Homebrew and installing all the necessary files:

   ```
   $ brew tap vapor/tap
   $ brew install vapor/tap/vapor
   $ brew install vapor-beta
   ```

4. Once this has finished, verify that the installation was successful. Type in the following command, and you should see a list of arguments:

   ```
   $ vapor --help
   ```

   Vapor is delivering a small toolbox as well, which is essentially putting together common controls for the SPM, for example.

Now we are ready to run our very first Vapor application!

Vapor in Action

After you have installed Vapor and understand its basic principles, let's install the API template to get started. Run the following command:

```
$ vapor new FirstApp
```

This command is telling Vapor to download the most recent version of their API starter template. It's a preconfigured set of files that are a good starting point for API applications. Follow the given steps:

1. Switch into the folder that contains FirstApp by typing the following:

   ```
   $ cd FirstApp
   ```

2. Now, let's create an Xcode project:

   ```
   $ open Package.swift
   ```

3. The preceding command will open the project for you automatically. You will now see the project and the structure you have learned about.

4. To run a Vapor application in Xcode you must make sure that you are running the "Run" target. It might default to another one. To run correclty it should look like this:

That's all for this chapter. Let's move to the summary.

Summary

In this chapter, you have learned the basic principles of Vapor and how it operates. You have seen Vapor's advantages over the other frameworks and why it is a great choice for microservices. After installing Vapor, you have run your very first Vapor application and have seen the result.

Please spend some time playing with Vapor in order to familiarize yourself with the framework. This chapter cannot cover all that Vapor can offer for you, but it should be a good starting point. You can visit `docs.vapor.codes` for more information. This chapter is introducing the relevant parts of Vapor to you, which you will need to write microservices. You should familiarize yourself with the official Vapor documentation, though, as this chapter cannot cover everything and the framework is constantly evolving.

In the next chapter, we are planning our e-commerce example backend in detail.

Questions

When you feel comfortable, answer the following questions to verify your understanding. The questions for this section are broader in nature and should lead you to study Vapor in more detail:

1. Add a new route to your FirstApp application that interacts with a new controller.
2. Add a new model to your application and integrate it into your controllers.
3. Build a simple pagination app in which the requests can contain parameters such as `sortBy` and `offset`.

4
Planning an Online Store Application

By now, you have learned about microservices in general and server-side Swift and Vapor. Now it is time to put all of that into practice and start building our example project. You are going to develop the backend for an e-commerce application. Let's pretend you have already made an iOS app that serves as the frontend, but you have not built the backend for it yet. In this chapter, you are going to plan the server application for your store. You may have worked on several backends before; you may have never touched a backend in your life. This chapter will catch you up, and you will come up with a concrete plan.

A programmer saying goes that you should spend 90% planning and 10% writing code. While reality does not always hold up to this, it is essential to plan well. By the end of this chapter, you should be able to set everything up and start coding.

You will explore the following sections:

- Application layout for an online store
- User Manager
- Product Manager
- Order Manager

Let's dive into it and plan!

Technical requirements

This section covers what you will need to have running on your machine so that you can write this microservice. The following components need to be installed:

- Vapor Toolbox
- Swift 5.2+
- Xcode 11+
- Docker
- macOS/Linux

We are also assuming that you have worked through the previous chapters. All code in this chapter will run alike under macOS and Linux.

The GitHub URL for this chapter is `https://github.com/PacktPublishing/Hands-On-Swift-5-Microservices-Development/tree/master/Chapter 4`.

Application layout for an online store

Every backend is different and has different requirements. In this section, you are going to learn how to design a microservice application for our online store example.

Let's start by discussing what you need for an online store. Let's assume that your iOS app has the following features:

- Show products in categories.
- Filter products according to their attributes.
- Put products in your basket.
- Check out your basket with a payment method.
- Log in.
- Register a new account.
- See all orders for a user.

 We could add a lot more functions to this list. However, this book is designed to teach you the basics, so you can write your applications using the methods and approaches used here.

You will now learn about the following topics:

- Frontend to API communication: The basics of app communications
- Authentification: How to secure a backend/application
- Database management: A few guidelines on how we will store data
- Cloud support: Embrace the cloud—it has a lot to offer

Frontend to API communication

The most common API architecture is REST. REST stands for **Re**presentational **S**tate **T**ransfer and means that every API call is independent of the state—previous API calls do not directly influence the current one. Stateless microservices are helpful, even necessary, in a setup where we have no guarantee *when* an API call succeeds or fails. So, we are building our store backend as a **REST API**.

REST APIs usually operate on HTTP; it is a common standard and easy to deal with. Through HTTP, we have a variety of methods we can use, and the ones we will use are POST, GET, PUT, DELETE, OPTIONS, and PATCH.

The HTTP protocol itself also offers a few ways to pass information *to* the server. It's either part of the URL (for example, /orders/42) or the body of a request (commonly known as the POST body).

JSON has become the default standard of modern API communication. Its format is easy to read and write and is usually sufficient for most use cases. Our online shop API will rely on JSON as well. There are various implementations for potential clients, so it is a safe bet to design an API with JSON as the primary input and output.

For our API, we will set the following standards for consistency:

- GET and DELETE endpoints take input in the form of query parameters (/getEndpoint?parameter=value).
- POST, PUT, and PATCH endpoints take input in the form of JSON-encoded strings.
- OPTIONS endpoints simply return a status code; they ignore all inputs.
- *ALL* methods can read from the URL itself (/get/order/:id) where the last part can be read.

Authentification

People need to be able to register and log in to our store. The microservices, particularly the order management service, will need to know the users' identity to save order information correctly.

You are going to look at authentication generically and then specifically for microservices.

Generic authentication

For a microservice, and generally every server application, to verify the user's identify, the client transmits a token to the server that contains a key that the server can associate to a specific user. The token is often transported through the headers of a request. A common way for traditional web applications is to save this kind of information in cookies; for mobile apps, you would save the token just in your local storage. In theory, the key that associates to a user could be merely the user ID in the database. This would be the case if you only saved the user ID in a cookie and transmitted this to the server with every request. Consequently, the browser (and user) could change the value and manipulate which user we are operating as. As you want to develop secure applications, do not only use the user ID as a token. Believe it or not, I have seen this happen in applications that were used by companies that should have known how this is done properly.

For the last two decades, people have mostly used what is called "sessions." It is essentially a database table that contains several random keys and associates information to them; the database can be in files or a relational database (SQL). So, in this case, we would tell the client a random key and save that key with the user ID in the session table. We would then be able to associate that key with the user we kept the key with.

If you only use one server, you could save your sessions locally in the RAM and, therefore, enjoy excellent performance. In a microservice setup, we cannot do that though because the services might (and probably will) run on different machines without access to a shared RAM.

Microservice authentication

Microservice setups usually have one microservice dedicated to authentification. The servers register and save the user information (such as email and password) and verify logins.

For the other microservices to verify requests, the following happens:

1. The user logs in with the authentification manager.
2. The authentification manager returns a security token.
3. Another microservice can verify this token with the authentification manager to verify the user's identity.

As you can imagine, it would be quite a bit of back and forth for every request to be verified with the authentification manager. Some microservices applications do this, though a lot more optimized. Cases in which this type of authentification is needed are banking transactions, for example. Whenever you want to be sure that you can block a user's access without any delay, you will need a real-time authentification system, as described earlier.

Another way to do authentification is if we use a fast key-value database system such as Redis, which is shared across all microservices. Then, tokens, user IDs, and access information can be accessed by all microservices alike. This, however, requires having a Redis server up and running, which is not always feasible or desirable as it adds complexity and cost.

JSON Web Tokens

In many other cases, however, we can use a more performant approach that does not compromise on security either: **JSON Web Tokens** (**JWTs**).

The approach differs only slightly from the preceding one:

1. The user logs in with the authentication manager.
2. The authentication manager returns a security token that contains the user information, encrypted.
3. Another microservice can now self-verify the token and get the relevant user information out of the token.

A JWT consists of three parts:

- Header: This describes the algorithm used for the signature as well as the nature of the token. In many cases, it looks similar to this: `{"alg": "HS256", "typ": "JWT"}`.
- Payload: Here we have the data we care about most, user information and timing information, for example, `{"exp": 1555701217, "uid": 1337, "name": "My Name"}`.

- Signature: This uses the preceding algorithm to sign the base64-encoded header and payload. The signature is the resulting hash string. The hash is generated with a private key that corresponds to a public key.

 Important: the header and the payload are readable for anyone who has the token. Do not ever save sensitive information in JWTs.

When a microservice receives a request with a JWT and needs to verify the user, the microservice can use the public key and verify that the signature has been signed by the correct auth server. If that is the case, the service can use the information from the payload safely since the signature has been validated.

Did you notice something? In this approach, a microservice can validate the JWT without having to interact with a database or the authentication server. It saves a lot of time and resources.

You might wonder now what to do when a user logs out or leaves the page—when does a JWT lose its validity? The answer is that in almost all cases you want to put an "expiration time" inside the payload of the JWT. Above the exp does it for us by defining the time when this JWT expires and should be rejected. So, a typical logout would look like the client deleting the existing JWT and thereby removing access.

Renewing JWTs

As JWTs expire (or lose their validity another way), we need a way for them to be renewed. One way would be to initiate the "login" process again. However, it requires us to have the login credentials ready. You do not want to save those in any way, for security reasons. The most common way to allow JWTs to renew is to provide two JWTs at once, as explained in the following.

Access token

The so-called "access token" refers to a JWT that has a short lifespan, usually between 5 and 60 minutes. During that time, the token is valid, and the user can use it. When it expires, the token has to be renewed. The reason this token has a short lifespan is that you can control it better. Every time the token is renewed, you can check again whether or not this user is still authorized to act with your app.

It's important to note that this is—obviously—not real time! But that's okay; for most cases, you do not need to block users in real time. If you do, set the lifespan to 30 seconds—that's still better than 0 seconds and gives you near-real-time control.

Refresh token

The refresh token is just another token (it can be JWT but doesn't need to be) that is used to refresh the access token. The refresh token has to be used with the authentication manager directly—not with any of the other microservices. This allows us to verify the user is *still* allowed to stay logged in. If you had to delete or block a user's access, you would flag the user so that your authentication manager would not renew the access token.

 The access/refresh token setup is not tied to JWT. I have seen implementations with this approach that did not use JWTs but operated, in essence, the same way.

Block access

Sometimes, you may need to block access for a particular user. Depending on the nature of your application, you may want this to take effect immediately or soon after you block the user. If you need it to happen quickly, you could do one of two things:

- Have very short lifespans for access tokens (such as 30-300 seconds)
- Have a blacklist of tokens

The first method might question whether it makes sense to even use this approach at all, but if you have a lot of requests, connecting to the authentication service only once every 30 seconds versus every request might make a big difference.

The second approach is something that could be offloaded to the load balancer. The load balancer would know which tokens to block and not grant access immediately.

Database management

While every microservice is unique and could have its own database design and conventions, let's agree on a few points that will unify the design of our microservices:

- The database engine is MySQL. If you wanted to use PostgreSQL, the principle remains the same.
- Every entity has a numeric ID. This is central to good database design; every entry in a table has to have a unique **Identifier (ID)**. For simplicity purposes, we keep it numerical and start with ID 1. Note: even big applications usually don't deviate from this approach. The field for this ID will always be called `id`. You could also use a **Universally Unique IDentifier (UUID)** for `id`—that is a matter of preference and relates to the purpose of the application.
- We use `camelCase` for names. This is solely preference, but it saves us from having to use underscores (_) between words and is, in my opinion, just as easy to read. An entity that associates products to orders would, therefore, be `OrderProduct` (as opposed to `Order_Product`). Entity names start with an uppercase letter whereas database tables start in lowercase. Note: some database systems, such as PostgreSQL, prefer `snake_case`.
- The database tables are plural. So, instead of `order`, we are using `orders`.

All of these points are mostly preference and can be adjusted to your liking.

Cloud support

The cloud is our friend, not our enemy! Some people want to develop applications as generically as possible, and it is certainly wise to not end up in a situation where only one vendor can deliver what you need. That being said, there is nothing wrong with embracing elements from the cloud even if they are a bit specific from one vendor to another.

For the application we are developing here, we are going to use the following elements from the cloud:

- Storage for product images
- Managed database servers for our databases
- Virtual servers to run our applications
- Docker-enabled container management to manage our containers
- Load balancing to redirect traffic

As you can see, this list is, compared to the offerings of cloud providers, fairly generic and you could easily switch from one provider to the next, or even set up your system if you wanted to.

The following table shows the names of the services you find on the most popular cloud providers, AWS, Azure, Google Cloud, and Digital Ocean:

Service	AWS	Azure	Google Cloud	Digital Ocean
Storage	S3	Blog Storage	Cloud Storage	Block Storage
Database	RDS	Azure Database for MySQL	Cloud SQL	Managed Databases
Virtual Servers	EC2	Azure Virtual Machines	Compute Engine	Droplets
Docker Management	ECS / EKS	ACS / AKS	Kubernetes Engine	Kubernetes
Load Balancer	Elastic Load Balancer	Load Balancer	Cloud Load Balancing	Load Balancer

As you can see, each one of the four cloud providers offers services that will fit our needs. Going forward, we will have an example setup with AWS; you could pick any of the ones listed here, though, to run the backend.

User Manager

Let's get started with our first service: **User Manager** (UM).

Our UM should allow us to do the following:

- **Sign Up**
- **Login (Get the Access Token)**
- **Forgot Password**
- **Verify Access Token**
- **Renew Access Token**

That's it—it's a lean and straightforward service but will be a central element for our application. The UM will verify incoming credentials (email and password) and then return an access—as well as a refresh—token to the client. With access and refresh tokens, the client can send requests to the other services and renew the access token when needed.

Models

This service saves only two models:

- User
- Address

The User-Entity contains every user itself, with the basic information. The Address-Entity contains associated addresses for users.

 You should set up and create another microservice for address management during the production phase. As our example is small in nature, we can include them with this server; for address validation and extended features, you should make it its own service though.

User

The user has the following variables:

- Email
- Password Hash
- First Name
- Last Name
- Last Login
- Status

You could add more attributes to a user, but, for our purposes, we will keep it simple. If you use our sample application as a starting point for your shop, you might want to add additional attributes to the user. But we will talk about this in more detail later. The status attribute will determine whether this user is active and can log in.

Address

The addresses we save will be limited to the US only, so the following fields are sufficient:

- Street
- Additional street information (such as apartment and floor)
- City
- Zip
- State

Now let's look at the **Product Manager (PM)**.

Product Manager

The PM serves as our central database and API for everything related to the products. Everything but the images we can save in our database for this service. The pictures we will keep in our cloud storage solution.

 To save a lot of files in the same folder can challenge a filesystem on a server. To keep microservices able to share the same storage, even as multiple instances of the same microservice are running, requires you to centralize the files.

Models

The following models are needed in our product service:

- Products
- Categories
- Product Categories

Products

A product will contain the following attributes:

- Name
- Description
- Price
- Categories
- Images

Category

Furthermore, we will save categories in this service. Categories will only have name as an attribute.

Product Categories

There will be an n:n relationship between categories and products, meaning we can have as many products in as many categories as we want.

The pivot model for us to connect products with categories will have the following attributes:

- Product ID
- Category ID

The two IDs for both the product and the category is all we need to connect the two.

Order Manager

The **Order Manager** (**OM**) is our third service for this project. It is the most advanced service as it will not only have various internal functions but also connect the other two services. PM and UM could technically exist by themselves in other projects. The OM, however, depends on the other two.

The following functions need to be covered:

- Take an order.
- Pay for an order.
- Update order status.
- Return all orders for a user.

While the list of functions is not very long, each one of them has aspects that will make it interesting and complex to implement them.

Models

For this service, we will need the following models:

- Order
- Order product
- Payment

Order

This model contains the necessary information on our order:

- Billing address (name, street, zip, city, and country)
- Shipping address (name, street, zip, city, and country)
- Status of the order
- Paid amount
- Total amount
- Tax amount
- Shipping amount

 Note: we are not saving the products associated with this order here; those will be in another model.

Order Product

Here, we are connecting `Order` with `Product`. To associate the two, we only need the IDs:

- Product ID
- Order ID
- Quantity
- Item amount (individual value)
- Tax amount (individual value)
- Total amount

We are saving the amount of one individual item as well as the tax for this one item. The total amount then is as follows:

```
total amount = quantity * (item amount + tax amount)
```

The total amount of `Order` will then be the sum of all `Order Product IDs`.

Payment

This is the model that will store any payment information for an order. Note that an order might have multiple payments, for example, a customer might pay with two different credit cards:

- Payment type (credit card, cash, PayPal, and so on)
- Amount (total value)
- Reference ID
- Order ID

The Reference ID is a value that we get from a third party, such as a credit card processor. The reason we want to save this is that we might need to issue refunds—and then we need this value.

API structure

The following diagram displays how our application will work conceptually:

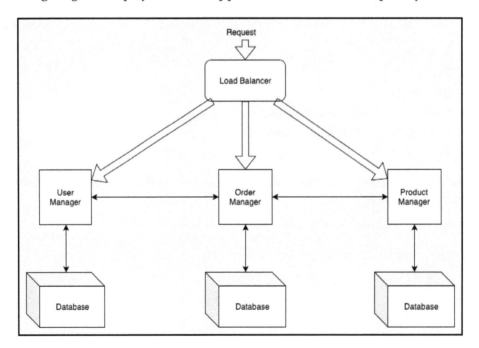

You can easily see the connections between the microservices and how each one has its own database. This setup could be hosted in the cloud as well as on dedicated servers and even on a single server if you needed it to.

Summary

In this chapter, you prepared and learned what our application needs from our backend. You saw how to structure the microservices and how they connect. By now, you should understand the whole concept behind the backend and feel comfortable implementing each service.

Further, you learned what each service will do and what models it will contain. We compared four cloud service providers that could serve as our hosting platform, and we analyzed the elements we need from the cloud.

Questions

Check your knowledge by answering and working through the following questions:

1. How do you verify that a user has access to a function of a microservice?
2. What is a good lifespan for an access token?
3. Why is JSON a good choice for the inputs and outputs of microservices?

5
Creating Your First Microservice

You made it! The theoretical part is mostly done, and we are now talking code! In this chapter, you will write your first microservice. However, before we write it, you will be introduced to the practical parts of a Vapor application. Using the Vapor framework will help you to write apps faster than if you were to start from scratch. By the end of this chapter, you will have written your first microservice and incorporated the necessary pieces.

In this chapter, you will learn how to develop a generic microservice that will serve as the basis for our online shop backend application. This will also be the basis for all the other services that we will write throughout this book. We will develop a template that will be used to create other services and that you could use for your own projects as well. By the end of this chapter, you will have written your first microservice!

At first, you will configure our package with all the necessary dependencies. Afterward, you will set up and learn how to incorporate models and controllers.

 A lot of the information in this chapter is based on decade-long practical experience. It is possible that you will find other ways, methods, and approaches that work better for you, and that is okay – take this as a starting point that sets you up well.

The following topics will be covered in this chapter:

- Starting a new service
- Using models
- Using controllers
- Using workers

Let's get started!

Technical requirements

This section covers what you will need to have running on your machine so that you can write this microservice. The following components need to be installed:

- Vapor Toolbox
- Swift 5.2+
- Xcode 11+
- Docker
- macOS/Linux

We are also assuming that you have worked through the previous chapters. All code in this chapter will run alike under macOS and Linux.

The GitHub URL for this chapter is `https://github.com/PacktPublishing/Hands-On-Swift-5-Microservices-Development/tree/master/Chapter 5`.

Starting a new service

In this section, we are going to set everything up for our first microservice. A microservice is essentially just like every other backend application; that is, it is only configured and set up to operate in a network of services. There are a couple of implications and best practices that make networking much more manageable. Because the service is not addressing humans, we can be a lot more mechanical in the way we design it.

We will look into the following topics:

- Version control: Keeping an excellent track of what we changed when
- Using the API template: An easy template to use for most services.
- Dependency management: Including the needed packages
- Configuration: Setting it up correctly
- Routes: How to expose the service to the world.

Let's explore!

Version control

This should not even be a discussion point, but, for the sake of completion, *always* save your code in some version control system such as git. While alternatives exist, I highly recommend that you get familiar with git if you aren't already. To host your git repositories, you should use an online cloud-based provider of your choice. GitHub is the most popular with attractive pricing models (including free models too!), but other providers such as GitLab or Bitbucket will do just as well. You do not want to save your code locally on your machine only: hard drives can break, and it will be much more peaceful for you to restore from the cloud.

 GitHub is the most popular git provider. Most server-side Swift projects are currently hosted on GitHub. Unless the owner (that is, Microsoft) changes their policies in dramatic ways, I would not expect that to change. GitHub offers free plans for open source projects.

A word about microservices and repositories – most cloud providers provide some way to deploy backend applications automatically. I recommend the following guidelines for storing your code:

- Use one repository for one microservice only.
- Have a master and a development branch at least.
- Use pull requests to update the master branch.
- The master is the branch that is deployed.
- Automatically deploy from the repository (master) to the server(s).
- Every project should have its own repositories.

It might be tempting to use one repository for multiple projects. In some very general use cases, this might work. However, in my experience, it happens fairly often that you need to customize just a little bit. Furthermore, unless the repositories are open, you might have to deal with various permission-setups, which is a lot easier if each project has its own repository.

So, go ahead and set up your accounts and prepare your repositories. Once you have done that, we can go on to look at how to use the standard API template of Vapor.

Using the API template

If everything is set up correctly, you can create the template by typing the following commands into your command line:

1. Create a new Vapor application:

    ```
    $ vapor-beta new template
    ```

    At the time of writing Vapor's CLI works with Vapor 4 only in beta. Once Vapor 4 is fully released you can also do the following:

    ```
    $ vapor new template
    ```

    Vapor's CLI will now automatically copy the standard API template. You can find the template at `https://github.com/vapor/api-template`; it is a good starting point for APIs.

2. Jump into the newly created folder:

    ```
    $ cd template
    ```

    The template compiles and builds as it is, but we want to modify it a little bit and get it to a good starting point for our own purposes. So, we will do the following:

    - Remove SQLite.
    - Add MySQL.
    - Add the JWT packages.
    - Add CORS middleware.

    By adding these packages, we are equipping the microservice with all that is needed to operate in a microservice architecture. You will learn how to add and remove packages in an upcoming section.

3. Compile the project. This will also load all the current dependencies:

    ```
    $ swift build
    ```

4. To open the project in Xcode, type the following:

    ```
    $ xed .
    ```

Alternatively, you could also open Xcode by opening `Package.swift`. In the terminal, you can do this as follows:

```
$ open Package.swift
```

Now that you have successfully compiled the template, let's take a look at the components of a Vapor application.

General file folders

We can keep the file structure of the template as it is; it is already providing a nicely organized hierarchy. The only folder you want to add is `Workers` on the same level as `Controllers`, so you should add it to `Sources/App/`. In this folder, we may put classes that act as *Workers* for us. In the *Workers* section, later on, you will learn in detail why we need such a folder.

Additionally, create another `Helpers` folder in `Sources/App/`. This folder is for extensions and functions that are not tied to our own classes but are either generic (global) or extended classes from other frameworks.

You can leave the remaining folders and files as they are. We will stick to a few guidelines, though, to keep things consistent:

- Filenames should be capitalized.
- There should be one class or struct per file.
- The class, function, or struct name should be the filename.
- Extension files use the + sign to label the original class. For example, the `Application+ImageRequest.swift` file would extend the `Application` class with functions related to image requests.

Go ahead and make any non-capitalized filenames capitalized (except for `main.swift`; the compiler requires this to be spelled in lowercase). Swift is not strict with the folders or filenames, but it will make it a lot easier to pick this project up later or have someone else work with it.

 During active development, it is entirely human to break some of these rules. Just make sure that you clean them up before committing them to a repository.

Now that you have set up the folders, let's set up our dependencies.

Dependency management

With server-side Swift projects, it frequently happens that you need to add or remove dependency packages. Let's explore an example of how that works next.

Adding and removing packages

We need to remove SQLite since we won't be using it:

1. Go ahead and remove the following line from `Package.swift`:

   ```
   .package(url: "https://github.com/vapor/fluent-sqlite-driver.git",
   from: "4.0.0"
   ```

2. Then, add a line in that same section:

   ```
   .package(url: "https://github.com/vapor/fluent-mysql-driver.git",
   from: "4.0.0"),
   ```

   This adds the MySQL Fluent package to the project. Note that this also adds the general Fluent package, so there is no need to add that as well.

3. Now you will need to change the following line:

   ```
   .target(name: "App", dependencies: ["Fluent", "FluentSQLiteDriver",
   "Vapor"]),
   ```

   You can change the preceding line to the following:

   ```
   .target(name: "App", dependencies: ["Fluent", "FluentMySQLDriver",
   "Vapor"]),
   ```

   This makes Fluent and FluentMySQL available to the project.

4. You can add the following packages in the same way now:

   - `https://github.com/proggeramlug/SimpleJWTMiddleware` the master branch

   You should end up with a `.target` line that looks like this:

   ```
   .target(name: "App", dependencies: ["FluentMySQLDriver", "Vapor",
   "SimpleJWTMiddleware"]),
   ```

5. After we have this setup, we can run the following:

   ```
   $ swift package update
   ```

Note that if you have done this all in Xcode, then Xcode will automatically update your dependencies.

This will cause Swift to update your dependencies. Note that it might take a minute or two to load all the packages. If you encounter any errors, then make sure you have spelled the package names correctly.

 In the GitHub folder for this chapter, you will find a fully working example of this service. Use it to compare it with your own version.

6. If you have not opened Xcode yet, you can do that now:

```
$ open Package.swift
```

After having set up the template, we are now ready to adjust the configuration.

Configuration

The API Standard Template comes with a `configuration.swift` file that contains one function as follows:

```
public func configure(_ app: Application) throws {
```

This function is called when the application starts up. We use it to add all the configuration that we need for the app, including middlewares, services, configuration, server, and more.

We want to add some middlewares, services, and configuration that we will certainly need. Let's do that next.

Middleware

Add the following middleware to your configuration:

```
app.middleware.use(CORSMiddleware())
```

The middleware we need are as follows:

- CORS: Respond to browser CORS requests.
- SimpleJWTMiddleware; however, we do not need to add it here as we will do that later on during the routes setup.

We do need to pass a JWKS to our application that will contain the appropriate keys, we can do that like this:

```
guard let jwksString = Environment.process.JWKS else {
        fatalError("No value was found at the given public key
        environment 'JWKS'")
    }
```

The `JWTKit` package provided by Vapor allows us to set JWT credentials in a variety of ways; this one is the easiest to set up.

So add the following line below the app.database.use() statement:

```
try app.jwt.signers.use(jwksJSON: jwksString)
```

If there is a problem with the JWKS this will prevent the application from starting and therefore not expose any security issue.

Let's set it up next.

CORS

This middleware is answering the `OPTIONS` request by merely returning it positively without doing anything else. Browsers send an `OPTIONS` request to hosts that are different from the originating file. So, for example, if you run your frontend under `https://www.domain.com` and your API from `https://api.domain.com`, then the browsers will send out an `OPTIONS` request because `www.domain.com` is not equal to `api.domain.com`. There is nothing wrong with this, and this handy middleware takes care of it for us.

 You can also forward requests going into `www.domain.com/api` to `api.domain.com` and, by doing so, prevent the requests from leaving the original domain, so browsers won't send this request either. It depends on the frontend design, though, and it does not hurt to install this middleware either way.

Error

This middleware converts all the errors and problems that occur in nicely formatted JSON messages. While you want to prevent this from happening as much as you can, this middleware converts it to the output we are using everywhere.

Services

Now, let's configure some of the services that we will need:

- Router
- DatabaseConfig
- Middleware
- Fluent

Other than the middleware, which we covered in the preceding paragraph, we can install each of these services as follows.

Router

The router is part of `Application`, by using the following line – it is already included in the template:

```
try routes(app)
```

The line calls the `routes(_ application: Application)` function to register the routes we want.

DatabaseConfig

For our database to know where to connect to, we need to configure the credentials:

```
guard let mysqlUrl = Environment.process.MYSQL_CRED else {
    fatalError("No value was found at the given public key environment
     'MYSQL_CRED'")
}
guard let url = URL(string: mysqlUrl) else {
    fatalError("Cannot parse: \(mysqlUrlString) correctly.")
}
app.databases.use(try DatabaseDriverFactory.mysql(url: url),
 as: DatabaseID.mysql)
```

You can see that, first, we check whether we have the minimum credential variable available. We need this to connect to the database; so, if we don't have it, we will get an error (which will prevent the application from starting). After we have verified it, then we have all we need to register the `MySQLDatabase` (that is, a `Service`) with that configuration.

If we want all of the queries to the database logged in the standard logger, we just need to pass an application to the `--log debug` argument. I have found this argument to be useful for debugging and understanding what is happening under the hood.

Fluent

Now that we have the database installed, we can install the migrations to Fluent, which will create our database tables for us:

```
app.migrations.add(CreateTodo())
```

Here we can repeat the line for every one of the `Model` classes that we want to be in the database. After registering the migrations, we should be done as the standard settings will cover all of the rest.

Our setup is now complete in regard to everything but the routes. Let's take a look at those next!

Routes

Routes are the endpoints of our API; they define what URL to call to trigger a server response. As they are, by nature, very service-dependent, there is not too much that we can prepare here. We want to define only one route that every service will share:

```
/*/serviceName/health
```

This URL will be used by our hosting infrastructure to ensure that the service is working correctly. In this case, we will also provide the controller function right within the `routes` function.

Write the following code into your `Routes.swift`:

```swift
import Fluent
import Vapor

func routes(_ app: Application) throws {
    app.get([.anything, "name", "health"]) { req in
        return "Healthy!"
    }

    // additional routes
}
```

In future services, we will need to replace the `"name"` variable inside the first route here. Since it is a manual process to create microservices and we should not fall into the habit of oversimplifying the setup process, this should not be a constant variable. Instead, it should be set manually every time you set up a new service.

Alright, next, let's look at models so that we can interact with a database.

Using models

Models are used whenever you need to store data and move it around. We will differentiate between two types of models, as follows:

- **Input and output (I/O) models**
- **Database (DB) models**

The difference between these two models is that I/O models mainly contain information only to pass it on. For example, a request has a payload (for example, the POST body) that contains information that should be stored. The data is parsed into an I/O model. To save this information, you need to convert the I/O model into a DB Model. You might be wondering why we don't combine the two into the same class or struct.

Well, unless it is a straightforward model – and I have not seen many of those – you almost always need to customize the inputs and outputs compared to what you have in the database. For example, consider timestamps: you save them in the database and they are usually saved as a sort of string that represents the time within the server's time zone. Now, you want to make it an output but you need to consider the user's time zone, which might be different to the time zone that the database is based on.

You could either modify the model to return a different value if it is asked for on request or – my preferred option – you could have a separate model that specifically deals with those cases. DB models can be pretty complicated and broad; only very occasionally will you want to output the entire model as it is.

Let's take a look at some examples:

- I/O models: Models that contain the information *from* and *to* the user
- DB models: Models that we use *to store data* in the database
- Returning DB models: Creating an I/O Model for a DB model
- Predefined models

I/O models

One typical model that almost every application encounters is the Login model. It holds all the data a user enters when logging in, for example, an email and password. In its more primitive form, it would look like the following:

```
struct LoginInput: Content {
    let email: String
    let password: String
}
```

When the user has logged in successfully, you will want to return some of the user information and then access and refresh the tokens. Notice that, here, you already wish for a different model than the user DB model itself, because you don't want to return the password hash.

So, the returning I/O model would look like this:

```
struct LoginOutput: Content {
    let userId: Int
    let email: String
    let firstname: String?
    let lastname: String?
    let accessToken: String
    let refreshToken: String
}
```

Generally speaking, you almost always want to define separate input and output models.

Let's take a look at DB models next.

DB models

We have defined I/O models in the preceding section, so now let's set the corresponding user model for this – that is, the DB models. Take a look at the following code:

```
final class User: Model {
    var firstname: String?
    var lastname: String?
    var email: String
    var passwordHash: String
    var lastLoginTime: Date?
    var registrationTime: Date
}
```

As you can see, this model has a lot more information, and we only request a fraction of it when logging in. We also need this model to be a subclass of `MySQLModel` so that it can be stored in our database. There is also some overhead we can avoid by not using this model publicly.

But what if you want to output the whole model in the request? Well, depending on the nature of the model, you *might* extend it by content and return the model as it is. It is cleaner and easier to maintain, however, to create a separate output model – even if it is 95% the same code. Consider that you might need to adjust to some client requests as well. For example, a specific client library (such as JavaScript or iOS) might expect you to have a particular format when returning the data. Through your output models, you can quickly satisfy that request.

And what if you want to output the user login as described previously? Let's take a look at how we can combine these two types of models next.

Returning DB models

To return the user model is relatively simple: create a new instance of the output model and assign the values to it. Thanks to Swift's extensions, you can do it like this:

```
extension UserOutput {
    init(withUser user: User, accessToken: String, refreshToken: String) {
        self.userId = user.id
        self.email = user.email
        self.firstname = user.firstname
        self.lastname = user.lastname
        self.accessToken = accessToken
        self.refreshToken = refreshToken
    }
}
```

To return the user, we now only have to call the following:

```
return UserOutput(withUser: user, ...)
```

We will complete these models in `Chapter 7`, *Writing the User Service*, when we write the User Manager Service.

Predefined models

You might be wondering whether you can and should predefine models for all your services together, meaning they would share the same models even though the services operate independently. There is no simple answer to this; it really depends on whether your services will share a lot of information. Some of your services might not require any shared models, whereas others would. In general, you will not have to copy DB models. By definition, they should stay unique within the architecture. Otherwise, you might want to reconsider your application design.

On the other hand, it might make perfect sense to define some I/O models that can be used across different services. One model that you would certainly need in most services would be the payload from the **JSON Web Tokens** (**JWTs**). It could look like this:

```
struct Payload: Content {
    var userId: Int
    var permissionLevel: Int
    // ...
}
```

With this model, every service can access the data from the JWT (with the help of some JWT packages). You can go ahead and put the model in the `Sources/App/Models/` folder and call it `Payload.swift`.

Let's now look at the controllers that will take data in and return outputs that the client, your app, can work with.

Using controllers

As we have already mentioned, a controller function is a function the router calls when a request comes in and addresses a particular path. It can look this simple:

```
router.get("hello") { req in
    return "Hello, world."
}
```

We can, of course, specify more than just that. Here are some examples:

```
router.post("hello", use: myPostFunction)
router.patch("hello", use: controllerClass.helloPatch)
```

You can see that we only need to specify a function for the router that can be called and that returns a `ResponseEncodable` object.

A lot of other classes can be made to conform to the
`ResponseEncodable` protocol. A simple string, for example, is extended
to be a valid return – just like in the preceding case.

Technically, we do not need controller classes because the router only needs functions.
Controller classes are, however, a common and clean way to group functions in logical
segments together. Additionally, we can pass the config of the routes themselves on to the
controller itself and have a self-maintained class that way.

For example, consider the following:

```
try router.register(collection: SampleController()) // sub-url: "/"
// or we want to have a sub-url
try router.grouped("sub").register(collection: SampleController())
// sub-url: "/sub/"
```

And within the controller, we define the routes as follows:

```
final class SampleController: RouteCollection {
    func boot(router: Router) throws {
        router.get(use: get)
        router.get(Int.parameter, use: getById)
        router.patch(Int.parameter, use: edit)
        router.post("new", use: add)
        router.delete(Int.parameter, use: delete)
    }
    // ...
}
```

Here, we are registering the class functions, `get`, `getById`, `edit`, `add`, and `delete`. All
functions are already registered within the sub-URL specified previously.

Interacting with models

Fluent makes it very easy to communicate with models. For our template, we just need to
keep the following things in mind:

- Every database interaction happens on the `eventLoop`.
- Define all models in the models folder. You can potentially create subfolders if
  you want to group some models together.
- Usually, you need two models – one for the DB and one for I/O. Combining the
  two can be dangerous.

Based on my own experience, I cannot emphasize enough how vital the third point is. You will be tempted to combine the two, but in almost all instances, you will end up having to rewrite your model numerous times because you have different requirements for I/O than for the DB.

Other than that, just stick to the way Fluent handles models and you should be fine.

File management

Microservices should be independent enough to not have to rely on the servicing server. This means that, if you take files (such as images) in and store them, then **always** store them in a cloud storage system. **Never** store them on the local file system (except for processing, but even this can almost always happen through the RAM).

If you need to return files, take advantage of cloud distribution systems (such as CloudFront or S3). Most of these systems will allow you to customize access if you have to restrict it, and they also provide caching functionality. Mostly, however, it takes the scalability required out of our microservice and saves your resources. They also have distributed data centers around the world that allow them to serve files much faster than you could. If you do need to return files yourself directly, then still receive them either from your database or from a cloud storage provider before returning them through your service.

In reality, most files will be media files, such as images or videos. Consider using a service like `imgix.com` to help you process them before returning them.

As this functionality is not required for every microservice, we are not adding it to the generic template. When we get to the product, you will see what the implementation looks like though.

SendGrid

Sometimes, you will probably need to send emails to your users. Instead of sending them through the SMTP yourself, you should use a service such as SendGrid. Sending quality emails that are compliant with anti-spam regulations is reasonably hard. SendGrid makes this easy by providing you with an easy-to-use API and properly formatted emails. Their costs are minimal, especially if you are just starting a project. The Vapor community also offers an easy-to-use package that helps you to integrate with SendGrid.

Similar to file management, we do not include SendGrid in our template because we only need it in one service.

In larger projects, you will want to create a generic "notification service" that manages all of your notifications for you. Whether this includes email, text, WhatsApp messages, or telegrams, you can manage individual user settings along with how they are formatted.

We have now set up the template with all the packages that we will need. Let's now take a look at the workers.

Using workers

A worker is a class or struct that performs tasks for us; it is usually a bit more complicated than what a controller would do. Examples of this include converting images, processing orders, and working through batches. In traditional server setups, you would do the same through *cron jobs*.

Depending on the nature of what your workers will do, you could wrap their functionality into a job with the vapor/jobs package. That way, you have automatic retries already given. You can check out the package here: https://github.com/vapor/jobs

And that's it – our template is ready! You can find the full working template in the GitHub repository for this chapter!

Summary

In this chapter, you have worked through creating a template API service that we will reuse for upcoming services. You have written the service and now understand what elements you will need and how they are connected.

You have learned how the template preconfigures common packages, how it sets up Fluent, the way it deals with information, and how it handles credentials. This has equipped you with the ability to write functional microservices that can operate together.

With this template, you are now equipped to work on the microservices for our online shop backend! In the next chapter, we will discuss the application structure and database design.

Questions

Answer the following questions to verify your understanding:

1. Why have we included SimpleJWTMiddleware?
2. How will you most likely run your microservices, and what server environment would you use?
3. Should you define models for your services all together or individually per service?

6
Application Structure and Database Design

After you created your own template for your services, let's now set up the entire project. This chapter will set you up practically so you can work on the backend structure. For a microservice application that involves running multiple applications (on each service) all at once, the setup is vastly different from monolithic development: in a monolithic application, you can test it all by just testing one application. In a microservice setup, you need to test multiple microservices interacting with each other.

The essence of this chapter is to get your system ready for microservice development. You will learn how an application should be structured and how to design your database. We will get really practical in this chapter and set up the folders we need for the chapters to come. You will also learn how to set up Git and Docker, essential tools for microservices. Last but not least, you will learn how to set up Vapor, the database, and our services on your machine. These preparations will pay off when developing the microservices in the next chapters as your system is ready to go.

We will look at the following aspects:

- Understanding project setup and folder structure
- Installing Git and Docker
- Setting up Vapor and the database
- Setting up our services

Let's do this!

Technical requirements

To complete this chapter, you should have the following setup:

- Swift 5 installed
- Vapor Toolbox installed
- Xcode 11+ installed
- macOS
- For Docker, you need the following:
  - Mac hardware must be a 2010 or newer model, with Intel hardware
  - macOS Sierra 10.12 and newer macOS releases are supported
  - At least 4 GB of RAM
  - VirtualBox prior to version 4.3.30 must **not** be installed

While all of this would work with Linux just the same, the illustrations in this chapter will show macOS.

The code files for this chapter can be found here: `https://github.com/PacktPublishing/Hands-On-Swift-5-Microservices-Development/tree/master/Chapter 6/Shop Backend/template`.

Understanding project setup and folder structure

Let's start by setting up the folders for our project. It is important for a microservice project to have a clean folder setup to keep everything organized. We will need folders for the following microservices:

- `OrderService`: Our order processing service, which processes the payment and saves the order
- `ProductService`: Our product service that delivers the product information
- `UserService`: Our user service that manages user accounts

Follow the steps given here:

1. Create a new folder for the project and name it `Shop Backend`. You can put this folder anywhere on your computer. You want to keep everything organized in one central place on your development machine.

2. Create a `template` folder and move the code of the template we created in `Chapter 5`, *Creating Your First Microservice* into it.

3. Create three empty folders called `OrderService`, `ProductService`, and `UserService`.

    By the end, the folder structure should look like the one given here:

It's mostly based on personal preference these days, but I prefer to not use spaces for actual project folders. Any computer can deal with it these days, but it doesn't look as nice when you are using your terminal or console, and it is printed as `Order\ Service`.

4. After you have copied the template in the template folder, go ahead and copy the template in the other three folders as well. You might wonder why we need to copy the same code in so many places. We will modify this code and work with it. The changes might be small in some cases, but you want to keep it organized and neat instead, even if it is the same code multiple times, rather than combine too many things and end up in a mess (believe me, I have done this myself often enough).

5. Go into your console and open the project folder. In case you are not used to working with the console a lot, the following commands will help you out:

`ls`	Lists all files and folders in the current folder
`cd <foldername>`	Opens a folder based on the given name
`pwd`	Prints out the folder you are currently in
`cd (no argument)`	Goes to your home folder

6. Go into the `Shop Backend` folder and then execute the `xed .` command in each of the project folders. This command will open the project in Xcode. You will be using the terminal/console a fair amount when dealing with services, so get used to it!

Now that the files are set up, let's set up Git and Docker so that we can save our code properly and publish our application through Docker.

Installing Git and Docker

Git and Docker are the two essential tools that we will be using to manage our code and our builds apart from our local machine. In this section, we will install them both and explore how they are helping us.

We will look at the following topics:

- Installing Git
- Installing Docker
- Using Docker with microservices
- Using Git and Docker

Let's get started!

Installing Git

Luckily, Git is in all likelihood already installed if you are using macOS. You can simply verify this by writing the following command in the terminal:

```
$ git --version
```

The result should look like this:

```
$ git --version
git version 2.21.0 (Apple Git-120)
```

If it does not look like this, you may have to install Git, which the preceding command will prompt you to do. When installing Xcode, which you should have done by this point, Git is also installed.

 If you are using Linux and you need to install Git, you can just do that by running `sudo apt install git-all` or `sudo dnf install git-all`, depending on your Linux flavor.

And that should be it—easy, right? Now, let's install Docker!

Installing Docker

In contrast to Git, Docker is not automatically installed with Xcode. To install Docker, go through the following steps:

1. Open
   `https://hub.docker.com/editions/community/docker-ce-desktop-mac` and download `Docker for Mac`. You will need to register to download Docker.

2. Double-click on `Docker.dmg` and go through the installation process. Once finished, you will see the Docker icon in your top bar:

3. Verify that everything is set up by running `docker version` in the Terminal. It should look like this:

```
[amlug@amlug:~$ docker version
Client: Docker Engine - Community
 Version:           18.09.2
 API version:       1.39
 Go version:        go1.10.8
 Git commit:        6247962
 Built:             Sun Feb 10 04:12:39 2019
 OS/Arch:           darwin/amd64
 Experimental:      false

Server: Docker Engine - Community
 Engine:
  Version:          18.09.2
  API version:      1.39 (minimum version 1.12)
  Go version:       go1.10.6
  Git commit:       6247962
  Built:            Sun Feb 10 04:13:06 2019
  OS/Arch:          linux/amd64
  Experimental:     false
```

And that was Docker! Let's explore why Docker and microservices are so connected.

Using Docker with microservices

Docker is a tool that allows applications to run in a virtual system, so a Linux application can run under macOS or Windows through Docker. Docker virtualizes the operation system on a kernel level, which is much more performant than, for example, VirtualBox if you are familiar with that.

Being able to run applications regardless of the actual host system is obviously a very useful feature for servers. Now we can run our application on pretty much any hardware! But there is actually more to it.

Docker allows us to configure a virtual system for our application. We can specify which programs we need to install, what permissions we need, and how everything should be set up. Docker starts the application and it is all just how we defined it to be (in so-called Dockerfiles). This is a very important feature of microservices. Remember that microservices are designed to operate independently. That also means we want to be able to scale them up and down as we please. If we want to start a few hundred instances of our service, we should not have to configure each one of them. And Docker is our solution for that; with it, we can simply define our system setup and start it as many times as we like.

After exploring Docker for microservices, let's look at Git and Docker in the context of our project.

Setting up Docker and Git with AWS and GitHub

By now, you should have installed Git and Docker already. The following two rules are essential for microservices when it comes to Git and Docker:

- Every service needs its own Git repository.
- Every service requires its own Docker repository.

Docker, just like Git, has repositories that save the history and current version of your builds. It will be the Docker repository that is used by your CI to update your microservices:

1. Go ahead and set up your repositories. If you need a starting point, check out AWS ECR: `https://aws.amazon.com/ecr/`
2. Set up a GitHub account (`https://github.com/`) for your Git repositories.
3. Set up an AWS account to host your project.

You can use any other "Git-and Docker-compatible" service; in my experience, AWS and GitHub are easy starting points that allow for growth easily. In AWS, you can set up the repositories within AWS **ECR (Elastic Container Registry)**.

Once you have AWS and GitHub set up, your projects can be connected to both GitHub and AWS, but we will cover that in `Chapter 14`, *Docker and the Cloud*.

Now that you have done the groundwork for GitHub and AWS, let's look at the Vapor and database setup.

Setting up Vapor and the database

At this point, Swift and Vapor are already installed and functional for you. If not, go back to `Chapter 3`. What's left to do is set up your local database environment. Since we are already using Docker, you can easily spin up a MySQL database through Docker. Follow the given steps:

1. Go into your terminal and run the following commands:

```
sudo mkdir /usr/local/opt/mysql
sudo mkdir /usr/local/opt/mysql/8.0
sudo chmod -R ug+w /usr/local/opt/mysql/
```

By executing the preceding commands, we are installing a local database folder that the Docker instance can access. It keeps us from losing our data when we close Docker.

2. Now, grant Docker permission to share information with that folder. Open the preferences for Docker:

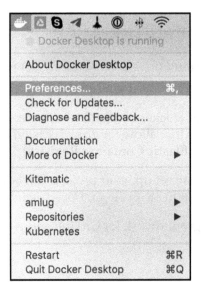

3. Add the folder we just created to the files under **File Sharing** and press **Apply & Restart**:

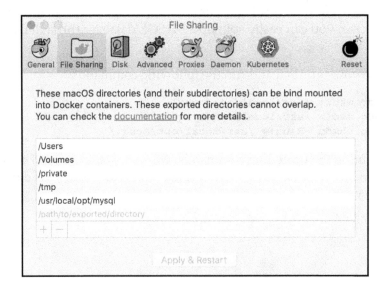

4. Now, we can start our MySQL server, and replace `your_password` with something you are more comfortable with. This is a local server and we are only using it for development purposes. See the following example:

```
docker run --restart always --name mysql8.0 -v
/usr/local/opt/mysql/8.0:/var/lib/mysql -p 3306:3306 -d -e
MYSQL_ROOT_PASSWORD=your_password mysql:8.0
```

5. Let's set up three users and three databases using the following code:

```
mysql -u root -p
mysql> CREATE USER 'service_users'@'localhost' IDENTIFIED BY
'password';
mysql> CREATE USER 'service_products'@'localhost' IDENTIFIED BY
'password';
mysql> CREATE USER 'service_orders'@'localhost' IDENTIFIED BY
'password';
mysql> CREATE DATABASE 'service_users';
mysql> CREATE DATABASE 'service_products';
mysql> CREATE DATABASE 'service_orders';
mysql> GRANT ALL PRIVILEGES ON service_users . * TO
'service_users'@'localhost';
mysql> GRANT ALL PRIVILEGES ON service_products . * TO
'service_products'@'localhost';
mysql> GRANT ALL PRIVILEGES ON service_orders . * TO
'service_orders'@'localhost';
mysql> FLUSH PRIVILEGES;
```

The preceding code creates three users for your database along with three databases and grants the users access to those databases. Each microservice will have its own user and database and this step makes sure they already exist.

6. Make sure you write down the passwords and usernames in a secure password manager. This is for development purposes only so you can (and maybe should?) use passwords you can remember easily.

Now that you have set up the database, we can set up our individual services.

Setting up our services

We will need three services set up for our backend, as seen in the previous chapters. It is time to set up the three services now. This section contains three parts:

- Setting up Dockerfiles
- Setting environment variables
- Running the entire application

Setting up Dockerfiles

A *Dockerfile* is used by Docker to create a new image. It contains the instructions you want Docker to execute to get to the final image. To set up Dockerfiles, follow the given steps:

1. Go into each service folder and open the `Package.swift` file.
2. Name the service accordingly (`UserManager`, `ProductManager`, or `OrderManager`).
3. Now create a `Dockerfile` file in each folder that contains the following commands:

```
FROM swift:5.1.2 as builder

# For local build, add `--build-arg env=docker`
# In your application, you can use `Environment.custom(name:
"docker")` to check if you're in this env

RUN apt-get -qq update && apt-get install -y \
  libssl-dev zlib1g-dev \
  && rm -r /var/lib/apt/lists/*

ARG env
RUN mkdir /root/.ssh/
RUN apt-get -qq update && apt-get install -y \
libssl-dev zlib1g-dev \
&& rm -r /var/lib/apt/lists/*
WORKDIR /app
COPY . .
RUN mkdir -p /build/lib && cp -R /usr/lib/swift/linux/*.so*
/build/lib
RUN swift package --enable-pubgrub-resolver resolve && \
    swift build -c release --verbose && \
    mv `swift build -c release --show-bin-path` /build/bin
```

```
# Production image
FROM ubuntu:18.04
ARG env
# DEBIAN_FRONTEND=noninteractive for automatic UTC configuration
in tzdata
RUN apt-get -qq update && DEBIAN_FRONTEND=noninteractive apt-get
install -y \
libatomic1 libicu60 libxml2 libcurl4 libz-dev libbsd0 tzdata \
&& rm -r /var/lib/apt/lists/*
WORKDIR /app
COPY --from=builder /build/bin/Run .
#COPY --from=builder /build/bin/*.so /usr/lib/
COPY --from=builder /build/lib/* /usr/lib/

ENTRYPOINT ./Run serve --hostname 0.0.0.0 --port 8080
```

The preceding file contains everything you need to potentially run a service in production. So, when Docker takes this file to generate an image that can spin into a server, this file gives Docker everything it needs to run our microservice. The file can be the same for each service; there is no difference.

 This Dockerfile keeps the source code in the image. In some instances, you might want to compile the executable and then only use it in a Docker image, without the source. You want to secure every Docker container no matter what, but not having the source with it might have other security-related reasons.

Most Vapor projects that are based on the Vapor template contain a web.Dockerfile that is equivalent to what we pasted above, you can choose to use that one or what we use above here.

Setting environment variables

To be able to start each service successfully, we need to pass the correct credentials to the application. Vapor uses environment variables, which are stored in the session of the Terminal. So, for you to set up your terminal for a specific service, you will do the following:

```
export MYSQL_CRED="mysql://service_users:your_password@localhost:3306/
service_users?ssl=false"
export JWKS="JWKS-Data"
```

With the first six statements, you are setting the environment variables needed by each service. Remember JWT from the first chapter? We are now setting the JWT data in form of JWKS and pass the value into a JWKS env variable here. You will see this in action in *Chapter 7: Writing the User Service*.

 It makes sense to save these commands in a text file that you can open and copy and paste out of. Vapor 4 uses .env files for this setup, similar to other frameworks as well.

Running the entire application

Now, how do we run the three services at once, you might ask? In essence, you need three terminal instances—one for each service. You can then run each service in a separate session. The only thing to consider is that you will need different ports for each service since you are running them on the same machine. You can do that by running each service like this:

```
./.build/debug/Run serve --port=8080
./.build/debug/Run serve --port=8081
```

This will spin up all services nicely, all at the same time. Now you have set up Docker and the environment variables and you have prepared yourself for running two applications at once.

Summary

In this chapter, you set up everything we need for the online shop backend folder. You created three projects based on our previously generated template, and you set up your database.

You learned how Docker and Git are essential tools for the development of microservices. Both are set up and you might already have an AWS account (or other cloud providers). You also learned how to set up Dockerfiles and have done that for our example project.

All you have learned and done in this chapter was the preparation needed to now write the first microservice of our example project in the next chapter.

Questions

Check your understanding by answering the following questions:

1. Why is it essential to use different repositories for Git and Docker for each service?
2. How are your services receiving credentials for the database and JWT?
3. How can you run multiple Vapor applications at once?
4. Advanced: push your Docker image into your Docker repository.

7
Writing the User Service

:Okay—let's start building the first service for our shop application! Everything should be set up at this point for you to start writing the services. What you learn in this chapter will equip you to build microservices within a bigger context. You will learn, step-by-step, what the code of a microservice looks like and how to interact with Vapor.

So far, we have been building up to this moment. You have learned the theory of how to build microservices and have prepared everything to get started. After you finish this chapter, you will be able to run your own, fully functional user manager service! It's the first microservice out of our example project and gives you a good idea of how to write your own user services. User services are very common across apps and websites, and the material of this chapter will hopefully help you with those as they come your way.

We are going to cover the following topics in this chapter:

- Setting up and taking the first step
- Exploring routes
- Exploring models
- Logging in and registering
- Managing users
- Understanding address management
- Starting the service

Let's get started!

Technical requirements

For this chapter, you will need the following software components up and running:

- Vapor Toolbox
- Swift 5
- Xcode 11+
- macOS or Linux

We will assume you are using macOS, but all this should work the same under Linux.

You can find all the code for this chapter at the following GitHub repository: `https://github.com/PacktPublishing/Hands-On-Swift-5-Microservices-Development/tree/master/Chapter 7/UserService`

Setting up and taking the first step

In this section, we will set up our environment. Everything that we need in terms of code and software will be prepared here.

For you to start writing this service, you will need to have the following pieces in place:

- A blank folder for this service
- A new Git repository available
- The microservice template we worked on in the previous chapters

If you have not completed any of the previous steps to have all three elements ready, please go back and finish those first. Microservices can be complex, and if not organized well, will end up in a mess.

This section will cover the following:

- Setting up the template
- Installing SendGrid
- Setting up **JSON Web Tokens (JWT)** and utility functions
- Setting up the database

Setting up the template

Let's start by setting up the template we created in the previous chapter. We don't need to rewrite what we have created before, and will simply use it as a basis for this service. We will now take the template we created and copy it into our current project folder. Then, we will modify it to fit our needs, which is to install SendGrid. Go through the following steps to do that:

1. Go into the folder for the user manager, as follows:

   ```
   $ cd ~/Shop\ Backend/UserService
   ```

2. Now, copy the template from the original folder into our new folder, like this:

   ```
   $ cp -r ../template/. . && rm -rf .build
   ```

3. Now, open up the `Package.swift` file by using the following command:

   ```
   $ open Package.swift
   ```

4. Change the `name` attribute in the `Package.swift` file to `UserService`.

Now that we have set up the template, we can customize it by adding a few packages and dependencies.

Installing SendGrid

It is common for users to verify their emails when signing up. We want our service to include this functionality. Configuring our own **Simple Mail Transfer Protocol (SMTP)** mail server for this is a complex task and would require us to comply with a lot of common rules for sending mail. It is easier to use a service that already does that so that we do not have to worry about it. Services of this kind include **Simple Email Service (SES)** from **Amazon Web Services (AWS)**, Gmail, Yahoo, and SendGrid. Since we want to customize the sender, we will use SendGrid, which offers a free plan for small projects. There is also a nice Vapor package we can use: https://github.com/vapor-community/sendgrid-provider.

To set up SendGrid, do the following:

1. Go to `https://sendgrid.com/` and create an account. Their free tier has plenty of room for us.

2. Install the Vapor package by adding the following line to your `Package.swift` file:

   ```
   .package(url: "https://github.com/skelpo/sendgrid-provider.git",
   from: "4.0.0")
   ```

3. Add `SendGrid` to your `.target` function.

4. Add the following lines to your `Configuration.swift` file within the `configure` function:

   ```
   guard let sendgridApiKey = Environment.get("SENDGRID_API_KEY")
     else {
           fatalError("No value was found at the given public key
             environment 'SENDGRID_API_KEY'")
       }
   let sendgridClient = SendGridClient(client: app.client, apiKey:
   sendgridApiKey)
   ```

   This code is adding an environment variable that provides the API key for SendGrid to the module.

5. Change the `try routes(app)` line to the following:

   ```
   try routes(app, sendgridClient)
   ```

6. Open `Routes.swift` and change the file lines, like this:

   ```
   import Vapor
   import SendGrid

   func routes(_ app: Application, _ sendgridClient: SendGridClient)
   throws {
   ```

After installing SendGrid, we need to set up a JWT and utility functions next.

Setting up a JWT and utility functions

Our template already contains all we need to set up a JWT properly. For our backend, we now need to create the actual keys for signing and verification. To do this, follow these steps:

1. Go to `https://mkjwk.org/` and create a new key pair for our backend. Select **2048** as **Key Size**, **Signing** as **Key Use**, **RS256** as **Algorithm**, and **backend** as the **Key ID**.
2. Press **Generate**.

   The result should look like this:

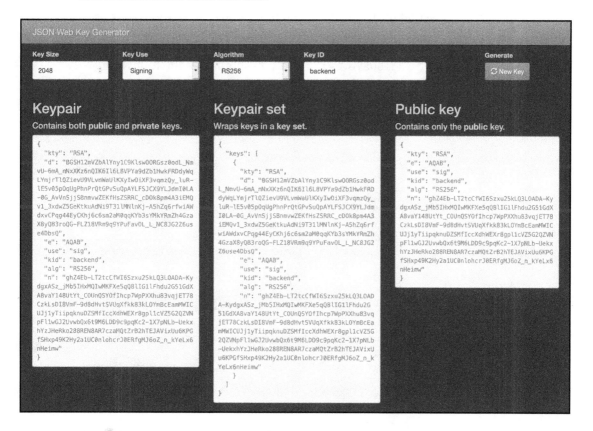

3. Store the content under **Keypair set** in a file within your Shop Backend folder and call it `keypair.jwks`. DO NOT PUBLISH THIS FILE.

> Generating keys can be done differently. This is simply an easy way to get started. Once you go into production, you should regenerate your keys using command-line tools, as mentioned on mkjwk.org.

4. Create an .env   file in the Shop Backend/UserService folder and write the following in it (you can add the .env file to your .gitignore file as well):

```
JWKS=<COPY_THE_KEYPAIR_AS_ONE_LINE_HERE>
```

And this is all we have to do. The SimpleJWTMiddleware has taken care of the rest for us.

Let's take a look at the actual middleware. Open the SimpleJWTMiddleware.swift file from https://github.com/proggeramlug/SimpleJWTMiddleware/blob/master/Sources/SimpleJWTMiddleware/SimpleJWTMiddleware.swift and you should see the following:

```swift
import Vapor
import JWT

public final class SimpleJWTMiddleware: Middleware {
    public init() { }

    public func respond(to request: Request, chainingTo next: Responder) ->
    EventLoopFuture<Response> {
        guard let token = request.headers.bearerAuthorization?.token.utf8
         else {
            return request.eventLoop.makeFailedFuture(Abort(.unauthorized,
             reason: "Missing authorization bearer header"))
        }

        do {
            request.payload = try request.jwt.verify(Array(token),
             as: Payload.self)
        } catch let JWTError.claimVerificationFailure(name: name,
          reason: reason) {
            request.logger.error("JWT Verification Failure: \(name),
             \(reason)")
            return request.eventLoop.makeFailedFuture(
            JWTError.claimVerificationFailure(
            name: name, reason: reason))
        } catch let error {
            return request.eventLoop.makeFailedFuture(error)
        }

        return next.respond(to: request)
```

```
        }

}
extension AnyHashable {
    static let payload: String = "jwt_payload"
}

extension Request {
    public var loggedIn: Bool {
        if (self.userInfo[.payload] as? Payload) != nil {
            return true
        }
        return false
    }
    public var payload: Payload {
        get { self.userInfo[.payload] as! Payload }
        set { self.userInfo[.payload] = newValue }
    }
}
```

Let's break this code down into smaller pieces.

The `SimpleJWTMiddleware` class is the actual middleware. We have a function that is responding to requests before they are passed to the controllers, as follows:

```
public func respond(to request: Request, chainingTo next: Responder) ->
EventLoopFuture<Response>
```

Within that function, we are first checking whether we have an `Authorization` token that is JWT-valid, as follows:

```
guard let token = request.headers.bearerAuthorization?.token.utf8 else {
            return request.eventLoop.makeFailedFuture(Abort(.unauthorized,
            reason: "Missing authorization bearer header"))
        }
```

If we do not have a valid JWT header, we will return an error, and the call never gets to the controllers. Afterward, we are checking if the given token is valid using the JWTKit functions provided by Vapor, as follows:

```
request.payload = try request.jwt.verify(Array(token), as: Payload.self)
```

The payload is defined here, as follows:

```
import Foundation
import Vapor
import JWT
```

```
public struct Payload: JWTPayload {
    public let firstname: String?
    public let lastname: String?
    public let email: String
    public let id: Int
    public let status: Int = 0
    public let exp: String
    public let iat: String
    init(id: Int, email: String) {
        self.id = id
        self.email = email
        self.role = role
        self.firstname = nil
        self.lastname = nil
        self.exp = String(Date().addingTimeInterval(
          60*60*24).timeIntervalSince1970)
        self.iat = String(Date().timeIntervalSince1970)
    }
    public func verify(using signer: JWTSigner) throws {
        let expiration = Date(timeIntervalSince1970: Double(self.exp)!)
        try ExpirationClaim(value: expiration).verifyNotExpired()
    }
}
```

Since this model is the same across all our services, we leave it as it is in the package.

In our `Configure.swift` file, you can see that we are configuring JWT globally, as follows:

```
try app.jwt.signers.use(jwksJSON: jwksString)
```

A **JSON Web Key Set** (**JWKS**) file is a very powerful way to define JWT keys and credential settings. So, here, we can simply pass it along as a string, and JWTKit will take care of the rest for us.

That is it! You have finished the configuration of the app for now. Let's continue by setting up the database.

Setting up the database

To set up the database, all we have to do is the following:

1. Add the following lines to the .env file:

```
MYSQL_CRED='mysql://service_users:password@localhost:3306/
service_users?ssl=false'
```

Make sure you have entered the correct password.

To use the `.env` file in Xcode, you need to adjust the schema to run in your project:

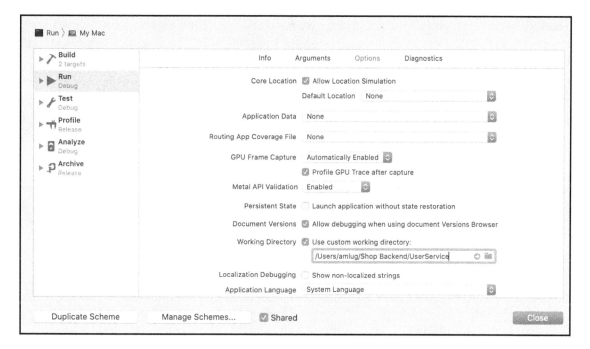

Now, when you run your project in Xcode, it will automatically read the `.env` file.

You have successfully set up the database for the service. Now, let's work on the routes.

Exploring routes

Our service needs to be reachable via URLs. Vapor's way of addressing that is by using a router. The router compares incoming request URLs to what we have told it to do and will execute the desired function. We need to do this for every service that is serving as a **Representational State Transfer (REST)** API.

Let's start by defining all the routes that we will need to cover. This service will serve three main purposes:

- User account management
- Login/verification
- Address management for user accounts

The following table lists all the routes that we need for that. The * stands for any character, to provide the ability to run multiple versions of the same API. The :variablename stands for placeholders that will be numeric IDs. All inputs and outputs are in JSON format:

Path	Method	Parameters	Output/Description
`/*/users/register`	POST	Email Password First Name (optional) Last Name (optional)	Error description or success message with the user profile.
`/*/users/login`	POST	Email Password	Error description or access and refresh token.
`/*/users/accessToken`	POST	Refresh Token	Error description or access token.
`/*/users` (Auth Required)	GET	(none)	Currently logged-in user.
`/*/users` (Auth Required)	PATCH	First Name (optional) Last Name (optional)	Updated user.
`/*/users` (Auth Required)	DELETE	(none)	No content if deleted correctly.
`/*/users/addresses` (Auth Required)	GET	(none)	List of all saved addresses.
`/*/users/addresses` (Auth Required)	POST	Street City ZIP	Adds a new address to the user.
`/*/users/addresses/:id` (Auth Required)	PATCH	Street City ZIP	Updates an existing address and returns the user profile.
`/*/users/addresses/:id` (Auth Required)	DELETE	(none)	Deletes an address and returns HTTP status 200.
`/*/users/health`	GET	(none)	Returns HTTP status 200 as long as the service is running.

As you can see, we require the users to authorize themselves for certain routes. Furthermore, we can see that we want to create three controllers, corresponding to the preceding three logical functions.

Let's see the process, as follows:

1. Create a file called `AuthController.swift` in `Controllers`.
2. Create a file called `UsersController.swift` in `Controllers`.
3. Create a file called `AddressesController.swift` in `Controllers`.
4. Open the `Routes.swift` file and replace the content with the following:

```
import Fluent
import Vapor
import SimpleJWTMiddleware
import SendGrid

func routes(_ app: Application, _ sendgridClient: SendGridClient)
throws {
    let root = app.grouped(.anything, "users")
    let auth = root.grouped(SimpleJWTMiddleware())

    root.get("health") { request in
        return "All good!"
    }
    //try root.register(collection: AddressController())
    //try root.register(collection: AuthController(sendgridClient))
    //try auth.register(collection: UserController())

}
```

You can see that we are registering routes that follow the pattern of `/*/users/`. A load balancer will be able to correctly lead a request such as `/v1/users/addresses` to our service because of this initial pattern.

The three controllers are commented out because have not created them yet. Uncomment them as we create them.

Also, we are only registering one direct route (`health`) because it is the only route we have that is not coming from one of our controllers. Due to the simplicity of this route, we just keep it as a callback function. Otherwise, we are using the `Application`'s feature to register a `RouteCollection`, which allows our controllers to register the needed routes themselves.

Note that we are passing the `SendGridClient` reference here. It is more performant to register those only once, and simply pass the reference to the controller.

We are returning an "`All good!`" message, along with HTTP status `200`, whenever `/*/users/health` is called. This is needed so that a load balancer knows that this service is still active and running. If the service crashes, the load balancer would know not to lead any traffic to this service any longer.

We have now configured the routes and created files for the controllers. Let's move on, by creating the models we need to store the users and their addresses.

Exploring models

As we have discussed in `Chapter 2`, *Understanding Server-Side Swift*, we are dealing with two types of models: database and **input/output (I/O)** models. We will now create both models and learn how to connect them to Fluent. This section will cover:

- Database models
- Connecting models to Fluent
- I/O models

Let's start with the database models.

Database models

Let's design and create our database models. We need them for Vapor to connect to the database and then return the information within those models.

As we are dealing with users and addresses, we need the following two database models, which we will cover in the next two sections:

- User
- Address

Let's start with the user!

User

We will be creating a user, so follow the steps given here:

1. Create a `User.swift` file in `Sources/App/Models/Database/` and enter the following content:

```
import Vapor
import Fluent

final class User {
    init() {
    }
    @ID(key: "id")
    var id: Int?
    @Field(key: "firstname")
    var firstname: String?
    @Field(key: "lastname")
    var lastname: String?
    @Field(key: "email")
    var email: String
    @Field(key: "password")
    var password: String
}
```

Database models will always have to be final. The class as we wrote it now is—so far—only a regular Swift class that contains a few attributes. For now, we have entered the following:

- `id`: A numeric number uniquely identifying the user.
- `firstname`: The user's first name.
- `lastname`: The user's last or family name.
- `email`: The user's email address.
- `password`: The user's password, though we will only save a hash code here.

The constructor simply takes an email and assigns an empty password. While constructors are used to create new instances, for Fluent, we will do a little more than just call the constructor. Consequently, we keep it simple and lean here.

2. A generic class cannot be a Fluent model, so go ahead and change the first line to the following:

```
final class User: Model
```

This is all it took for this class to be a valid Fluent model now. But we are not quite ready yet, as we want to use this class for a bit more than simple data storage.

3. Add the following properties to the class:

```
static let schema = "users"

@Timestamp(key: "createdAt", on: .create)
var createdAt: Date?
@Timestamp(key: "updatedAt", on: .update)
var updatedAt: Date?
@Timestamp(key: "deletedAt", on: .delete)
var deletedAt: Date?
```

The first property entity is defining the name of the database table. Fluent needs to have this variable in order to name the database table correctly.

The other three properties are storing information about when the model was created, modified, and deleted. We are using property wrappers to define the keys and the event, which sets the timestamps. We will pick up these keys in the migration later.

4. To initiate a user and set the password properly, add the following constructor:

```
init(_ email: String, _ firstName: String? = nil, _ lastName:
String? = nil, _ password: String) throws {
        self.email = email
        self.firstname = firstName
        self.lastname = lastName
        self.password = try BCryptDigest().hash(password)
    }
```

We are now setting the first and last names, as well as the password.

The password is using a simple hash function here. For production setups, you should use more advanced methods of storing password hashes.

Finally, we want to be able to store the user information in the payload for our JWT.

That's it! Our `User` model is complete! Let's continue with the `Address` model.

Now, let's see in the next section how to add an address.

Address

Let's add an address by following these steps:

1. Create an `Address.swift` file in `Sources/App/Models/Database/` and enter the following content:

```
import Vapor
import Fluent

final class Address: Model {
    static let schema = "addresses"
    @ID(key: "id")
    var id: Int?
    @Field(key: "street")
    var street: String
    @Field(key: "city")
    var city: String
    @Field(key: "zip")
    var zip: String
    @Timestamp(key: "createdAt", on: .create)
    var createdAt: Date?
    @Timestamp(key: "updatedAt", on: .update)
    var updatedAt: Date?
    @Timestamp(key: "deletedAt", on: .delete)
    var deletedAt: Date?
    init() {
    }
}
```

You can see that we are also storing the basic properties (`street`, `city`, `zip`) in the class. Just as with `User`, we have given `Address` the correct dependencies and customized the table name through `schema`.

 To keep it simple, we are assuming that we only need the street, ZIP, and city as properties for an address. In a real-world application, you would certainly want to use more properties (such as country, and so on) to specify an address. Check out this article to learn more: `https://www.mjt.me.uk/posts/falsehoods-programmers-believe-about-addresses/`.

We do want an address connected to a `User`, so we will create a `userId` property that saves the user's ID.

2. Add the following lines after the `zip` property:

```
@Field(key: "userId")
var userId: Int
```

3. Adjust the constructor to look like this:

```
init(street: String, city: String, zip: String, userId: Int) {
    self.street = street
    self.city = city
    self.zip = zip
    self.userId = userId
}
```

Since `userId` is not optional, we always need it when creating a new instance. This is by design so that no addresses can exist without a user connection.

This function is now taking the `userId` field and connects it to the `User.id` property. That way, the two models are connected, both logically and in the database.

Connecting models to Fluent

We have now created all the models we need. Do you recall that Vapor uses Fluent as its database system, as seen in `Chapter 3`, *Getting Started with the Vapor Framework*? Let's connect our models with Fluent now.

Some frameworks detect models automatically. Since Vapor and Swift are aiming for the best performance, all models have to be declared in the `Configuration.swift` file.

1. Go back into the `Configure.swift` file and enter the following lines of code to register our models for Fluent:

```
app.migrations.add(CreateUser())
app.migrations.add(CreateAddress())
```

2. Now, create a new `CreateUser.swift` file in `Sources/App/Migrations/` and fill it out, like this:

```
import Fluent

struct CreateUser: Migration {

    func prepare(on database: Database) -> EventLoopFuture<Void> {
        return database.schema("users")
            .field("id", .int, .identifier(auto: true))
            .field("firstname", .string)
            .field("lastname", .string)
            .field("email", .string, .required)
            .field("password", .string, .required)
            .field("createdAt", .datetime)
            .field("updatedAt", .datetime)
            .field("deletedAt", .datetime)
            .create()
    }

    func revert(on database: Database) -> EventLoopFuture<Void> {
        return database.schema("users").delete()
    }
}
```

3. Next, we need to do the same with the address. Create a `CreateAddress.swift` file in the same folder and fill it out, like this:

```
import Fluent

struct CreateAddress: Migration {
    func prepare(on database: Database) -> EventLoopFuture<Void> {
        return database.schema("addresses")
            .field("id", .int, .identifier(auto: true))
            .field("userId", .int, .references("users", "id"))
            .field("street", .string, .required)
```

```
                        .field("zip", .string, .required)
                        .field("city", .string, .required)
                        .field("createdAt", .datetime)
                        .field("updatedAt", .datetime)
                        .field("deletedAt", .datetime)
                        .create()
            }

            func revert(on database: Database) -> EventLoopFuture<Void> {
                return database.schema("addresses").delete()
            }
        }
```

You can see very well from these two examples how to create database tables through Fluent. A class that is conforming to the `Migration` protocol will have two functions: `prepare(on database: Database) -> EventLoopFuture<Void>` and `revert(on database: Database) -> EventLoopFuture<Void>`. `prepare` is used to create the database table and `revert` is used to delete it. For both models, we are creating the database tables by defining the fields. Note that we are picking up the keys we defined in the property wrappers of the preceding models.

4. Now, run the following code:

```
$ swift build && vapor run migrate
```

We build the app, and the database tables will be created now.

After we have created the database models, we need to focus on the I/O models next.

I/O models

I/O models are the models we need to take input in or return output to the responders. They are a bridge between the database models and the user request. As we have discussed in Chapter 6, *Application Structure and Database Design*, they are closely linked to the database models but should be their own class or struct.

We need models for the following components:

- Access token
- Refresh token
- Response models
- Input models

Access token

The access token is also referred to as the payload. The access token is the signed payload we want to get across, together with the headers. In our case, we want to save the ID, first name, last name, and email.

The `SimpleJWTMiddleware` package provides the `Payload` class for us already; we do not need to define it. However, let's take a look at it, as follows:

1. Open the `Payload.swift` file from `https://github.com/proggeramlug/ SimpleJWTMiddleware/blob/master/Sources/SimpleJWTMiddleware/Payload. swift` and look at the following content:

```
import Foundation
import Vapor
import JWT

public struct Payload: JWTPayload {
    public let firstname: String?
    public let lastname: String?
    public let email: String
    public let id: Int
    public let status: Int = 0
    public let exp: String
    public let iat: String
    init(id: Int, email: String) {
        self.id = id
        self.email = email
        self.firstname = nil
        self.lastname = nil
        self.exp = String(Date().addingTimeInterval(
          60*60*24).timeIntervalSince1970)
        self.iat = String(Date().timeIntervalSince1970)
    }
    public func verify(using signer: JWTSigner) throws {
        let expiration = Date(timeIntervalSince1970:
Double(self.exp)!)
        try ExpirationClaim(value: expiration).verifyNotExpired()
    }
}
```

Notice that `firstname` and `lastname` are optional. They are not always existent in the `User` model and do not have to be here as well.

To store the information needed to verify the JWT, we also need to add the expiration time, as well as the creation time, of the token.

2. Notice these three variables:

```
let status: Int = 0
let exp: TimeInterval
let iat: TimeInterval
```

These three properties contain the information needed to verify the JWT.

3. To verify, the payload has the following function:

```
func verify(using signer: JWTSigner) throws {
        let expiration = Date(timeIntervalSince1970: self.exp)
        try ExpirationClaim(value: expiration).verifyNotExpired()
    }
```

The verification is very simple in this case: if the expiration date (exp) is not in the past, the token is valid. You could add further verification claims and check the token against other criteria as well.

For us to issue a token now, we need to have a constructor that uses the correct information from the User class and sets the correct internal values.

4. Check out the following constructor to the class:

```
init(id: Int, email: String) {
        self.id = id
        self.email = email
        self.firstname = nil
        self.lastname = nil
        self.exp = String(Date().addingTimeInterval(
          60*60*24).timeIntervalSince1970)
        self.iat = String(Date().timeIntervalSince1970)
    }
```

We are using the current time (Date()) and are building the exp and iat variables from those. The rest of the values are simply copied from the user. Note that we are leaving information out (password, most importantly) from the user profile. You could technically use the whole User model as the payload, but because of sensitive information—such as the password— you should never do so.

 The iat variable is not used at all in our service. It might be required by the client, though, to verify when a token is about to expire.

Alright. You have now seen all we need for the access token. Let's now look at the refresh token.

Refresh token

A refresh token is very similar to the access token. We do not need any user-specific information, except for the ID. The reason is that the refresh token is only used to get a new access token. The refresh token is never sent to any service except for the user service. The expiration of a refresh token is longer than an access token, so the default expiration time will be longer.

Create a `RefreshToken.swift` file in `Sources/App/Models` and insert the following content:

```
import Vapor
import JWT

struct RefreshToken: JWTPayload {
    let id: Int
    let iat: TimeInterval
    let exp: TimeInterval
    init(user: User, expiration: TimeInterval = 24 * 60 * 60 * 30) {
        let now = Date().timeIntervalSince1970
        self.id = user.id ?? 0
        self.iat = now
        self.exp = now + expiration
    }
    func verify(using signer: JWTSigner) throws {
        let expiration = Date(timeIntervalSince1970: self.exp)
        try ExpirationClaim(value: expiration).verifyNotExpired()
    }
}
```

This code contains the `struct` for the `RefreshToken` so that we can issue it. `RefreshTokens` allow users to refresh their `AccessToken` without having to re-submit the password or email.

Notice that the `RefreshToken` struct conforms to `JWTPayload`—just as the payload shown previously does.

The `verify` function is the same as for the access token, and the function of `iat` and `exp` remains the same as well.

Response models

As discussed in an earlier chapter, you will almost always have I/O models. As a reminder, these models represent the data of the database model, but only the data we need for a specific use case.

Because these models are small in nature, we can put them all in the same file. If you wanted to create separate files, you could do that too. All I/O models are dependents of `Content` so that they can be returned as JSON. To mark them as response models, we call them `NameOfClassResponse`.

Go through the following steps:

1. Create a `UserResponse.swift` file in `Sources/App/Models/Responses/` and insert the first model, as follows:

```
import Vapor

struct UserResponse: Content {
    let id: Int?
    let firstname, lastname: String?
    let email: String
    let addresses: [AddressResponse]?
}
```

The `UserResponse` model is used whenever we want to return a `User`. So, it contains the information we want to be seen whenever a user is returned. As this service is only returning users who have authenticated themselves, we can include information such as the email address. If we ever wanted to return a public user list, we would create another model that only contains the first letter of the last names, or something similar.

Notice that we are referencing `AddressResponse` and not `Address` here. The reason is that we want to use `AddressResponse` instead of `Address` to properly use response models only.

All properties of a `Content` struct or class have to be compliant with `Content` as well.

When the user is returned, we may want to include a status indicating that the request was successful.

2. Go ahead and create a new `UserSuccessResponse.swift` file with the following content:

```
import Vapor

struct UserSuccessResponse: Content {
    let status: String = "success"
    let user: UserResponse
}
```

Note that this struct is referencing our `UserResponse` struct.

We also need to return the access and refresh tokens when someone logs in.

3. Enter the following struct in another file that you call `LoginResponse.swift`:

```
import Vapor

struct LoginResponse: Content {
    let status = "success"
    let accessToken: String
    let refreshToken: String
    let user: UserResponse
}
```

Lastly, we need to return a new access token whenever it is returned.

4. We then need the address response. Create an `AddressResponse` file and enter the following content:

```
import Vapor

final class AddressResponse: Content {
    var id: Int?
    var street: String
    var city: String
    var zip: String
    var userId: Int
    var createdAt: Date?
    var updatedAt: Date?
    var deletedAt: Date?
}
```

We are using all properties from `Address` here since we might need them.

5. Add the final file, `RefreshTokenResponse.swift`, with the following content:

```
import Vapor

struct RefreshTokenResponse: Content {
    let status = "success"
    let accessToken: String
}
```

All `status` properties are already defined as `"success"`. The reason is that if an error occurs, we are not returning these structs, so they will—by definition—only be returned in case of success.

After defining the response models, let's start defining their counterpart: the input models!

Input models

The input models will take in all the information we need to process a request. We only need three models:

- `AddressInput`: When passing along address information.
- `NewUserInput`: When registering a new user.
- `EditUserInput`: When editing an existing user.
- `LoginInput`: When logging in.

Go through the following steps to create the models:

1. Create an `AddressInput.swift` file in `Sources/App/Models/Inputs/` and insert the first model, as follows:

```
import Vapor

struct AddressInput: Content {
    let street: String
    let city: String
    let zip: String
}
```

The model only reflects the properties that we need from the model. It conforms to the `Content` protocol.

2. Create a new `NewUserInput.swift` file, as follows:

```
import Vapor

struct NewUserInput: Content {
    let firstname: String?
    let lastname: String?
    let email: String
    let password: String
}
```

Again, we only take the `firstname`, `lastname`, `email`, and `password` properties. To register a new user, that is all we need.

3. Create a `RefreshTokenInput.swift` file with the following content:

```
import Vapor

struct RefreshTokenInput: Content {
    let refreshToken: String
}
```

Renewing the access token only requires the refresh token (because all we need is saved in that token), so it's the only property of that struct.

4. Create an `EditUserInput.swift` file with the following content:

```
import Vapor

struct EditUserInput: Content {
    let firstname: String?
    let lastname: String?
}
```

We only let the client change the first and last names, so we only need those two.

When users want to log in we need to capture their information.

5. Finally, create a `LoginInput.swift` file with the following content:

```
import Vapor

struct LoginInput: Content {
    let email: String
    let password: String
}
```

And that's it. Let's connect the response models to their models now!

Connecting response models to the database model

Now that we have our response models ready, we can connect them to the models behind them.

Create the models by following these steps:

1. Open `UserResponse.swift` and add the following function to the class:

```swift
init(user: User, addresses: [AddressResponse]? = nil) {
        self.id = user.id
        self.firstname = user.firstname
        self.lastname = user.lastname
        self.email = user.email
        self.addresses = addresses
    }
```

The function takes in a user and, optionally, addresses to assign them to its properties.

2. Now, include the following function in `AddressResponse.swift`:

```swift
init(_ address: Address) {
        self.id = address.id
        self.street = address.street
        self.city = address.city
        self.zip = address.zip
        self.userId = address.userId
        self.createdAt = address.createdAt
        self.updatedAt = address.updatedAt
        self.deletedAt = address.deletedAt
    }
```

The function takes an address and assigns its values to the response's values.

We have now created and connected all models, so let's start writing the controllers to make our service functional!

Logging in and registering

The main function of the user service is for users to register and log in. In this section, we will cover all functions of the `AuthController`, which addresses all the routes needed for access management.

The following sections will cover this:

- Preparations
- Registration
- Login
- Refresh Access Token

Let's begin by preparing our service.

Preparations

Logging in and registering are the two main functions of our service. We need to prepare a little bit to get them working correctly. In this section, we will make sure we have all that need to create these functions.

You should have created the `AuthController.swift` file already. So let's go through the next few steps to get the logic implemented:

1. Open this file in the editor (Xcode).
2. Write the following class:

```swift
import Vapor
import Fluent
import SimpleJWTMiddleware
import SendGrid

final class AuthController: RouteCollection {

    private let sendGridClient: SendGridClient
    init(sendGridClient: SendGridClient) {
        self.sendGridClient = sendGridClient
    }
    func boot(routes: RoutesBuilder) throws {
    }
}
```

Remember: Every controller is only a collection of functions, so it can be a struct or a class. In this case, we want it to be a `RouteCollection` so we can register our own routes. For that, we need to add the `func boot(routes: RoutesBuilder)` function. You can now uncomment the respective line in `Configure.swift`.

3. Write the empty functions of the routes that we need to cover, as follows:

```
func register(_ request: Request) throws ->
EventLoopFuture<UserSuccessResponse> { }

func login(_ request: Request) throws ->
EventLoopFuture<LoginResponse> { }

func refreshAccessToken(_ request: Request) throws ->
EventLoopFuture<RefreshTokenResponse> { }
```

You can see that we are taking in one argument: `Request`. Through `Request`, we can then parse the body of the request.

All three functions are returning the previously defined response models packed in an `EventLoopFuture`.

Before we can start filling in the logic, we now need to connect those three functions to the routes. All three of our routes are `POST` routes, so we can simply call `routes.post` to register them.

4. Write the following lines within the `boot` function:

```
routes.post("register", use: register)
routes.post("login", use: login)
routes.post("accessToken", use: refreshAccessToken)
```

In the first line, we are registering a `register` route, which comes after everything that was previously attached to `routes`. In this case, the full path looks like this: `/*/users/register`. The route takes in a JSON body, which can be parsed to `NewUserInput`. If the JSON body does not fit this struct, Vapor will automatically throw an error and output it to the requester. The route is connected to the `register` function.

The second line is registering `login` and connecting it to the `login` function.

The third line is equivalent to the first line, merely defining the route `accessToken` and connecting it with our input model and the `refreshAccessToken` function.

Alright. Let's begin filling in those functions, starting with registration.

Registration

When a user registers, we mainly need to make sure the entered data is correct (valid) and there is no conflict (already registered). We are receiving the `Request` and a `NewUserInput` instance when the function is called.

Go through the following steps to add the registration logic.

1. First, we need to parse the input and create a `User` instance. We can do that by simply calling the following:

    ```
    let user_ = try request.content.decode(NewUserInput.self)
    let user = try User(user_.email, user_.firstname, user_.lastname,
    user_.password)
    ```

    Note that `user_` is of `NewUserInput` type.

    Next, we need to make sure the user is not already registered. This is quite simply asking Fluent for all users who already exist with that email and checking whether the count is bigger than zero. Remember that Fluent is always returning `EventLoopFuture`, which means we need to work with an `EventLoopFuture` that is not the return type we need for this function.

2. Insert the following code after the last line in the function:

    ```
    return User.query(on: request.db).filter(\.$email ==
    user.email).count().flatMap { all in
            if all > 0 {
                return
    request.eventLoop.makeFailedFuture(Abort(.badRequest, reason: "This
    email is already registered."))
            }
            return user.save(on: request.db).transform(to: user)
        }
    ```

    Okay. The first line is creating an `EventLoopFuture<Int>` that returns the count of all users where `email == user.email`. If the count is bigger than 0, we abort and throw an error explaining that the email already exists in the system. Otherwise, we return the `User` instance we previously created. Notice that the return of the count-Future (`EventLoopFuture<Int>`) turns into an `EventLoopFuture<User>` because of the `map` function. If you are not clear about this transformation, go back to `Chapter 3`, *Getting Started with the Vapor Framework*, to learn about how `EventLoopFutures` works.

The route handler function demands that we return a `UserSuccessResponse`, and so far, we only checked if this user exists already. So, we still have to save the user and build the return struct.

3. Add the following code directly after the last } from the previous code snippet:

```
.map { user in
        return UserSuccessResponse(user: UserResponse(user:
        user))
    }
```

We are changing the `EventLoopFuture<User>` we made before and creating another Future that will be executed right after. The `EventLoopFuture` is built with `user.save(on: request.db)`, and this is the future that will save `user`.

Finally, we want to output the information and send a nice email to the user.

4. Add the following code to the file—again, directly after the last }:

```
.flatMap { (userResponse) in
        let subject: String = "Your Registration"
        let body: String = "Welcome!"
        let name = [user.firstname, user.lastname].compactMap({
        $0 }).joined(separator: " ")
        let from = EmailAddress(email: "info@domain.com",
        name: nil)
        let address = EmailAddress(email: user.email,
        name: name)
        let header = Personalization(to: [address], subject:
        subject)
        let email = SendGridEmail(personalizations: [header],
        from: from, subject: subject, content: [[
            "type": "text",
            "value": body
            ]])
        return self.sendGridClient.send([email], on:
        request.eventLoop).transform(to: userResponse)
    }
```

In the first two lines, we define the content of the email. You can customize and extend those as you wish. From *line 3* to *line 7*, we are building the `SendGridEmail`. SendGrid offers a lot of features, and I would encourage you to check them out. In this case, we are simply forming a normal email, without HTML formatting.

In the last line, we are then using our `sendGridClient` instance to send the email, which is returning an `EventLoopFuture` of a different type. The last `.transform(to: user)` ignores the future type and returns an `EventLoopFuture<User>` with the original instance included, which is what we want.

You made it! You have built your first, sophisticated controller function using models, futures, extensions, and SendGrid! Pat yourself on the back and keep going!

Now that we have covered registration, let's work on login so that users can get their access tokens.

Login

For a user to log in, our controller needs to verify the credentials and then issue two JWTs: the access token and the refresh token. Luckily, pretty much all of this is done through existing providers and middleware.

Let's add the logic for the login function:

1. Add the following code to the `login` function:

```
let data = try request.content.decode(LoginInput.self)
return User.query(on: request.db).filter(\.$email ==
data.email).all().flatMap { users in
        if users.count == 0 {
                return request.eventLoop.makeFailedFuture(
                  Abort(.unauthorized))
        }
        let user = users.first!
        var check = false
        do {
                check = try Bcrypt.verify(data.password,
                  created: user.password)
        }
        catch {}
        if check {
        }
        return request.eventLoop.makeFailedFuture(
          Abort(.internalServerError))
}
```

We are first parsing the incoming data into a `LoginInput` struct. Then, we are looking for that user based on the email. If we don't find it, we return an error. If we do find it, we go ahead and verify the password.

Note that the password check is in a `do {}` block. We cannot throw an error within a `flatMap` callback, and have to isolate this call here.

2. Add the following line after `if check {`:

```
let userPayload = Payload(id: user.id!, email: user.email)
```

This line is creating our payload based on the user. Check out the `Payload` model if you want to customize this part. Next, we need to create the two tokens, for which the `JWT` package has a simple `sign` function.

3. Add the following lines to the function:

```
do {
    let accessToken = try request.application.jwt.signers.
    sign(userPayload)
        let refreshPayload = RefreshToken(user: user)
        let refreshToken = try request.application.jwt.signers.
        sign(refreshPayload)
}
catch {
    return request.eventLoop.makeFailedFuture(Abort(.
    internalServerError))
}
```

First, we are creating the access token with the previously created payload. Afterward, we are creating the refresh token based on the user.

Finally, we need to create the `LoginResponse` and fill in the details. Part of the `LoginResponse` is the `UserResponse`, so let's create that one first.

4. Create the `UserResponse`, as follows, after `let refreshToken ...`:

```
let userResponse = UserResponse(user: user)
```

If you need the addresses of a user right after logging in, you can fill them out here. For our purposes, we will leave this empty for now.

5. Now, create the `LoginResponse`, like this:

```
return user.save(on: request.db).transform(to:
LoginResponse(accessToken: accessToken, refreshToken: refreshToken,
user: userResponse))
```

We just have to return the `LoginResponse` as a future, so we are using Vapor to create one. And that's already it! The `login` function is ready.

6. Lastly, add the following `else` so that we can return a proper user if the password is not correct:

```
else {
    return
request.eventLoop.makeFailedFuture(Abort(.unauthorized))
}
```

Now we need to set up the function that allows users to refresh their access token with the refresh token.

Refresh access token

To refresh the access token, all the user has to do is pass the refresh token to us and we can verify it and, if everything is okay, return a new access token:

1. Fill out the function with the following code:

```
let data = try request.content.decode(RefreshTokenInput.self)
let refreshPayload:RefreshToken = try
request.application.jwt.signers.verify(data.refreshToken, as:
RefreshToken.self)
return User.query(on: request.db).filter(\.$id ==
refreshPayload.id).all().flatMap { users in
        if users.count == 0 {
                return request.eventLoop.makeFailedFuture(Abort(
                .badRequest, reason: "No user found."))
        }
        let user: User = users.first!
}
```

We are taking the input and parsing it into a `RefreshToken`, while also verifying it. Then, we load the user from the token and, if it exists we can go ahead.

2. Write the following code before the last `}`:

```
let payload = Payload(id: user.id!, email: user.email)
var payloadString = ""
do {
    payloadString = try request.application.jwt.signers.
     sign(payload)
}
catch {}
return user.save(on: request.db).map { _ in
    return RefreshTokenResponse(accessToken: payloadString)
}
```

This now creates a new `Payload`, an access token, and returns it to the user.

> If you wanted to implement some blocking mechanism, here you can verify that the user is *still* allowed to have access.

After finishing login and registration, let's now deal with the user data so that users can update their profiles.

Managing users

Let's now cover some user functions we need in our service to provide the client with enough ability to manage the user's profile. We want to cover three routes in this section:

- Profile (GET `"/*/users"`): This route is merely returning the logged-in user.
- Update (PATCH `"/*/users"`): This route saves new information about this user.
- Delete (DELETE `"/*/users"`): This route deletes the current user.

Also, we need to create a controller first.

The following four sections will implement the `UserController` class:

- Preparations
- Profile
- Update
- Delete

Let's discuss these in the following sections.

Preparations

The preparations here are straightforward. All we need is a class that will register the correct routes and connects them to our internal functions.

Go through the following steps:

1. Write down the following code in the `App/Sources/Controllers/UsersController.swift` file:

```swift
import Fluent
import Vapor

final class UsersController: RouteCollection {
    func boot(routes: RoutesBuilder) {
    }
    func profile(_ request: Request) throws ->
     EventLoopFuture<UserSuccessResponse> {
    }
    func save(_ request: Request) throws ->
     EventLoopFuture<UserSuccessResponse>     {
    }
    func delete(_ request: Request) throws ->
     EventLoopFuture<HTTPStatus> {
    }
}
```

The class is implementing `RouteCollection` as well so that we can register the routes accordingly. The three empty functions are representing the three routes we are about to register. Note that we are returning `UserSuccessResponse` whenever we are dealing with the user data. We have to return something else with the `delete` function as the user won't exist anymore; the HTTP status is a great way of confirming the deletion.

2. Register the three routes in the `boot` function, as follows:

```swift
routes.get("profile", use: profile)
routes.post("profile", use: save)
routes.delete("user", use: delete)
```

Now, we are prepared and are ready to start writing the controller functions. Let's start with a profile.

Profile

This route is the easiest to implement. We know that the user is logged in already and we also have a function that will return the user for an authenticated request.

So, all we have to do is write down the following line in the function:

```
return User.query(on: request.db).filter(\.$id ==
request.payload.id).all().map { users in
            return UserSuccessResponse(user: UserResponse(user:
            users.first!))
        }
```

That's it. We are using the `id` user from the `payload` that `SimpleJWTMiddleware` is handing to us.

You might wonder why we want to write such a call at all if everything we return is already in the JWT. Sometimes, you will want to verify the JWT is still accurate. Imagine the user is changing their name, but the JWT does not get updated. In an online shop setup, such as in our example case, you will want to verify this before submitting an order.

That was quick and easy, Now, let's create the `update` function.

Update

The `update` function is also straightforward and not very complex. Just as in the `profile` function, we can grab the `User` instance through our `request.payload.id`. We then change what we want to change, and save it.

Go through the following steps:

1. Write the following code in the `update` function:

    ```
    let content = try request.content.decode(EditUserInput.self)
    return User.query(on: request.db).filter(\.$id ==
    request.payload.id).first().flatMap { user in
    }
    ```

    This is parsing the incoming content and is getting us the `User` instance.

2. Change the attributes, and then write the following code after the last statement:

```
let user = user!
if let name = content.firstname {
    user.firstname = name
}
if let name = content.lastname {
    user.lastname = name
}
```

In our case, we only care about adjusting the first and last name. You can, of course, add as many attributes as you want to. Notice that we have `firstname` and `lastname` as optional attributes in our `EditUserInput` struct. So, we need to see if they are set before we can assign them to the user.

3. Write the following line of code to save the user:

```
return user.update(on: request.db)
```

"Doesn't this last line return `EventLoopFuture<User>` ?", you might wonder. That is correct; we are not entirely done yet. We need to map this to the correct return type.

4. Write down the following code, right after the last):

```
.map { _ in
        return UserSuccessResponse(user: UserResponse(user:
user))
    }
```

So, the whole line looks like this:

```
return user.update(on: request.db).map { _ in
        return UserSuccessResponse(user: UserResponse(user:
user))
    }
```

And that's it: the `update` function is complete. Now, let's work on the `delete` function.

Delete

It happens: users may want to delete their account, as sad as it is. And if they do, we want to make sure they can do so correctly. For our case here, we need to delete two types of models: the addresses attached to the user, and the user itself.

1. Let's grab the user as we did before, then write down the following line in the `delete` function:

```
return User.query(on: request.db).filter(\.$id ==
request.payload.id).first().flatMap { user in
        }
```

Now, we need to collect all addresses and delete them. Remember that we wrote a convenience function that allows us to grab addresses directly from the `user` model.

2. Write down the following line after `{ user`:

```
if let user = user {
        return Address.query(on: request.db).filter(
        \.$userId == user.id!).delete().flatMap {
            return user.delete(on: request.db).
            transform(to: .ok)
        }
    }
    else {
        return request.eventLoop.makeFailedFuture(
        Abort(.badRequest, reason: "No user found!"))
    }
```

This will delete all the addresses we found for the user. To get the instance back, we can add a `.transform(to: user)` to the line, and we will have an `EventLoopFuture<User>` instance again. Fluent allows us to delete a user from here on by simply adding `.delete(on: request.db)` to that future. And finally, we need to return an `EventLoopFuture<HTTPStatus>`, which we can do with `transform` again.

3. Modify the line to look like this:

```
return user.delete(on: request.db).transform(to: .ok)
```

You can see how we are chaining various Fluent functions together that are all doing what we want them to. And that's it: the user is deleted now.

We are using the Fluent *soft delete*, which means the models are still in the database but are marked as deleted. If you want to change that so that they are deleted, just modify `delete()` to `delete(force: true)`.

Alright—we have now finished all functions for the `UsersController`. Let's deal with address management next.

Understanding address management

The address management for our service is a traditional REST API. Addresses can be read, added, edited, and deleted. All of this needs to be done only for the user who is logged in and, therefore, in the JWT.

The following routes will be covered:

- Get addresses (`GET /*/users/addresses:`) This route is merely returning all addresses belonging to the user.
- Create addresses (`POST /*/users/addresses`): This route creates a new address for the user.
- Update addresses (`PATCH /*/users/addresses/:id`): This route updates addresses with a specific ID.
- Delete addresses (`DELETE /*/users/addresses/:id`): This route deletes addresses with a specific ID.

We will cover the following sections:

- Preparing the controller and routes
- Getting addresses
- Creating addresses
- Updating addresses
- Deleting addresses

Let's go through each one.

Preparing the controller and routes

Similar to the `UsersController.swift` file, we can start by filling out the rough structure of the classes.

Go through the following steps:

1. Write the following lines into the
    `Sources/App/Controllers/AddressesController.swift` file:

    ```swift
    import Fluent
    import Vapor

    final class AddressesController: RouteCollection {

        func boot(routes: RoutesBuilder    ) {
        }
        func addresses(_ request: Request) throws ->
         EventLoopFuture<[AddressResponse]> {}
        func create(_ request: Request) throws ->
         EventLoopFuture<AddressResponse> {}
        func update(_ request: Request) throws ->
         EventLoopFuture<AddressResponse> {}
        func delete(_ request: Request) throws ->
         EventLoopFuture<HTTPStatus> {}
    }
    ```

    So far, this is almost identical to the `UsersController` class.

2. Enter the following lines to register our routes in the `boot` function:

    ```swift
    routes.get("", use: addresses)
    routes.post("", use: self.create)
    routes.patch(":id", use: self.update)
    routes.delete(":id", use: delete)
    ```

    Just as before, the base route (`/*/users/addresses`) is already given to this function, so we don't have to write all this down. You should be very familiar with the first two lines and understand what they do.

    The third and fourth lines are adding a new element: `:id`.

    When you write down the paths for a route, you have done this so far by just writing it as a string, such as `users`. Technically, you can specify a path in a few different ways, though. One way is to supply a `PathComponent` of a `RouteComponent`. That could look like this:

    ```swift
    router.get("a/b/:id", use: func) // "/a/b/:id"
    ```

Any class that conforms to a `Parameter` can be used as a `RouteComponent`. In our case, we simply want to pass on the ID of the address, so the parameter is of the type `Int`.

You might wonder how it is possible that both routes result in the same URL. Remember that it is always tied to the `HTTP` method. We are registering the routes for `PATCH` as well as `DELETE`. The URL itself would not be able to be called without specifying the `HTTP` method. However, we often tend to assume that it is a `GET` call, if not specified otherwise.

Okay—now, let's fill out the functions.

Getting addresses

Returning all addresses for a user is simple. You might have guessed it already, but we have some nice helper functions that make this easy. The whole body of this function is only one line.

Write down the following line:

```
return Address.query(on: request.db).filter(\.$userId ==
request.payload.id).all().map { addresses in
            return addresses.map { AddressResponse($0) }
        }
```

Since we are returning an `EventLoopFuture<[AddressResponse]>`, we do have to modify the result from Fluent. Note that this function is only called after the user has been verified, so we can assume that the payload ID is authentic.

Next, let's work on the `create` function.

Creating addresses

To create an address, we will have to get the authorized user first, then build the new address, and then save it.

Go through the following steps:

1. Write the following line into the `create` function:

```
let content = try request.content.decode(AddressInput.self)
```

This should be very familiar to you by now; we are simply parsing the incoming content.

2. Next, build the address, like this:

```
let address = Address(street: content.street, city: content.city,
    zip: content.zip, userId: request.payload.id)
```

Remember that Vapor already ensured that the user content passed on is conforming to AddressInput.

While Vapor is making sure that the content of our input is matching our struct, Vapor does not know specific rules. If you wanted to make sure that a ZIP code is at least five digits long, you would need to enter that in the controller.

3. Finally, we need to save the address and return the UserSuccessResponse, as follows:

```
return address.save(on: request.db).map { _ in
        return AddressResponse(address)
    }
```

And that's it! Easy, right? Now, let's move on to the next function: Update Address.

Updating addresses

Updating the address is fairly similar to how we updated the user. The main difference is that we are saving a model that is *connected* to the user.

Go through the following steps:

1. Start by writing down our standard line, like this:

```
let content = try request.content.decode(AddressInput.self)
```

2. Now, grab the ID from the router, like this:

```
let id = try request.query.get(Int.self)
```

This ID is of type Int (not optional), and it has to be present. If the requester tries to send something other than Int, the Router will reject the call.

Next, we need to find the correct address in the database. We know the ID of the address, and we know the user ID of the user who owns this address. So, we will simply make both conditions for the database query that Fluent is generating.

3. Write down the following `return` function:

```
return Address.query(on: request.db).filter(\.$id ==
id).filter(\.$userId == request.payload.id).all().flatMap {
addresses in
}
```

The first part should look familiar: We are building a `QueryBuilder` address with Fluent. Next, we filter out the ones that match our ID, and then, we also filter out the ones that match the user ID.

You might be wondering why we want to filter out the ones that match our user ID, and not just compare the user ID later on with the address that we find. You really could do both, and it would be fine. However, by adding the user ID as a filter to the query, we are utilizing the database server's CPU and RAM to filter out, and not our own. This also means we don't have to output another error message and make sure it works. We can simply assume that we only get the results we want.

4. Add the following code to the `callback` function after the `addresses in` line:

```
if addresses.count == 0 {
        return request.eventLoop.makeFailedFuture(
        Abort(.badRequest, reason: "No address found!"))
    }
    let address = addresses.first!
```

While we can offload the user ID verification, Fluent might not find any rows and return an empty array. In this case, we do want to abort and return an error. Note that this also happens if the user ID does not match; we are not differentiating the cause.

5. Next, add the following lines after the `let address ...` statement:

```
address.street = content.street
address.city = content.city
address.zip = content.zip
```

This is simply updating the resulting address. We know, based on our database layout, that we will only have one result in the array if we get to this point. So, we grab it and store it in `address`. Then, we assign new values from the `AddressInput` struct.

6. Finally, we need to save the address and return the `AddressResponse`, as follows:

```
return address.save(on: request.db).map { _ in
            return AddressResponse(address)
    }
```

We are done with the `update` function. Now, let's finish the service with the `delete` function.

Deleting addresses

The `delete` function matches the `update` function until we save or delete the address.

Go through the following steps:

1. Fill out the following for the `delete` function:

```
let id = try request.query.get(Int?.self)
        return Address.query(on: request.db).filter(
        \.$id == id!).filter(\.$userId == request.
        payload.id).all().flatMap { addresses in
            if addresses.count == 0 {
                return request.eventLoop.makeFailedFuture(
                Abort(.badRequest, reason: "No address found!"))
            }
        }
```

All of this is identical to the `update` function.

2. Now, add a return call, right before the last }, like this:

```
return addresses.first!.delete(on: request.db).transform(to: .ok)
```

We are grabbing the first address of the array—the only address that we have in there. Then, we tell Fluent to delete it and return a simple `OK HTTPStatus`.

And that's it! We are done writing the service—yay! So, let's earn the fruits of our hard work, and start the service.

Starting the service

You've made it! We now need to compile the service and start it. To do that, run the following commands:

1. Run `swift build`.
2. Run `./.build/debug/Run`.

If you run into any problems after running `swift build`, you should check the following:

- Did you make any little spelling mistakes? As you know, Swift doesn't forgive those.
- Is Swift able to pull all the correct dependencies?

Otherwise, if you run the second command and the service quits very quickly, be sure to check the following:

- The credentials are correctly in the environment. See in the preceding sections for how to do that.
- The database server is reachable and configured.

If you have any doubts about working through this chapter, you might want to check out the code on GitHub and compare it.

Excellent! We have written, compiled, and started our first service for the example case! Now, let's summarize.

Summary

In this chapter, you have learned how to write a microservice based on the template we created in the previous chapters. You have planned the routes and written the entire code base for the service. We started by configuring and defining the routes of this service. We then started writing helper functions and extensions. We also wrote the I/O and database models and finished by writing the functions of the controllers.

Now, you have learned how to write an extended microservice that is the first block of our shop backend use case. This is also important because you can use this service in other applications.

You should be proud of yourself; this is a big step. Also, this service can be the starting point for many other web projects. In the next chapter, we will cover how microservices will communicate with each other, and you will learn how to test microservices.

Questions

Test your knowledge and understanding by working on the following tasks:

1. Extend the user service so that new users need to confirm their email first.
2. Save the last login time to a user's model.
3. Complete the address model by adding attributes such as `Country`, `LAT`, `LNG`, and `State`.
4. Advanced: Write admin functions to allow an admin user (you have to define what that is) to edit another user's addresses and profile.

8
Testing Microservices

You have probably tested software before. If you have not, don't worry: this chapter will cover all you need to know about testing microservices. But in all likelihood, you have run your own software before, which is the most basic kind of testing. Different kinds of testing tools allow us to make sure that software is doing what it should. After reading this chapter, you will have a basic understanding of how to test server-side Swift applications and specifically microservices. Testing microservices is different from testing a monolithic application as defined in Chapter 1, *Introduction to Microservices.* Instead of just testing one application, you need to test every service and—and this makes it so special—the services working together. If, for example, three microservices are working together, an error in one of them might cause the others to *appear* not to be working either. In a perfect world, with enough money and time, you could test every service for every possible case but that is rarely the case, even in well-funded projects. The approach should be geared to restrict errors by design. For starters, using Swift over any dynamically typed language will certainly make sure you are always looking at the correct type of variable. But let's get into this chapter by looking into the following topics:

- Understanding unit tests
- Trying functional tests via Postman
- Using isolation as a feature
- Testing multiple services together

Technical requirements

The code files for this chapter can be found here: https://github.com/PacktPublishing/Hands-On-Microservices-with-Swift-5/tree/master/Chapter 7/UserService.

Understanding unit tests

Let's start with the most often-discussed way of testing software: unit tests. You are most likely familiar with them: they are based on the concept of testing one function at a time and making sure it reacts correctly to every possible and reasonable input. This way of testing is essential when we develop individual functions that have a great impact on the microservice. So, if we have a function that performs some major logical implementation in our application, this is certainly the most reliable way to ensure it works correctly.

Let's look at the following topics:

- Defining unit tests
- Setting up Xcode
- Unit tests for microservices

Okay, are you ready to dive into this? Let's get started with unit tests!

Defining unit tests

Before we get into this, let's quickly define what unit tests are and what they should accomplish:

- **Isolated:** Every unit test should test only one function.
- **Repeatable:** Whether you run the test once or 10 times, the result should remain the same.
- **Pass/Fail:** The test either passes or fails.
- **Self-validating:** The results should be easily understandable.

From the preceding definitions, it becomes clear that we can use unit tests only for a few functions. For example, functions that are used for the routers (controllers) might not be good candidates because they are often connected to a database and that almost always involves increased complexity. But a lot of the functions that our controller functions are using are perfect candidates, for example, the function to validate whether or not the input is a valid email? That's a perfect candidate.

Defining functional tests

Functional tests test the end-user functions of an application. They are concerned with whether or not the user (or client) is receiving what is expected.

Since Vapor is built using Swift and Swift is naturally closely tied to Xcode, we can take full advantage of the Xcode testing tools. You might have worked with them already for app development. So, let's now set up our Xcode.

Setting up Xcode

To start, you need to set up a test target within your `Package.swift` file. All Vapor projects have such a target by default, so you probably don't need to do anything:

1. Go into the folder of a Vapor project.
2. Open the project in Xcode.
3. Look at `Package.swift`.

    It looks like this:

    ```
    .testTarget(name: "AppTests", dependencies: ["App"])
    ```

When we create an Xcode project with `xed.`, the test target is correctly created and usable within Xcode.

Within Xcode, you can find the example test file for every Vapor project, as shown in the following screenshot:

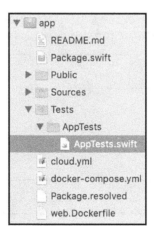

The content of the `AppTests.swift` file is the following:

```
import App
import XCTest

final class AppTests: XCTestCase {
    func testNothing() throws {
        // Add your tests here
        XCTAssert(true)
    }

    static let allTests = [
        ("testNothing", testNothing)
    ]
}
```

The `XCTestCase` class is what Xcode is looking for to automatically run tests. The basic principles here are as follows:

- Every test class contains a group of tests, mostly connected by the underlying functionality.
- Every function that starts with `test` is a unit test.
- `XCTAssert` functions check the result of a given variable. The function asserts (hence the name) whether a given expression is true.

All `XCTAssert` functions will exit with an error if the condition they check is not met. The following assert functions are available for you:

`XCTAssert(expression)`	Checks whether the result of the expression is `true`
`XCTAssertTrue(expression)`	Checks whether the result of the expression is `true`: Technically, this is equivalent to the first function, but Apple chose to provide this one as well.
`XCTAssertFalse(expression)`	Checks whether the result of the expression is `false`
`XCTAssertNil(expression)`	Checks whether the result of the expression is `nil`
`XCTAssertNotNil(expression)`	Checks whether the result of the expression is not `nil`

XCTAssertEqual(expression1, expression2)	Checks whether expression1 is equal to expression2
XCTAssertNotEqual(expression1, expression2)	Checks whether expression1 is not equal to expression2
XCTAssertGreaterThan(expression1, expression2)	Checks whether expression1 is greater than expression2
XCTAssertGreaterThanOrEqual(expression1, expression2)	Checks whether expression1 is greater or equal than expression2
XCTAssertLessThan(expression1, expression2)	Checks whether expression1 is less than expression2
XCTAssertLessThanOrEqual(expression1, expression2)	Checks whether expression1 is less than or equal expresion2
XCTAssertThrowsError(expression)	Checks whether expression throws an error
XCTAssertNoThrow(expression)	Checks whether expression does not throw an error
XCTFail()	Fails immediately

All of these functions also take extra arguments to describe the error message, the file, and the line for further debugging.

For example, let's assume you have the following function:

```
func checkPassword(_ password: String) -> Bool
```

Passwords have to be longer than 8 characters and contain one number and a special character. The unit test for that function could look like this:

```
func testPasswordFunction() throws {
        // These passwords should be accepted:
        XCTAssertTrue(checkPassword("abcadefgh1A!"))
        XCTAssertTrue(checkPassword("aFcade+gh1A"))
        // These passwords should be rejected:
        XCTAssertFalse(checkPassword("asdf")) // too short
        XCTAssertFalse(checkPassword("abcadefgh1A"))
        // no special character
```

```
    XCTAssertFalse(checkPassword("abcadefghA!"))
    // no number character
}
```

 If a test fails, Xcode will then tell us exactly which test it is.

Great, we have covered the basics. Now let's look at unit tests for microservices.

Unit tests for microservices

For the most part, unit tests are the same whether it is a monolithic application or a microservice application. Due to their defining nature, unit tests are not ideal as the only tool to test software; however, we should definitely use unit tests for individual functions that provide some isolated features. The difference is that unit tests look at an individual function only. This is certainly useful but it does not test the software as a whole. Examples of good unit tests include the following:

- Input validation
- Output validation
- Name/string parsing
- Date/time-related functions
- Function chains

 The entire Vapor framework is tested with unit tests. Because the framework has a lot of connected functions, it makes sense to validate each function individually.

In a lot of other cases, however, testing becomes much more difficult, which is why functional tests are just as important for web applications.

Functional tests versus unit tests

As with so many things in life, there is no such thing as the "better testing approach." You will need both functional tests and unit tests. Unit tests are validation for functions individually, and functional tests test your application as a whole. That being said, there are pros and cons to both approaches.

Unit test pros and cons

The pros of unit testing are as follows:

- It can validate a function 100%.
- It finds errors quite easily.
- Tests are quickly executed and repeated.

The cons of unit testing are as follows:

- It cannot easily test database operations.
- It struggles to dynamically test functions.

It is worth noting that web applications specifically are almost always doing something with a database, which is why relying on unit tests can be fatal.

Functional test pros and cons

The pros of functional testing are the following:

- It can validate semi-real users' requests, meaning requests that are very close to what actual user requests look like.
- It can validate the general functionality of a service/application.
- It is not specific to the internal functions of an application.
- It can validate new releases and verify whether specific client versions are still compatible.

The cons of functional testing are the following:

- It does not help much with finding errors.
- It may interfere with existing data when testing database inserts.
- Problems may not be related to the current test.

Functional tests struggle to pin down the issues rather than helping you to reproduce it. Since functional tests are always from the user's perspective, the resulting errors are usually not debugging-friendly. The biggest benefit for functional tests, after using unit tests for individual functions, is to validate new releases of your software. Before you deploy an update for your service, you can use functional tests to validate that all public features are operational and working as expected.

Now, let's set up Postman to get started!

Trying functional tests via Postman

There are a lot of good tools to perform functional tests. Functional testing involves testing the application from a user's perspective. Software pretends to be a human and sends human-like requests to other software. The test is said to be successful or failed based on the returned responses. This also means that functional tests are not specifically checking individual functions but functional operations of the application. In this section, we will look at the Postman tool, a free tool that provides a rich library of features and functions that allow the testing of websites but also specifically APIs.

Let's check it out:

- Installing Postman
- Setting up Postman

Installing Postman

To install Postman, follow the given steps:

1. Go to `https://www.getpostman.com/` and download the newest version. You will see that Postman offers a variety of helpful features for API development but, for now, we mainly care about its testing abilities.

2. Unzip the downloaded archive and move `Postman-file` into your `Applications` folder.
3. Click the **Download** button and install it when it is loaded.

Now, let's set it up!

Setting up Postman

To set up Postman, follow the given steps:

1. Start the previously installed Postman file.
2. When starting with Postman for the first time, you are asked to create a free account. As Postman offers quite a few helpful tools for server developers, I recommend you sign up and proceed.

Testing with Postman

Okay, let's get practical now! In this section, we want to test our previously created user management service (`Chapter 7`). If you have not followed along with the chapter, go ahead and grab the source files from the GitHub repository for this chapter:

1. Start your service and create a user in our service by executing the following command:

```
curl -X POST -H "Content-Type: application/json" \
--data '{"email": "email@domain.com","password": "test123"}' \
http://localhost:8080/v1/users/register
```

Exchange `email@domain.com` for your own personal email, so you can see an email coming in. The console should show you the following:

```
{"status":"success","user":{"id":10,"email":"email@domain.com",
 "addresses":[]}}
```

Now we have a user in the database

2. Open Postman and create a new collection:

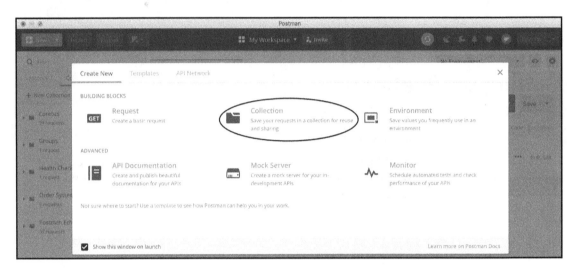

3. Call it `User Service Testing` and create an empty variable, `TOKEN`:

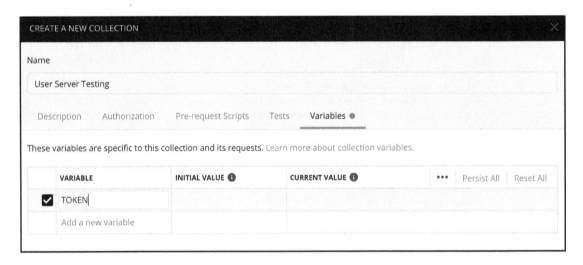

4. Go into the **Authorization** tab and set the authorization type to **Bearer Token**. Then, enter `{{TOKEN}}` in the **Token** text field:

5. Create a new request in that collection and call it `Auth`:

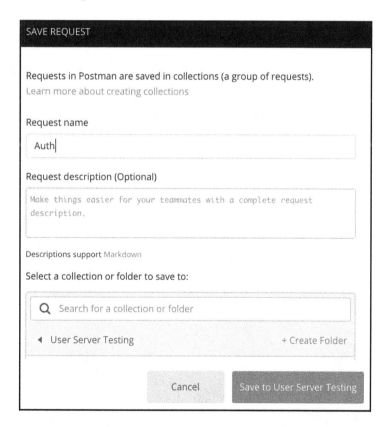

6. Fill out the URL and add a header, **Content-Type**, which should be
   `application/json`:

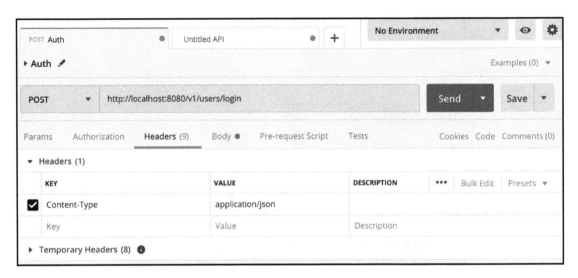

7. Now, fill in the body we need to log in; it is the same code we used earlier to
   register:

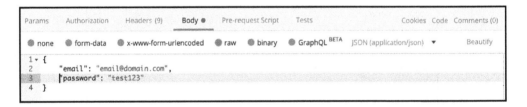

8. Go ahead and press **Save** (to save the request) and then **Send** to test it. The result should be similar to this:

Body Cookies Headers (4) Test Results   Status: 200 OK Time: 386 ms Size: 1.3 KB   Save   Download

Pretty   Raw   Preview   JSON ▾   ⇄   🗑 Q

```
1 ▾ {
2       "status": "success",
3       "refreshToken": "eyJraWQiOiJ1c2VyX21hbmFnZXJfa21kIiwiY3JpdCI6WyJleHAiLCJhdWQiXSwidHlwIjoiSldUIiwiYWxnIjoiUlMyNTYifQ
          .eyJpZCI6MTAsImlhdCI6MTU2MzcyODM0OS4wMjA0ODExLCJleHAiOjE1NjYzMjAzNDkuMDIwNDgxMX0.OQDdyXJbNtGqdnRHylWMRcLCuJCpID4GgR-p
          -jk5RHLwef-ivInJJU6XZLKIeUNTpUDkHjYT8UNVGKmwKXnbpA5q6IdIZPDzhT1MH0TKdh
          -fpMJOUraCMUI_LoNKiZPmZhmZKOL4joliRsCEJ0l8K2OK5F708SqOqaECbL8kf0LbFALtR3w2NZtoALoIY50qKn4CQqwcsH6wGdQdefzXzVCYy1aEMq3wO
          SMj14uCxvVCGR7YswuvV9H6w822Q-0a_N2eat1xGn5AgdIol6DxD8-SZdC79k8m_ova7LSZRNTXLFcFVAMGsK5DJSYuTCJG3yc2X7M-Gxi6sg4LX-2JJQ",
4       "accessToken": "eyJraWQiOiJ1c2VyX21hbmFnZXJfa21kIiwiY3JpdCI6WyJleHAiLCJhdWQiXSwidHlwIjoiSldUIiwiYWxnIjoiUlMyNTYifQ
          .eyJlbWFpbCI6ImVtYWlsQGRvbWFpbi5jb20iLCJpZCI6MTAsImV4cCI6MTU2MzczMTk0OS4wMTYzMiwic3RhdHVzIjowLCJpYXQiOjE1NjM3MjgzNDkuMD
          E2MzJ9.SLeVH-wZKedQfqKpEnPgQy08mc-wIrJpbclEw3
          -XFRLbOJBi2XPEBEJ9HT8bDL4pklJ9aQt0gyh1ZQc4VHcqtvj613wXFaVYYNYeOWZ0KW6eklhIIeMcbmLTDSxyGu9lSCpD
          -8a8G2Ivm6ibV08J8ti1lE1udG_JSf96ZJpWRous2CkUFsUcb-GS5OOgnaKypcxMVqmFqEBendHspKcNAvf7b2T5j1TtDz8Cl0ukHuoqKbqlqP3NkG_b_NA
          -C2fm2_v90HzvMbXZQh_80ODb2ZQrdtAzxJwCkO6_ONCjDYmSjRo4ay9p88vS194S8KcTO6If-viJLTmMCDjU2PSguQ",
5 ▾     "user": {
6           "id": 10,
7           "email": "email@domain.com"
8       }
9   }
```

This verifies that our service is working as intended and that we can work with Postman. Note: We are already testing our service.

9. Next, create an environment as shown in the following screenshot:

11. Call it `User Service` and add an empty variable, `TOKEN`, again.

12. Select the environment in your main window:

13. Now add the following code to the **Tests** tab in your **Auth** request:

```
pm.environment.set("TOKEN", pm.response.json()["accessToken"]);
pm.test("success value existent", function () {
    pm.expect(pm.response.json().status).to.eql('success');
});
```

We are doing two things here:

- The first line sets the environment variable, `TOKEN`, in our Postman collection. It will enable us to use the generated access token for all other calls.
- The second line is the actual test. Here we are verifying that we have `status == "success"` in the return JSON.

14. Save the request.

15. Create a new request and call it `Check Status`. This call will only verify that our **JSON Web Token (JWT)** setup is working as intended. We will send the created access token back to the server and have the server verify it.

    The URL is `http://localhost:8080/v1/users` and it is a simple `GET` call. Since we have the authorization set up in the collection already, we don't need to do anything else for this call to have the right headers.

16. Enter the following test into the **Tests** tab:

```
pm.test("success available", function () {
    pm.expect(pm.response.json().status).to.eql('success');
});
```

Your request should look like this now:

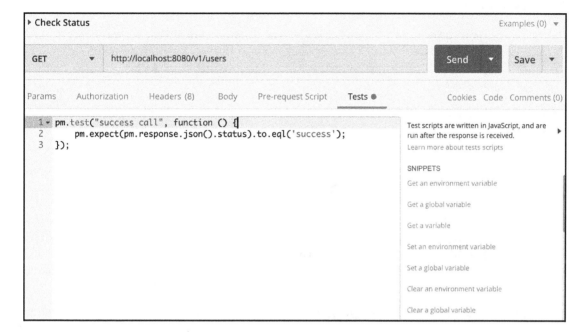

17. Save the request and then hit **Send**. The output should look like this:

And that's it! You have successfully created a collection and an auth request for that collection and then created another request that uses the token to test another call.

You should go ahead, for your own training, and create test requests for all endpoints of the user service.

 You can also run the entire collection, instead of testing each request individually. I would also encourage you to read through some of the features of Postman—it is a powerful tool to test your APIs.

Now that you have learned how to interact with Postman, let's look at how isolation is a helpful feature for testing.

Using isolation as a feature

The beauty of microservices is that they are, by definition, as isolated as possible. Consequently testing microservices can be very simple and comprehensive without much work. What the unit test is to the whole software is what a functional test is to a microservice setup. The benefit of testing is that each service can be tested without looking at the other services. That allows us to find any errors before they even surface.

Let's look at a few examples of where you can see this benefit.

Reusable services

In Chapter 7, *Writing the User Service,* you developed a user management service. You wrote this service only once, but you may be able to use it in different projects. Once you have finished all applicable tests, you will not have to rewrite them for projects using this service in the future.

Controlled testing

Because of isolation, it is a lot easier to define tests (or, as some recommend, define tests before writing the code). Every microservice can be tested by itself and without the others. Compared to monolithic applications, this is helpful to identify general problems. For example, testing the user service from Chapter 7 does not impact any of the other services we are about to write. And likewise, testing any of the services coming up will have no impact on the user service.

Let's now explore how to test multiple services together.

Testing multiple services together

Testing different microservices together can be quite challenging. Not only may they have to interact with each other but they also cause different changes (mostly in the databases) whenever you run a test that involves multiple services.

 For efficiency purposes, you should have tested each service thoroughly before you test them together. Bugs and errors are caught significantly easier in isolation than in a multi-service setup. Trust me, it saves you hours and days of work.

Let's dive into it by looking at the following topics:

- Configuration
- What to test?
- Testing locally
- Testing in a development environment
- Testing in production

Configuration

Having multiple services depend on each other is a situation we are trying to avoid as much as possible. Whenever you need to connect two services, though, you need to make sure to configure them correctly. Do not statically enter a URL for a service. Assume we have two services:

- Order service: Managing orders in the shop system
- Product service: Managing products in the shop system

Let's say you want the order service to confirm the prices with the product service and you save the product service URL in a variable. Do not do this:

```
let productServiceUrl = URL(string: "https://api.mybackend.com/
v1/products")
```

This will backfire when you want to test in a different environment. Instead, you should use environment variables during the `configure` function call when starting up your app:

```
public func configure(_ config: inout Config,_ env: inout Environment,
 _ services: inout Services) throws {
    let productServiceUrl = URL(string: Environment.get(
     "PRODUCT_SERVICE_URL")
    // now pass this variable into any controller or service you need
}
```

This way, you are making sure you can control what the service is trying to call when you are testing. In a production setup, meaning a setup that runs with real users and customers, you would have this variable defined to point at the production URL, such as `https://api.mybackend.com/v1/products`. On the other hand, you can also set it locally to just another port like this:

```
export PRODUCT_SERVICE_URL="http://localhost:8081/v1/products"
```

Let's look at what to test in the following section.

What to test?

We do not need to test everything with multiple services. Perform testing on what needs to be tested because it depends on another service. You will notice that you will naturally want to avoid making services depend on each other too much; take note whenever you do need to and write functional tests for those cases.

Popular cases include the following:

- Verifying information with another service, such as verifying the prices for products
- Submitting information to another service, such as logging, tracking, or spreading data
- Consolidating information to help the client output the correct information directly instead of sending requests to various services; so, one service would gather information from other services instead of leaving it to the client to do so

Testing can happen locally, in a development setup or in production. Let's look at local tests first.

Testing locally

The easiest and most efficient way to test services is by testing them locally. In practical terms, it means you need to start each service and assign a different port to each. Then, you can run your tests (via Postman, for example) to verify each service is doing what it should do. In macOS, this looks like having multiple Terminal instances open and running a service in each. Vapor allows you to specify the port you are using by using the −p attribute when running the service, as in the following example:

```
./.build/debug/Run -p 8081
```

In another Terminal, you could run this:

```
./.build/debug/Run -p 8082
```

Now, we only have to make sure that we have configured our services to work with the correct URLs and we are good to test.

Now that you have learned how to test multiple services together, let's summarize this chapter.

Summary

In this chapter, you learned how to test microservices. We started by looking at unit tests and what the pros and cons are. Afterward, we looked at functional tests and how they go hand in hand with unit tests. Then, we looked at how to test microservices and how to do that with the help of Postman.

By now, you have learned how to write your own test suites for APIs and verify that everything is working as expected.

You created a test collection for the user service we wrote in `Chapter 7` and verified its functionality. In the next chapter, we will write the next microservice, a product management service, for our example case.

Questions

Answer the following questions or work through the problems to solidify your understanding. For some of these, you need to work through the external documentation of Postman:

1. What is the fundamental difference between unit tests and functional tests?
2. How can unit tests and functional tests work together?
3. Write Postman tests for all endpoints of the user service.
4. Write more sophisticated tests when verifying the responses (for example, check that the token contains the correct information).
5. Write unit tests verifying the JWT functions in the user service are working correctly.

Product Management Service 9

Alright—you have already written your first microservice in Chapter 7, *Writing the User Service*, and you have learned how to test microservices in Chapter 8, *Testing Microservices*. Now, we are going to write our next microservice: **Product Management Service (PMS)**!

The PMS will be an important service in our setup, but it will be very different from the **User Management Service (UMS)**. In this chapter, you are going to learn how to write microservices that verify authentification and provide some limited admin management functions. This is the second microservice in our example shop application and will bring us closer to having the application run fully. It will also show you another way microservices can interact with each other since this service is less complex than the UMS. By the end of this chapter, you will have built a second microservice that interacts within the context of the application and serves as the content provider for products.

In this chapter, we will cover the following sections:

- Setting up the project
- Developing routes
- Writing the models we need
- Writing the controllers we need
- Testing the service

Let's get started!

Technical requirements

This section covers what you will need to have running on your machine so that you can write this microservice. The following components will need to be installed:

- Vapor Toolbox
- Swift 5.2+
- Xcode 11+
- macOS/Linux

We are also assuming that you have worked through the previous chapters and know how to write a Vapor microservice. Going through the creation of this microservice will focus on the *new* elements, not what was covered in Chapter 7, *Writing the User Service*. All code in this chapter will run on macOS and Linux alike.

The GitHub URL for this chapter is `https://github.com/PacktPublishing/Hands-On-Microservices-with-Swift-5/tree/master/Chapter 9/ProductService`.

Now, let's start by setting up the project.

Setting up the project

In this section, you will be instructed on how to set this service up before we start coding the main elements. Setting up this service is a good bit easier than the previous service, the UMS. We are not sending emails, nor are we issuing **JSON Web Tokens** (**JWTs**). Remember that JWTs are issued by our UMS, so all we have to do is validate that they are actually issued correctly and have not been tampered with. We will need a database in which to store the product and category information, which—just as before—is going to be MySQL.

What we will do is basically the following:

- Manage models that represent the products and categories.
- Verify that a user is authorized to modify products or categories.

This section covers the following:

- Setting up the template
- Setting up JWT verification
- Setting up the database

Let's start with the template.

Setting up the template

Let's start setting up the template we created in Chapter 5, *Creating Your First Microservice*. We don't need to rewrite what we created before, and will simply use it as a basis for this service. Follow these steps:

1. Go into the folder for the product manager, as shown here:

   ```
   $ cd ~/Shop\ Backend/ProductService
   ```

2. Now, copy the template from the origin folder into our new folder:

   ```
   $ cp -r ../template/. . && rm -rf .build
   ```

3. Now, open up the Package.swift file, like this:

   ```
   $ open Package.swift
   ```

4. Change the name to ProductService.
5. Now, install all dependencies and build the project, as follows:

   ```
   $ swift package update
   ```

6. Open the project in Xcode, like this:

   ```
   $ xed .
   ```

Now that we have set up the template, we can start using it. The PMS does not require any additional packages. We do want to verify certain requests to allow admin users to manage the products, so let's go ahead and set up JWT verification.

Setting up JWT verification

Thanks to our JWT packages we installed with the template, we do not need to do much here. For convenience, let's create a setup file, just as we did in Chapter 7, *Writing the User Service*. To do so, follow these steps:

1. Create a setup file in the folder, like this:

   open .env

2. Open your **JSON Web Key Set (JWKS)** file, which should be saved in your folder above the project folder.
3. Copy the entire JWKS content into one line and paste it into the .env file, like this:

   ```
   JWKS='<copy the value from the jwks>
   ```

   And that's it. We do not need the private key as we are only validating the JWT. Whenever a request comes in and it needs to be verified, the JWTMiddleware will automatically check if the JWT payload is correctly signed by using the public key. If you need to familiarize yourself with this, you might want to go back to Chapter 3, *Getting Started with the Vapor Framework*.

Now that we have set up JWT, let's get the database configured.

Setting up the database

Go ahead and create a new user and a database in your local database setup. If you need a reminder on how to do this, check out Chapter 3, *Getting Started with the Vapor Framework*. Name the user service_products, and the database should also be named service_products.

To set up the database, all we have to do is the following:

Add the following lines to the .env file:

```
MYSQL_CRED='mysql://service_products:password@localhost:3306/
service_products?ssl=false'
```

 Make sure you have entered the correct password.

We have completed setting everything up now: the template, JWT, and the database. This completes our preparations so that we can now work on the routes.

Developing routes

These services need to be reachable via URLs, just as with the user service. Remember that Vapor's way of addressing that is by using a router. The router compares incoming request URLs to what we have told it to do and will execute the desired function. We need to do this for every service that is serving as a **Representational State Transfer (REST)** API.

For this service, we will need routes that cover the following features:

- Getting categories
- Getting products
- Updating, creating, and deleting products
- Updating, creating, and deleting categories

The last two features—updating, creating, and deleting products and categories—are of course reserved for administrators and require JWT verification with the correct user level. The other two features—getting (reading) categories and products—are open to the public.

Note that we will need the following functions as well for the first two features.

For categories:

- Filter based on the name and ID
- Paging: Only 10 categories per page

For products:

- Filter based on the name, category, price, and ID
- Paging: Only 10 products per page

 You might wonder why we need paging. Even if we only serve a small number of categories and products at first, we still want to be able to support thousands of entries, if needed. We do that by never delivering the entire list but only parts of it. It's a good practice to have because it prepares for the future well.

The list of routes appears in the following table:

Path	Method	Parameters	Output/Description
`/*/products/categories`	GET	Options: `name, id,` `page`	Returns a list of categories, limited to the page and filter settings.
`/*/products/categories` (Auth Required)	POST	Name	Creates a new category.
`/*/products/categories/:id` (Auth Required)	DELETE	(none)	Deletes the category identified by the ID.
`/*/products/categories/:id` (Auth Required)	PATCH	Name	Updates a category based on the ID and sets the name.
`/*/products`	GET	Options: `categoryId,` `name, id,` `page`	Returns a list of all products that match the filters.
`/*/products`	POST	Name Description Category ID Price	Creates a new product.
`/*/products/:id`	PATCH	Name Description Category ID Price	Updates the product located under the ID with the given information.
`/*/products/:id`	DELETE	(none)	Deletes the product under the ID.

 Note how much simpler the route structure is compared to our previous service.

For the routes to work, we will need to create the controllers and link them correctly. To do this, follow these steps:

1. Go into your `Sources/App/Controllers` folder.
2. Create a `ProductsController.swift` file.
3. Create a `CategoriesController.swift` file.
4. Open `Routes.swift` and enter the following content:

```
import Fluent
import Vapor
import SimpleJWTMiddleware

func routes(_ app: Application) throws {
    let root = app.grouped(.anything, "users")
    let authorized = root.grouped(SimpleJWTMiddleware())
```

```
root.get("health") { request in
    return "All good!"
}
let productsController = ProductsController()
let categoriesController = CategoriesController()
root.get("categories", use: categoriesController.get)
authorized.post("categories", use: categoriesController.new)
authorized.patch("categories/:id", use:
 categoriesController.edit)
authorized.delete("categories/:id", use:
 categoriesController.delete)
root.get("", use: productsController.get)
authorized.post("", use: productsController.new)
authorized.patch(":id", use: productsController.edit)
authorized.delete(":id", use: productsController.delete)
}
```

Let's go through the function quickly.

We are creating instances of our controllers. In contrast to the UMS, we are not just passing the controller as a `RouteCollection` into the `Router` but we are defining our routes ourselves. The reason is that we have some routes that require authentification and other routes that do not.

Next, we are defining all the routes from the preceding table. The routes that require user permissions are using the `authorized` variable to force the request through our `SimpleJWTMiddleware`.

Now, we have declared the routes. A user could now call the routes, and our application would at least know they exist and where to forward them to technically. Before we can write the logic in the controllers, let's take a look at the models we need first.

Writing the models we need

As we discussed in `Chapter 2`, *Understanding Server-Side Swift*, we are dealing with two types of models: database and **input/output (I/O)** models. You will now create both models and learn how to connect them to Fluent.

This PMS service features two models:

- Products
- Categories

Products are in categories, but in this (simplified) service, a product can only be in one category at a time. If you feel confident enough, you are welcome to extend this so that products could be in multiple categories.

In the next two sections, we will do the following:

- Create database models: the models we need to store our information in the database.
- Create I/O models: the models we need to take data in or return data to the client.
- Create the payload model: the model we need to work with our JWT.

Let's create the database models first.

Creating database models

To create database models, go through the following steps:

1. Create a `Category.swift` file in `Sources/App/Models/Database`.
2. Insert the following code:

```swift
import Vapor
import Fluent

final class Category: Model {
    static let schema = "categories"
    @ID(key: "id")
    var id: Int?
    @Field(key: "name")
    var name: String
    init() {
    }
    init(name: String) {
        self.name = name
    }
}
```

You can see that this class is very simple, only containing the name and the ID of a category.

3. Create a `Product.swift` file in `Sources/App/Models/Database`.

4. Insert the following code:

```
import Vapor
import Fluent

final class Product: Model {
    static let schema = "products"
    @ID(key: "id")
    var id: Int?
    @Field(key: "name")
    var name: String
    @Field(key: "description")
    var description: String
    @Field(key: "price")
    var price: Int
    @Field(key: "categoryId")
    var categoryId: Int
    @Timestamp(key: "createdAt", on: .create)
    var createdAt: Date?
    @Timestamp(key: "updatedAt", on: .update)
    var updatedAt: Date?
    @Timestamp(key: "deletedAt", on: .delete)
    var deletedAt: Date?
    init() {
    }
    init(name: String, description: String, price: Int,
     categoryId: Int) {
        self.name = name
        self.description = description
        self.price = price
        self.categoryId = categoryId
    }
}
```

The product is also kept simple. In a real-life service, we would add many more attributes, but for this example, we are covering all we need.

Note that we are storing `price` as an `Int`. The reason is that while it seems intuitive that a `price` might be a `Float` or `Double`, the reality is that money will never be less than cents (0.01). So, storing in the smallest possible unit will be helpful to prevent rounding issues when saving in a database. Also, note that we are not defining a currency; we are assuming it is USD for now. Storing a `Double` or a `Float` can be tricky; JSON, the system, and the database are not always perfectly aligned with how to interpret a number. Storing in an `Int` or a `String` is, generally speaking, safer.

For the last function, we are connecting `categoryId` to the `Category` table in the database. This will prevent us from having products without categories.

Now that we created our database models, let's see how we can utilize them with our object models.

Creating I/O models

The I/O models are as simple as the database models. Go through the following steps:

1. Create a `CategoryInput.swift` file in `Sources/App/Models/Inputs`.
2. Enter the following lines in that file:

```
import Vapor

struct CategoryInput: Content {
    let name: String
}
```

3. Now create a `ProductInput.swift` file in `Sources/App/Models/Inputs` with the following content:

```
import Vapor

struct ProductInput: Content {
    let name: String
    let description: String
    let price: Int
    let categoryId: Int
}
```

We only need two kinds of input: `Categories` and `Products`, the two database models we are dealing with. Whether they are new or updated does not impact our models here, so two models in total will suffice. Note that we are leaving out the ID from the models because it is either non-existent (new model) or will be passed through the URL (see the preceding *Developing routes* section).

4. Create a `CategoryResponse.swift` file in `Sources/App/Models/Responses`.
5. Enter the following lines into that file:

```
import Vapor

struct CategoryResponse: Content {
    let id: Int
```

```
        let name: String
    }
```

6. Create a `ProductResponse.swift` file in `Sources/App/Models/Response` with the following content:

```
import Vapor

struct ProductResponse: Content {
    let id: Int
    let name: String
    let description: String
    let price: Int
}
```

Here, as well, we only need two kinds of responses: one for categories and one for products. Both responses feature all variables found in their classes.

After setting this up, we only need to register the models in the config, as follows:

7. Open `Configure.swift` in `Sources/App/`.

8. Adjust the file to reflect the following lines:

```
app.migrations.add(CreateCategory())
app.migrations.add(CreateProduct())
```

9. Lastly, we need to create the migrations we just referenced. Create a `CreateCategory.swift` file in `Sources/App/Migrations` with the following content:

```
import Fluent

struct CreateCategory: Migration {
    func prepare(on database: Database) -> EventLoopFuture<Void> {
        return database.schema("categories")
            .field("id", .int, .identifier(auto: true))
            .field("name", .string, .required)
            .create()
    }

    func revert(on database: Database) -> EventLoopFuture<Void> {
        return database.schema("categories").delete()
    }
}
```

10. And the final file for this section is `CreateProduct.swift` in `Sources/App/Migrations` with the following content:

```swift
import Fluent

struct CreateProduct: Migration {
    func prepare(on database: Database) -> EventLoopFuture<Void> {
        return database.schema("products")
            .field("id", .int, .identifier(auto: true))
            .field("name", .string, .required)
            .field("description", .string, .required)
            .field("price", .int, .required)
            .field("categoryId", .int, .required)
            .field("createdAt", .datetime)
            .field("updatedAt", .datetime)
            .field("deletedAt", .datetime)
            .create()
    }

    func revert(on database: Database) -> EventLoopFuture<Void> {
        return database.schema("products").delete()
    }
}
```

This is all we need for the database models. Let's work on the payload next.

The payload model

The payload model is the model that is generated out of the JWT that we might receive. The model comes with the `SimpleJWTMiddleware`, so we do not need to define it ourselves here. The code is covering the same fields as the payload from our UMS from Chapter 7, *Writing the User Service*. Naturally, the JWT that the other service creates needs to correspond to what we are getting here. The `SimpleJWTMiddleware` will then call the `verify` function. Because we only need JWT for administrators in this service, we check the status of the user, and if it is not 1 (which means an admin user) we will throw an error. This is effectively protecting the service from any non-admin users changing products.

And that is it! We have created all the models—for the database, as well as I/O—we need for this service. Now, we can start writing the controllers we need. Since the controllers depend on the models, they are the last thing to write.

Writing the controllers we need

Controllers are the logical parts of a Vapor application. A controller converts input to an output. We just defined the I/O models as well as the database models, so we have everything we need to write the controllers.

We have already created the two controller files needed. Now, let's work through each one of them, as follows:

- Writing `CategoriesController`: This controller will manage the categories.
- Writing `ProductsController`: This controller will manage the products.

We will start with `CategoriesController`.

Writing CategoriesController

Let's go through these steps to write our `CategoriesController`:

1. Open `CategoriesController.swift` in `Sources/App/Controllers`.
2. Write the following lines of code:

```
import Fluent
import Vapor

final class CategoriesController {
}
```

As this controller is not registering the routes itself, it does not need to be a `RouteCollection` instance, therefore we are just using a simple class.

 Some people prefer to use `structs` instead of `classes`. The reality is that it will not make a big difference for a controller of this kind, but you might want to learn more about `classes` and `structs`.

Let's fill in the functions for our routes now.

3. Enter the following function in the class:

```
func get(_ request: Request)throws ->
EventLoopFuture<[CategoryResponse]> {
    return Category.query(on: request.db).all().map { cats in
        return cats.map { CategoryResponse(id: $0.id!,
        name: $0.name) }
```

```
        }
    }
```

We simply load all entries of `Category` from the database, convert it to our response model, and return it to the requester. No filters or other operations are needed.

4. Enter the following code into the class for the `new` function:

```
func new(_ request: Request)throws ->
EventLoopFuture<CategoryResponse> {
        let input = try request.content.decode(CategoryInput.self)
        let category = Category(name: input.name)
        return category.save(on: request.db).map { _ in
            return CategoryResponse(id: category.id!,
            name: category.name)
        }
    }
```

This should not look unfamiliar to you as we wrote similar code in Chapter 7, *Writing the User Service*. We create a new `Category` instance, and then save it and return it as a `CategoryResponse`.

5. Let's work on the `edit` function now. Enter the following code:

```
func edit(_ request: Request)throws ->
EventLoopFuture<CategoryResponse> {
        let id = try request.query.get(Int?.self)
        let input = try request.content.decode(CategoryInput.self)
        return Category.query(on: request.db).filter(\.$id ==
        id).all().flatMap { categories in
            if categories.count == 0 {
                return request.eventLoop.makeFailedFuture(
                Abort(.badRequest, reason: "No product. found!"))
            }
            let category = categories.first!
            category.name = input.name
            return category.save(on: request.db).map { _ in
                return CategoryResponse(id: category.id!,
                name: category.name)
            }
        }
    }
```

In this function, we are now first getting the `id` parameter. Using it, we can get the correct category. Note that we want to make sure we actually find the category and return an error otherwise. Afterward, we set the name of the category, save it, and return a new `CategoryResponse`.

6. Add the `delete` function by adding the following code:

```
func delete(_ request: Request)throws ->
EventLoopFuture<HTTPStatus> {
        let id = try request.query.get(Int.self)
        return Category.query(on: request.db).filter(\.$id ==
        id).delete().map { _ in
            return .ok
        }
    }
```

Here, we need the id again, and then use Fluent's `delete` function to delete the entry in the database. We are only returning a status code here as we have deleted the entry, and a `CategoryResponse` would make no sense.

And that is all we need for the categories.

Writing ProductsController

The `ProductsController` is similar in nature to the `CategoriesController` but has a very different function to return a list of products. We want to be able to filter products based on their name, category, or ID. But let's get started with the basics, as follows:

1. Open `ProductsController.swift` in `Sources/App/Controllers`.
2. Enter the empty class into that file, as follows:

```
import Fluent
import Vapor

final class ProductsController {
}
```

So far, so good. Now, let's get started with the main function.

3. Enter the following function into the class:

```
func get(_ request: Request)throws ->
EventLoopFuture<[ProductResponse]> {
        let querybuilder = Product.query(on: request.db)
```

```
        return querybuilder.all().map { products in
            return products.map { ProductResponse(id: $0.id!,
            name: $0.name, description: $0.description,
            price: $0.price) }
        }
    }
```

This should look familiar to you. The only difference to everything we have done thus far is that we save the QueryBuilder instance (Product.query(on: request) is returning that) in a variable before we use it.

4. Add the following lines after the querybuilder instance is created:

```
if let categoryId = try request.query.get(Int?.self,
 at: "categoryId") {
            querybuilder.filter(\.$categoryId == categoryId)
        }
```

We check if a categoryId parameter (GET parameter) is present, and if that is the case, we add a filter to the QueryBuilder. Now, if the categoryId parameter exists, we are only looking for products in that category id.

5. Add the following lines after the preceding code:

```
if let query = try request.query.get(String?.self, at: "query") {
            querybuilder.group(.or) {
                $0.filter(\Product.$name ~~ query)
                    .filter(\Product.$description ~~ query)
            }
        }
```

Here, we check whether we have a query parameter and if so, we filter by name. If you are not familiar with SQL, we essentially let the database search for all models that contain query in their name.

6. Lastly, add the following lines after the preceding code:

```
if let idsString = try request.query.get(String?.self, at: "ids") {
            let ids:[Int?] = idsString.split(separator: ",").map {
            Int(String($0)) }
            querybuilder.filter(\.$id.field ~~ ids)
        }
```

This code uses the IN function of MySQL. The filter will only return products whose IDs are in the array provided. For the array, we use the ids parameter and make it into an array by splitting it whenever a comma appears.

You might wonder why we don't just ask for an individual ID. We could, but we will need this function later within another microservice. Whenever you want to verify or check multiple products, it is very helpful to do so in one call, not in multiple calls.

Let's take care of the other **create, read, update, and delete (CRUD)** functions now.

7. Add the new function, like this:

```
func new(_ request: Request) throws ->
EventLoopFuture<ProductResponse> {
    let input = try request.content.decode(ProductInput.self)
    let product = Product(name: input.name,
     description: input.description, price: input.price,
     categoryId: input.categoryId)
    return product.save(on: request.db).map { _ in
        return ProductResponse(id: product.id!,
         name: product.name, description: product.description,
         price: product.price)
    }
}
```

This is very similar to the new function for the preceding categories. We take all the parameters, pass them into a Fluent model, let Fluent save the model, and return it as a ProductResponse.

8. In the same spirit, add the edit function, like this:

```
func edit(_ request: Request) throws ->
EventLoopFuture<ProductResponse> {
    let input = try request.content.decode(ProductInput.self)
    let id = try request.query.get(Int?.self)
    return Product.query(on: request.db).filter(\.$id ==
     id).all().flatMap { products in
        if products.count == 0 {
            return request.eventLoop.makeFailedFuture(
             Abort(.badRequest, reason: "No product. found!"))
        }
        let product = products.first!
        product.name = input.name
        product.description = input.description
        product.price = input.price
        product.categoryId = input.categoryId
        return product.save(on: request.db).map { _ in
            return ProductResponse(id: product.id!,
             name: product.name, description: product.description,
```

```
                          price: product.price)
              }
        }
   }
```

There is nothing that should surprise you at this point. We are updating a product with new information and returning the updated model.

9. Last, but not least, add the `delete` function, as follows:

```
func delete(_ request: Request)throws ->
EventLoopFuture<HTTPStatus> {
        let id = try request.query.get(Int?.self)
        return Product.query(on: request.db).filter(\.$id ==
        id).delete().map { _ in
            return .ok
        }
   }
```

Again, almost identical to the function we used for categories, but that is okay: it's not wrong for code to be simple, especially as microservices thrive on simplicity.

Alright—the controllers are ready, and that completes our service in terms of logic and models! Now, we want to apply our knowledge about writing tests to make sure it works.

Testing the service

Testing this service is relatively simple. We can skip unit tests as we are not writing functions suited for those. It makes more sense to write a Postman test suite that will test the API endpoints. In Chapter 8, *Testing Microservices* you learned how to do that. So, let's apply that here, as follows:

1. Open Postman and create a new test suite.
2. Set up authentication so that we can test the admin functions as well.
3. Go through the preceding routes and add a test for each one of them.
4. Let Postman test this service and verify that it works as expected.

You can find the entire test suite in the GitHub repository for this chapter: `https://github.com/PacktPublishing/Hands-On-Microservices-with-Swift-5/tree/master/Chapter 9/ProductService`

Now that we have tested this service, let's summarize what we have learned.

Summary

In this chapter, we wrote the second microservice for our example application. In contrast to the first service, we only validate a JWT without creating one. You have identified the routes needed. Then, you created the I/O models as well as the database models. Afterward, you wrote the corresponding controllers and developed the functions needed for our routes. Lastly, you wrote functional tests for this service and verified its functionality.

Now, we have two running microservices, and we will want to see them in action together. The next chapter will go through how microservices can and should communicate with each other.

Questions

To make sure you understood everything in this chapter, answer the following questions:

1. Why do we not need to sign a JWT in this service?
2. Add a new filter that only returns the product within a given price range.
3. Expert: Add a way for products to be connected to more than one category (this will drastically improve but also complicate this service).

10
Understanding Microservices Communication

Microservices are designed and intended to operate as independently as possible. Still, they need to talk to each other once in a while. In this chapter, you will learn what good communication between microservices looks like and what you should avoid. Microservices sometimes have to communicate with each other; for example, when it comes to validating or aggregating information. Imagine that one microservice needs to get data from another one to then visualize it. The first microservice could, of course, access the database directly, but this might threaten the integrity of the second microservice. This is also dangerous because of the database's structure changes, or even the database itself, which means that the first microservice won't be able to operate anymore. So, for the first database to retrieve reliable information, it will need to communicate with another, but in an effective way. In this chapter, you will explore what cases warrant communication, what this communication entails, and how to structure it within a service.

After completing this chapter, you will have a solid foundation that you can use to connect your microservices.

In this chapter, we will cover the following topics:

- Understanding when to communicate
- Exploring good communication
- Message Systems
- API calls
- Leveraging Swift

Let's dive in!

Technical requirements

You will need the following software components up and running to complete this chapter:

- Vapor Toolbox
- Swift 5
- Xcode 11+
- macOS or Linux

We will assume that you are using macOS, but the code should work the same under Linux.

You can find all the code for this chapter in the GitHub repository: `https://github.com/PacktPublishing/Hands-On-Swift-5-Microservices-Development/tree/master/Chapter 7/UserService`.

Understanding when to communicate

Let's face it – your microservices will, sooner or later, communicate with each other. In this section, we will explore when they should communicate and what should be communicated. The cases in which microservices can communicate with each other can be limited to the following cases:

- Data verification
- Data processing
- Data aggregation
- Data management

Notice that they all start with *Data*? That is actually an important hint: microservices usually only communicate with each other for internal purposes. This means that the request that is sent from one service to another almost never happens synchronously with a user request but rather through internal jobs, such as cron jobs.

For example, let's say we want to verify some user input, such as an order. The order contains products, and those products have prices. Of course, we want to verify those prices with the service that created the prices.

For example, the following is the input that we get from the user:

```
{
"items":[
    {
        "id": 1,
        "name": "Product",
        "price": 1000,
        "quantity": 3
    },
    {
        "id": 1,
        "name": "Product",
        "price": 100,
        "quantity": 1
    }
],
"coupons": [
    {
        "code": "ABC",
        "percentage": 10,
        "amount": 310
    }
],
"total": 3100,
"coupon": 310,
"due": 2790,
"creditCardToken": "asdfasdfasdf"
}
```

Naturally, we want to make sure the prices the user is sending (and seeing) are the same as the ones we are using. To keep loading times minimal, we won't send this out as the user request comes in. Instead, we will queue this job and do it slightly later.

We'll explore all the aforementioned cases in the following sections.

Understanding data verification

Verification is the process in which user inputs are taken in and then verified against something that is saved elsewhere. An example of this is an online shop. When you order, meaning the request goes to the Order Processing Service, the prices of the products need to be validated, and the coupons and payment methods need to be confirmed. All of this *can* happen synchronously as the request comes in, but this could be problematic if any of those services have issues and are not available.

Let's take a look at what's happening in detail.

First, the user submits the order. Then, the Order Processing Service receives the request, which may look something like the following:

```
{
"items":[
    {
        "id": 1,
        "name": "Product",
        "price": 1000,
        "quantity": 3
    },
    {
        "id": 1,
        "name": "Product",
        "price": 100,
        "quantity": 1
    }
],
"coupons": [
    {
        "code": "ABC",
        "percentage": 10,
        "amount": 310
    }
],
"total": 3100,
"coupon": 310,
"due": 2790,
"creditCardToken": "asdfasdfasdf"
}
```

This request is essentially the entire order with everything that we need:

- All the products the user wants to buy, including their prices
- The total amount the user is expecting
- The total amount that the user has in coupons
- The due amount
- The payment information (such as a credit card token) so that the order can be paid right away

Technically, we could process this request as it is and not even calculate it. You might be wondering why the request would look like this, so let's take a look.

Users expect to see everything they're paying for on one page. So, the final checkout page will contain everything that you can see in the request, including all the totals. Why do we want to submit this to our order service now? Because we can verify that what the user *sees* is also what we *know*. Now, we can reliably tell whether what the user has on their screen is actually what it should be.

Let's be very clear about this: we never trust user input. When a request comes in, we need to validate and verify every single number. However, it is helpful for non-malicious users to know when there is a discrepancy.

Let's get back to the flow of the order. Now, we save the request. This step just means we are taking in the order as it is and saving it. The reason we're doing this is that we want to have a record of what the user requested, regardless of what happens next. Afterward, we return to the user with an "order received" message.

The user request is complete, and the user is not actively waiting for us at this stage. However, we need to do some work in the background. Here, we need to request the prices for every product from the product service and verify they are accurate. Then, we need to calculate the total for each row and add them together for the total amount of the order. Next, we need to go through the coupons and verify they exist and are applicable. If they are, then we have to add all their amounts together for the total coupon amount. Then, we subtract the total coupon amount from the total amount. This is the number the user has to pay. This is also the number that is in the request, so we need to verify that it is correct.

If we found a problem (for example, a coupon is no longer valid), we need to notify the user and let them know. The easiest solution could be canceling the order, but you could also offer alternatives (such as paying for a higher amount).

If everything is okay and the total due amount matches what the user is expecting, then you can charge their credit card.

Now that the order has been verified, it can be processed and sent to shipping.

Throughout this process, we are communicating at least twice with other services:

- When getting the item's prices
- When charging the user's credit card

Depending on our structure, we may have additional services (for example, for coupons), but there are at least two other services involved. We absolutely do not want those requests to happen as the order comes in, which means we don't want to verify the prices immediately as the requests come in. This would mean making the user wait and could cause problems. If our product service is down (for whatever reason), we cannot take the order in, and the same goes for the payment provider. Just imagine that there's a problem with one of those services and you've missed out on orders. It would be preferable to have the orders and process them later if you have to.

 It is common for credit card payments to be preauthorized. This is usually something that happens *before* you submit an order and it happens with the payment provider directly. This will confirm to you that the credit card has enough available balance and increases the likelihood of the order being processed. We will see this in action in the next chapter.

Now that we know how data verification is done, let's look at how the data is processed.

Understanding data processing

Now that we've covered data verification, let's talk about data processing. The data that you have stored might interact with more data. For example, to stay within the store example, your order details need to be submitted to the fulfillment center. The goal here is that the stored data is being processed in one of the following ways:

- Transferring data to another service for further processing (passing it down the chain)
- Using another service to process the data and then receiving the results (for example, image or video processing into a target format)
- Updating the information "on file" from another service (for example, updating currency rates on file)

The technical implementation of these services will look very different, depending on what the processing part is meant to do. You do want to stick to some rules, though:

- Process data in an asynchronous manner.
- Expect the other service to fail (implement retries).

Now that you have learned the basics of data processing, let's check out how data is aggregated.

Understanding data aggregation

In a microservice architecture, often, your information is spread across different services. You have products in one service, orders in another service, and shipping information in yet another service. But what if you want to provide a holistic view of a customer? What if you want to have some statistics on how often certain products have been bought?

In those cases, you want to aggregate the data, meaning you want to collect the data from other services and bring it together in one place. The aggregated data should usually be a copy to ensure you're not getting the data from another service that you can then update locally. For example, a microservice is returning a list of orders with money amounts and dates. Instead of maintaining your own local database, you should replace it every time it comes from the other service.

That might mean you need to set up procedures to update aggregated data or add to it continually. Depending on the nature of the data, this might be very complex.

Let's look at an example. Let's say you have orders in your database that have a total value and timestamp and you want to aggregate them by date.

The following is what the response from your order processing service may look like:

```
[
    {
        "id": 1,
        "totalValue": 10,
        "date": "10-10-2019"
    },
    {
        "id": 2,
        "totalValue": 15,
        "date": "10-10-2019"
    },
    {
        "id": 3,
        "totalValue": 25,
        "date": "10-11-2019"
    },
    {
        "id": 4,
        "totalValue": 10,
        "date": "10-12-2019"
    }
]
```

This is a simple list of orders, not aggregated in any way. Here, you can see that two orders were made on the same day but that they haven't been formatted nicely so that someone can easily see how many orders came in each day. Due to this, our aggregation service wouldn't try to aggregate them by day. The desired result should look like this afterward:

```
[
    {
        "date": "10-10-2019",
        "totalValue": 25,
        "orders": 2
    },
    {
        "date": "10-11-2019",
        "totalValue": 25,
        "orders": 1
    },
    {
        "date": "10-12-2019",
        "totalValue": 10,
        "orders": 1
    }
]
```

Can you see that we have a list of days with the number of orders instead?

This kind of aggregation is very common and should happen through your microservices. Of course, you might argue that the client can perform tasks of this kind as well. While this is true for smaller datasets, once there are gigabytes and terabytes of data, the server will be much better equipped to perform aggregations.

Now that we've looked at data aggregation, we are going to see how data is managed.

Understanding data management

Conceptually, data management is very similar to data aggregation. We want to control data in other services based on one service. An example of this would be a request to delete a user account. Imagine a data system as complex as Facebook. You can easily tell that this would not just be a short call to update the database. Specifically deleting entries can have their own challenges (legally and organizationally) and requires a lot of interaction with many services.

Let's imagine you have a user request to delete all of that user's content in your online shop. Here, the user's client (such as an app or website) sends the delete request to the user service. The user service will realize that other services need to be notified as well and sends delete requests to them. A fair few services may need to be notified, which is why you should perform this kind of task in a background queue that processes asynchronously (such as a cron job).

In this section, we explored what data management should look like with multiple microservices. We learned about the four components of data processing: **Data verification**, **Data processing**, **Data aggregation**, and **Data management**. Now, let's take a look at what good communication looks like.

Exploring good communication

A good microservice structure also enjoys good communication between microservices. In Chapter 1, *Introduction to Microservices,* we discussed that microservices should operate as independently as possible and therefore limit communication to each other as much as they can. In this section, we are going to look at cases where communication between microservices is actually appropriate.

We will explore the following topics:

- Asynchronous communication: What is asynchronous communication and how is it useful?
- What to avoid: Things not to do when communicating.

Let's start with asynchronous communication.

Asynchronous communication

There is always an exception to this rule, but please do make it a rule: Don't send synchronous requests within your user-facing API services – make everything asynchronous whenever feasible. To explain this a bit better, let's take a look at an example.

You have a user-facing service that is called UserService. Within that service, you need to verify the user's address from AddressService. Because UserService is user-facing, meaning clients (users) are requesting information from it, it should respond as quickly as possible. For it to respond as quickly as possible, we should implement the address check asynchronously, detached from the user request. This means that user requests will never be combined with an internal call to AddressService.

The user will always get a quick answer. For this to work, we need to have some kind of state information being returned to the user. For example, when requesting a user object that has not been verified yet, it could return `status: pending`.

The reasons you want to avoid synchronous requests are simple:

- The other service (`AddressService`, in this example) might be down.
- The other service might have made changes you are unaware of.
- The other service might take longer and cause either you or your client to time out.

If you are using asynchronous requests and the service is down, you can simply retry and notify the developer of a potential problem.

You might be wondering if this rule still applies even if you yourself are maintaining the service in question. Yes, absolutely. You will make mistakes, things will change, and you will forget to update the dependent services.

Let's look at what asynchronous communication looks like in Swift:

- When receiving requests, consider the following:

There's nothing here that you wouldn't do for a normal web API. Treat any *internal* calls just like you would treat public calls. Adding an extra level of security is all you have to do in most cases. It might make sense for you to define an internal subroute just for calls that are not really public. This could look something like the following:

```
let root = routes.grouped(.anything, "internal")

try root.register(collection: InternalController())
```

Now, you can do everything that could work internally in that controller.

- When sending requests, consider the following:

Thanks to SwiftNI (see Chapter 2, *Understanding Server-Side Swift*, for more details), sending asynchronous requests is very easy. The following code shows what sending a request may look like:

```
return client.post(
                    url,
                    headers: [
                        "Authorization": "Basic \(
                            credentials.base64EncodedString())",
                        "Content-Type": "application/json"
```

```
            ]
    ) { request in
            let body = try JSONEncoder().encode(json)
            request.http.body = HTTPBody(data: body)
    }
```

This is all you have to do to make the request run on SwiftNIO's `EventLoop`.

Now that we've explored asynchronous communication, let's look at what to avoid.

What to avoid

So far, you have learned about *how* to communicate between microservices. Now, let's discuss what to *avoid*. The list of things to avoid goes hand in hand with what to do:

Communicating at all: Less is more; this is very true when it comes to this. If you want to avoid communicating in the first place, try to think creatively around having to communicate. For example, instead of verifying a user session with an auth service, you can use JWT to verify the requests decentrally, as we discussed in `Chapter 1`, *Introduction to Microservices*. Another example would be storing some information in an internal cache; for example, you are only requesting an update every so often but keeping an internal cache.

Synchronous communication: We have talked about this already, but let me say it again: avoid this at all costs. It will cost you more time and energy later on to fix this. The only acceptable exception to the rule is if you're working with live data and communication is critical; for example, a payment confirmation.

Multi-service communication: You might find yourself in a situation where you need to communicate with multiple microservices in your system. Try to avoid this as this adds a lot more complexity. Often, you can work around this.

Chained requests: Imagine that service A requests something from service B but service B needs to connect to service C first. Not only will this take a while to execute, but it also invites all kinds of trouble. To avoid this, you should have B deal with C asynchronously with a local database cache of what it needs from C.

In this section, we have learned what good communication looks like between microservices. Specifically, we looked at asynchronous communication and what to avoid when implementing communication. With this knowledge, we can start looking at message and event systems.

Understanding Message and Event Systems

By now, you might be wondering *how* we are actually connecting microservices together well. The most intuitive and simple answer is that we're providing a (REST) API. There are, however, ways for systems to communicate that are not public but solely internal. They can be classified into one of two groups:

- Message Systems
- Event Systems

We will explore both topics in this section.

Let's dive in and start with Message Systems!

Message Systems

Message Systems are part of your infrastructure and allow messages to be sent across the system. This means a microservice can send a message to another service through this system. The question is, how is that different from just using the API a service offers?

A messaging system typically offers the following benefits:

- Reliable transmission, since a message needs to be confirmed by the receiver
- Retries if the transmission fails
- Warnings and crash detection
- Queuing

Each of these benefits comes in very handy as your system grows. If a microservice is down, the API won't be available either. Your dependent services either need to have their own retry systems in order to communicate, or they can rely on a message system.

Now, let's look at how the event system works.

Event Systems

Generally speaking, Event Systems are similar to message systems. The main difference is that, in a Message System, you have a *sender* and a *receiver*, while in an Event System, you have a *sender* and a *topic/event*. Services can subscribe to topics or events and will be notified every time a sender sends a message to that topic or event.

The important difference here is that the sender has no control over the message that's been sent. Once a message has been sent, the sender will not know who received the message when, or at least not in most event systems.

The use case for such a system is obviously different from a message system. Some popular use cases are as follows:

- End user notification
- Mass data events (such as social media)
- Statistics and metrics

So far, you've learned what message and Event Systems are and how they can benefit your application, as well as their differences and which one to pick for what situation. Now, let's take a look at REST and WebSocket APIs.

REST and WebSocket APIs

A lot of APIs use REST as their way of exposing the API. REST's main advantage is that there is no state. Every request is isolated. For microservices to communicate with each other, this isn't a bad idea. You never know when you need to communicate, and when you do need to communicate, it is usually single queries asking for or sending information.

On the other hand, you might have heard about WebSockets. They are the simple idea of *sockets* being used in a public space. Sockets are a very basic way of how computers communicate with each other. Typically, they don't define the interface for you, but they do allow you to send raw bytes of data. The main difference between socket connections and REST connections is that sockets have a state. When you connect to another service through a (web) socket, you are opening the connection, communicating, and then closing the connection afterward.

We'll explore this in a bit more in detail in the following sections:

- Advantages of WebSockets: When to use them and how
- Defining the interface: How to communicate in a structured way
- Advantages of REST: Why REST is a good starting point

Let's start with the advantages of WebSockets.

Advantages of WebSockets

WebSockets are primarily used for live data. Messengers such as the ones from Facebook (Facebook Messenger and WhatsApp) use WebSockets to send data from the clients to the server and back. Since everything happens with active connections, WebSockets are much more performant in sending a lot of data back and forth compared to (REST) APIs.

Let's say you have to receive 100 items from the server but mark every item as "read" when you receive it. Now, to complicate things, let's say we want to make sure that two clients are not getting the same item, so we have to request them individually and confirm them individually. In an HTTP API, this would look like this:

- Request 1 item.
- Mark it as "read".
- Request 1 item.
- Mark is as "read".
- (Repeat 100 times).

This would result in 200 calls that are going back and forth, as well as 200 connections that are being opened and closed every time. With WebSockets, we only send the information back and forth in one connection. It is much faster and also less resource-intensive.

Now that we've learned about WebSockets, let's look at how to define the interface.

Defining the interface

Whether you use WebSockets or REST APIs, you want to clearly define the interface or the format of communication. You need to define exactly what a microservice is expecting and what it is returning. Both sides need to know what is being expected, including cases that are not always present. Let's take a look at an example:

A login request may look like this:

```
{
    "email": "test@domain.com",
    "password": "test123"
}
```

The normal login response looks like this:

```
{
    "accessToken": "ABCDEFG",
    "refreshToken": "ABCDEFG"
}
```

However, it may also return an error stating that the user gave the wrong password. In this case, the response would look like this:

```
{
    "status": 400
    "errorCode": "invalidLogin",
    "errorMessage": "The submitted login was invalid."
}
```

The following are a couple of important notes on error messages:

- Rely on HTTP status codes for the overall coding process. There's no need to introduce your own status code unless you have a specific reason to. You can and may want to include the same HTTP code in the body of the message as well, though, if it makes sense to do so.
- Use your own error code (such as in the preceding example) to clearly identify the issue. This is what the client will use to deal with the error properly.
- You can include an error message, but don't rely on it being shown to the user. The user may have a different interface language than what is in your code.

Now that we've looked at how to define the interface, let's look at the advantages of REST.

Advantages of REST

Building a REST API makes a lot of sense for applications that use stateless data. This is usually the case for most apps and general data. You might have cases that require real-time data (for example, Uber's car tracking, Facebook Messenger, and so on), in which case REST might not be the ideal choice. However, in many cases, REST is usually a solid choice.

Let's discuss some of the advantages in detail:

It makes asynchronous complications possible: This is not the case with WebSockets, which require synchronously going back and forth since WebSocket connections are usually not closed until the client disconnects. REST allows you to send requests without them being connected to each other continually.

Easily adapts to the database structure: Usually, a database consists of entities that are in a database table. Each entity type can get its own endpoint in your REST API and make it easy to be addressed. In some cases, you can also automatically generate the API endpoints.

The common standard in many services: Because REST is easy to implement and interact with, it is commonly used in many services you might encounter, such as payment processors (Stripe), tax-related services (`Taxjar.com`), accounting (such as Freshbooks) and many more.

So far, we've looked at the advantages of REST and WebSockets and what they can offer, as well as how to structure communication. Now, let's look at how Swift can help us with microservices.

Leveraging Swift

As you already know, Swift is great for microservices. However, there are a couple of features that apply specifically to Swift and make it very convenient to develop microservices. Swift, as a language, is quite young, so many popular features in other languages were not readily available in Swift when it started out. In this section, we will look at some of the Swift-specific features that can help with writing microservices.

We'll explore the following two features of Swift:

- **Shared libraries**: The ability to write a library that can be used by more than one service.
- **Generic functions and classes**: Save yourself time by utilizing Swift's features.

Let's start with shared libraries.

Shared libraries

As we mentioned previously, you'll want to define the protocol and the format for your microservices clearly. It's handy if you can do this by defining a common library that contains structs, protocols, and classes that you need for that purpose. For example, let's take a look at the following output:

```
{
    "email": "test@domain.com",
    "password": "test123"
}
```

Now, let's create a struct that represents that output:

```
struct LoginResponse {
    var email: String
    var password: String
}
```

As you can see, the output can be parsed into the struct. `email` and `password` are two variables that exist in both and so the struct can either read or write the preceding output.

Now, this struct can be used in all microservices that communicate with this specific function. Similarly, we can define the error message:

```
struct LoginErrorResponse {
    var status: Int
    var errorCode: String
    var errorMessage: String
}
```

You'll notice that these structs we just defined can easily be placed in a shared library that can be used by the following:

- All microservices that need to receive information
- The microservices sending this information
- The client interacting with this information

Such a library will ensure that your services will effectively communicate with each other and reduce errors.

Now, let's take a look at generic functions and classes.

Generic functions and classes

Generic functions and classes allow you to define a class or a function without specifying their type. You may have used them already. An example of generic functions and classes is as follows:

```
func add<T>(_ a: T, _ b: T) -> T {
    return a + b
}
```

This is, of course, a very simple example. However, you can use the same principles to create a function, like this:

```
Func loadModel<T: MyModelType>(_ id: Int, on container: Container) ->
EventLoopFuture<T?> {
    return T.query(on: request.db).filter(\.$id == id).first()
}
```

Here, you can see that we are able to load *any* model with one function. The same principle can be applied to a whole class:

```
final class ModelController<M: MyModelType> {
}
```

With that, we can now create controllers for all our models without having to rewrite the same code. We can have one controller serve multiple endpoints and different models. This saves you time and effort and reduces errors.

 Generic functions can also be found in other languages, such as Java and C#. However, there are few *native* languages that have such powerful features while remaining easy to learn and work with.

Now, we can wrap this chapter up.

Summary

In this chapter, you learned the basics of how microservices need to communicate with each other.

You learned which cases warrant communication between services and what to communicate. Then, we looked at how to define interfaces for services and discussed the two main protocols: WebSockets and REST.

Lastly, we took a quick look at some perks Swift offers that allow us to write code once but use it again, either through libraries or generic functions.

In the next chapter, we will apply the knowledge we have gained in this chapter by writing the order processing service.

Questions

To validate your understanding of this chapter, answer the following questions:

1. When should microservices communicate with each other?
2. What are the two main ways/protocols microservices can use to communicate with each other?
3. How can Swift be helpful in facilitating communication between microservices?
4. Describe three scenarios in which your shop application has to implement communication between services.

Order Management Service

11

After writing the **user management service** (**UMS**) and the **product management service** (**PMS**), let's now connect the two and write the **order management service** (**OMS**).

In this chapter, you will learn how to write a microservice that connects to another microservice to verify the information and then process data asynchronously. You will apply the knowledge from `Chapter 10`, *Understanding Microservices Communication*, to have this service validate the data. By the end of this chapter, you will have written the final piece of our example app: a microservice that connects the other two.

We will cover the following sections in this chapter:

- Getting started
- Creating our routes
- Creating our models
- Creating our controllers
- Connecting to the PMS
- Adding payment methods

Let's begin!

Technical requirements

This section covers what you will need to have running on your machine so that you can write this microservice. The following components need to be installed:

- Vapor Toolbox
- Swift 5.2+
- XCode 11+
- macOS/Linux

We are also assuming that you have worked through the previous chapters and know how to write a Vapor microservice. Going through the creation of this microservice will focus on the *new* elements, not what was covered in `Chapter 7`, *Writing the User Service*. Further, we will assume you are using macOS going forward. All features would work the same under Linux, however. You can find the code for this chapter on GitHub: `https://github.com/PacktPublishing/Hands-On-Swift-5-Microservices-Development/tree/master/Chapter 11/OrderService`.

Now let's start by setting up the project.

Getting started

In this section, you will be instructed on how to set this service up before we start coding the main elements. Setting up this service is a good bit easier than the previous service, the UMS. We are sending emails, but we are not issuing JWTs. What we will do is basically the following:

- **Take in orders from the user:** The service needs to take in orders that are coming from the user, usually through your app or frontend. The order requests contain the items the user wants to buy along with shipping and billing information.
- **Verify the prices in the orders:** In microservices, the databases are not shared. So the OMS does not know the prices of the products since they are in the PMS. In order to verify an order, we have to connect to the PMS and get the price list after an order was received.
- **Wait for payments to come in:** After an order is taken, we need to wait for payment. Some payments may be almost instantaneous, like credit cards. Other payments, like sending a check or wiring money, can take a few days.
- **Process the order when payment is complete:** When the order is complete, we need to start shipping. In our case, we simply mark the order as shipped, but it might involve more in the future when you extend this service.
- **Let the user see order history:** Users typically want to see what they have ordered in the past, so there should be a function providing that for them.

This section covers the following:

- Setting up the template
- Setting up JWT verification
- Setting up the database
- Configuration

In each of these sections, we are going to prepare our microservice template to be used for this service. We will customize the settings, add the middleware we need, and configure the database. In the last section, we will configure the `configure` function Vapor calls.

Let's start with the template.

Setting up the template

Let's start setting up the template we created in the previous chapter. The template we created in Chapter 5, *Creating Your First Microservice,* is a great start for this service. But we need to customize it. We simply use what we created before as a basis for this service. Follow these steps:

1. Go into the folder for the product manager, shown as follows:

   ```
   $ cd ~/Shop\ Backend/OrderService
   ```

2. Now copy the template from the origin folder into our new folder, using the following command:

   ```
   $ cp -r ../template/. . && rm -rf .build
   ```

3. Now open up the `Package.swift` file using the following command:

   ```
   $ open Package.swift
   ```

4. Change the name to `OrderService`.
5. Now Xcode will install all the dependencies, and we can build the project.

Now that we have set up the template, we can start using it. The product management service does not require any additional packages. We do want to verify specific requests to allow admin users to manage the products, so let's go ahead and set up a JWT.

Setting up JWT verification

For this service to connect the right user to the order, we need to be able to identify who is sending the request. As we discussed in Chapter 7, *Writing the User Service,* we are using a JWT for identification. In this service, we simply need to verify the payload against its signature. Luckily, the provided packages will do that for us.

Thanks to the JWT packages we installed with the template, we do not need to do much here. For convenience, let's create a setup file just like we did in `Chapter 7`, *Writing the User Service*. Follow these steps:

1. Edit the `.env` file in the folder:

   $ open .env

2. Open your `jwks.json` file, which should be saved in your folder above the project folder. It looks like this:

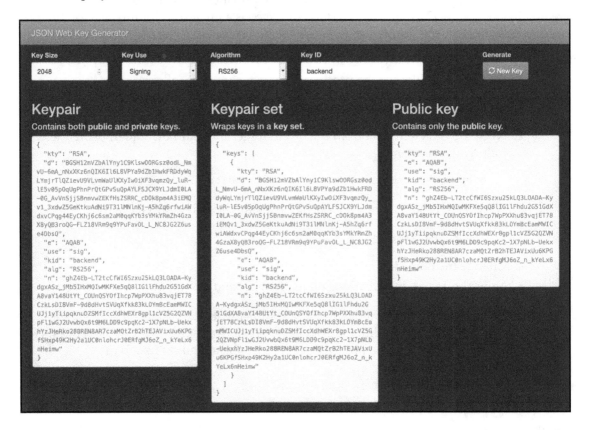

3. Copy the `jwks.json` in one line.
4. Paste it into the setup file as follows:

   ```
   JWKS='<copy the value from the jwks>
   ```

And that's it. We do not need the private key as we are only validating the JWT. Whenever a request comes in, and it needs to be verified, the JWT middleware will automatically check if the JWT payload is correctly signed by using the public key. If you need to familiarize yourself with this, you might want to go back to Chapter 3, *Getting Started with the Vapor Framework*.

Now that we have set up the JWT, let's get the database configured.

Setting up the database

Go ahead and create a new user and a database in your local database setup. If you need a reminder, check out Chapter 3, *Getting Started with the Vapor Framework*. Name the user service_orders and the database also as service_orders.

To set up the database, all we have to do is the following:

1. Add the following lines to the .env file:

    ```
    MYSQL_CRED='mysql://service_orders:password@localhost:3306/
    service_orders?ssl=false'
    ```

Make sure you have entered the correct password.

Let's look at the configuration next.

Configuring Vapor

The configuration of this service is quite simple. All you need to do is add our migrations and set up the database.

Open Configure.swift and adjust the function to the following:

```
import Fluent
import FluentMySQLDriver
import Vapor

func configure(_ app: Application) throws {
    guard
        let jwksString = Environment.process.JWKS
        else {
```

```
            fatalError("No value was found at the given public key
                environment 'JWKS'")
        }

    guard
        let urlString = Environment.process.MYSQL_CRED
    else {
        fatalError("No value was found at the given public key
            environment 'MYSQL_CRED'")
    }

    guard
        let url = URL(string: urlString)
    else {
        fatalError("Cannot parse: \(urlString) correctly.")
    }

    app.databases.use(try DatabaseDriverFactory.mysql(url: url),
     as: DatabaseID.mysql)
    app.middleware.use(CORSMiddleware())
    app.middleware.use(ErrorMiddleware(()))
    try app.jwt.signers.use(jwksJSON: jwksString)
    app.server.configuration.supportCompression = true
    app.migrations.add(CreateOrder())
    app.migrations.add(CreateOrderItem())
    app.migrations.add(CreateOrderPayment())
    try routes(app)


}
```

Notice that we are registering three `migrations` here? You will create the corresponding classes later in this chapter. Also, the `routes` function is called, which we will configure right after this section.

That's all we need here.

You have successfully set up the service, you have configured the database and the middleware, and you have created the references for migrations and routes. Now let's work on the routes.

Creating our routes

Like the other services, our OMS needs to be callable publicly. We do that by setting up routes that allow the user, and other services, to call this service. The routes we set up in this section will do this for us.

This service does most of its work behind the scenes and not publicly. For the end user (or consumer), the following two actions are important:

- Submit a new order.
- Retrieve the history of orders.

For an administrator, we need to do the following:

- Get the list of all orders
- Add payment to an order

The following table list the orders:

strong>Path	strong>Parameters	Output/Description	
`/*/orders` (Auth required)	POST	Expected Total Order Items	Submits an order from an end-user/consumer
`/*/orders` (Auth required)	GET	-	Returns all orders of the user from the JWT
`/*/orders` (Auth required, admin level)	GET	-	Returns all users
`/*/orders/payment/:id`	POST	Payment Information	Submits a payment for the order

So, there are not a whole lot of routes. Let's get them implemented. Follow these steps:

1. Go to `Sources/App` and open `Routes.swift`.
2. Enter the following code:

```
import Fluent
import Vapor
import SimpleJWTMiddleware

func routes(_ app: Application) throws {
    let currentVersion = app.grouped(.anything, "orders")
    currentVersion.get("health") { req in
        return "All good."
    }
    let protected = currentVersion.grouped(SimpleJWTMiddleware())
```

```
let orderController = OrderController()
protected.post("", use: orderController.post)
protected.get("", use: orderController.listMine)
protected.get("all", use: orderController.list)
protected.post("payment", ":id",
  use: orderController.postPayment)
}
```

The first lines should be very familiar to you. We are then utilizing JWTMiddleware to protect our routes. In this service, we have no public routes. After that, we define the routes from the preceding table. The code will do nothing but register the routes when executed, but it will tell the Vapor Router where to direct calls that come to specific URL endpoints.

Alright, we have created the routes that allow the user to call this service. For this service to start working, we need to work on the controllers and the models. The controllers will need the models to work because the models will contain all our information. So let's work on the models.

Creating our models

In this service, we need to store the incoming orders in the database. The models we are creating in this section are representing that information in Swift through Fluent. Additionally, we also need to create input and output models that help us transfer the information from and to the user.

We have the following models to consider:

- Order: This represents the order from a consumer.
- OrderItem: This is an item within an order.
- OrderPayment: This is a payment posted for an order.

When it comes to payments, make sure you always provide enough flexibility for different payment types and amounts. People are usually not as well-versed as we would like them to be for our services.

Let's go through the following sections:

- Configuring database models: Creating the models that correspond with the database.
- Writing input models: All our inputs put into structs.
- Writing output models: The model corresponds to the database models, so that the user gets them formatted as we specify.

Here we go!

Configuring database models

Our database models live in their usual folders: `Sources/App/Models`. Follow the steps given below:

1. Open the `Sources/App/Models/Database` folder, either in Finder or Xcode, and add a new `Order.swift` file, and enter the following code for the file:

```
import Fluent
import Vapor

final class Order: Model {
    static let schema = "orders"
    @ID(key: "id")
    var id: Int?

    @Field(key: "totalAmount")
    var totalAmount: Int

    @Field(key: "paidAmount")
    var paidAmount: Int

    @Field(key: "userId")
    var userId: Int

    @Field(key: "status")
    var status: Int

    @Timestamp(key: "createdAt", on: .create)
    var createdAt: Date?
    @Timestamp(key: "updatedAt", on: .update)
    var updatedAt: Date?
    @Timestamp(key: "deletedAt", on: .delete)
    var deletedAt: Date?
    @Field(key: "firstname")
```

```
var firstname: String
@Field(key: "lastname")
var lastname: String
@Field(key: "street")
var street: String
@Field(key: "zip")
var zip: String
@Field(key: "city")
var city: String
@Children(for: \OrderItem.$order)
var items: [OrderItem]

init() { }
init(
    id: Int? = nil,
    totalAmount: Int,
    paidAmount: Int = 0,
    status: Int = 0,
    firstname: String,
    lastname: String,
    street: String,
    zip: String,
    city: String) {
    self.id = id
    self.totalAmount = totalAmount
    self.firstname = firstname
    self.lastname = lastname
    self.street = street
    self.paidAmount = paidAmount
    self.status = status
    self.zip = zip
    self.city = city
    }
}
```

The code you see is the entire model for the order in a Fluent model. We start by declaring it as a model subclass, to then define our attributes:

- id: This is the ID in the database.
- totalAmount: This is the total amount of the order. This number is in dollar cents.
- paidAmount: This is the total amount that is already paid.
- status: This is the status of the order.
- firstname: This is the first name of the customer.
- lastname: This is the last name of the customer.

- `street`: This is the customer's street.
- `zip`: This is the customer's zip code.
- `city`: This is the customer's city.

> The address, as well as the customer information, is, of course, oversimplified, so you would need to add more information (such as country, state, and so on) for this to work well.

The order contains everything we need for us to store the order. You might wonder why we are saving the address here as well, as it is also in the user service. There are two reasons for this:

- The user might change his or her address in the future. However, this order was still sent to the old address, and we need to have an accurate record of sending it.
- This way, we don't need to load the address from the user service. Remember, avoiding communication at all is critical here.

2. Create another file, `OrderItem.swift`, and enter the following content:

```swift
import Fluent
import Vapor

final class OrderItem: Model, Content {
    static let schema = "orderItems"
    @ID(key: "id")
    var id: Int?

    @Field(key: "unitPrice")
    var unitPrice: Int

    @Field(key: "totalAmount")
    var totalAmount: Int
    @Field(key: "productId")
    var productId: Int

    @Field(key: "quantity")
    var quantity: Int
    @Parent(key: "orderId")
    var order: Order

    @Timestamp(key: "createdAt", on: .create)
    var createdAt: Date?
    @Timestamp(key: "updatedAt", on: .update)
    var updatedAt: Date?
```

```
@Timestamp(key: "deletedAt", on: .delete)
var deletedAt: Date?
init() { }

init(
    id: Int? = nil,
    totalAmount: Int,
    unitPrice: Int,
    quantity: Int,
    order: Order) {
    self.id = id
    self.totalAmount = totalAmount
    self.unitPrice = unitPrice
    self.quantity = quantity
    self.order = order
  }
}
```

Similar to the preceding `Order` class, we are storing all we need for an individual item:

- `id`: The id in the database
- `totalAmount`: The total amount of this row (`quantity` x `unitPrice`)
- `unitPrice`: The individual price of this item
- `quantity`: The quantity
- `order`: The corresponding order

We are storing everything we need to recreate the order at a given point in time. If the price of a product changes in the future, we still have the price for this order saved here.

3. Create the third and final database model by creating another file, `OrderPayment.swift`, and enter the following content:

```
import Fluent
import Vapor

final class OrderPayment: Model, Content {
    static let schema = "orderPayments"
    @ID(key: "id")
    var id: Int?

    @Field(key: "totalAmount")
    var totalAmount: Int
    @Parent(key: "orderId")
    var order: Order
```

```
@Field(key: "method")
var order: String

@Timestamp(key: "createdAt", on: .create)
var createdAt: Date?
@Timestamp(key: "updatedAt", on: .update)
var updatedAt: Date?
@Timestamp(key: "deletedAt", on: .delete)
var deletedAt: Date?
init() { }

init(
    id: Int? = nil,
    totalAmount: Int,
    method: String,
    order: Order) {
    self.id = id
    self.totalAmount = totalAmount
    self.method = method
    self.order = order
}
}
```

The payment entries save the following attributes:

- `id`: The id in the database
- `totalAmount`: The total amount of this payment
- `method`: A String describing the method, for example, "cash"
- `order`: The corresponding order

We are not specifying the payment method; we are leaving it open so that the administrator can enter "credit card," "cash," or something else.

Now we also need to create migration files so that Vapor will automatically create our tables.

4. Create a new `CreateOrder.swift` file in `Sources/App/Migrations`, and enter the following code:

```
import Fluent

struct CreateOrder: Migration {
    func prepare(on database: Database) -> EventLoopFuture<Void> {
        return database.schema("orders")
            .field("id", .int, .identifier(auto: true))
            .field("totalAmount", .int, .required)
```

```
                        .field("paidAmount", .int, .required)
                        .field("userId", .int, .required)
                        .field("status", .int, .required)
                        .field("firstname", .string, .required)
                        .field("lastname", .string, .required)
                        .field("street", .string, .required)
                        .field("zip", .string, .required)
                        .field("city", .string, .required)
                        .field("createdAt", .date)
                        .field("updatedAt", .date)
                        .field("deletedAt", .date)
                        .create()
        }

        func revert(on database: Database) -> EventLoopFuture<Void> {
            return database.schema("orders").delete()
        }
    }
```

The migration creates all the attributes for the order.

5. Create a new `CreateOrderItem.swift` file, and enter the following code:

```
import Fluent

struct CreateOrderItem: Migration {
    func prepare(on database: Database) -> EventLoopFuture<Void> {
        return database.schema("orderItems")
                .field("id", .int, .identifier(auto: true))
                .field("totalAmount", .int, .required)
                .field("unitPrice", .int, .required)
                .field("productId", .int, .required)
                .field("quantity", .int, .required)
                .field("orderId", .int, .required)
                .field("createdAt", .date)
                .field("updatedAt", .date)
                .field("deletedAt", .date)
                .create()
        }

        func revert(on database: Database) -> EventLoopFuture<Void> {
            return database.schema("orderItems").delete()
        }
    }
}
```

This code contains the migration to create the order item from above.

6. Create yet another file, the `CreateOrderPayment.swift` file, with the following code:

```swift
import Fluent

struct CreateOrderPayment: Migration {
    func prepare(on database: Database) -> EventLoopFuture<Void> {
        return database.schema("orderPayments")
            .field("id", .int, .identifier(auto: true))
            .field("totalAmount", .int, .required)
            .field("method", .string, .required)
            .field("orderId", .int, .required)
            .field("createdAt", .date)
            .field("updatedAt", .date)
            .field("deletedAt", .date)
            .create()
    }

    func revert(on database: Database) -> EventLoopFuture<Void> {
        return database.schema("orderPayments").delete()
    }
}
```

This last migration creates the table for order payments, with the preceding corresponding fields. All three migrations direct Fluent on which fields to create. The fields correspond 100% to the preceding models, as you can see.

And that is it for the database models. Let's move onto the input models.

Writing input models

Input models define the user input the service is receiving from the user or client. It is important to differentiate the database models as they may vary in what they contain. Just like we defined the input models for the product management service as well as the user management service, we need to define the correct models here.

We have to write input models for the following purposes:

- Order submission: The content of an order
- Payment submission: The information needed for the payment
- Product information: The information we retrieve from the PMS

Follow these steps to create the input models:

1. Open the `Sources/App/Models/Input` folder, create
   an `OrderItemInput.swift` file, and insert the following code:

   ```
   import Vapor

   struct OrderItemInput: Content {
       var productId: Int
       var unitPrice: Int
       var quantity: Int
   }
   ```

   It is very straightforward, and we have everything we need to take in an item for the order.

2. Create an `OrderInput.swift` file, and insert the following code:

   ```
   import Vapor

   struct OrderInput: Content {
       var totalAmount: Int
       var firstname: String
       var lastname: String
       var street: String
       var zip: String
       var city: String
       var items:[OrderItemInput]
   }
   ```

   This now contains more general information about the order. Notice that we are referencing the `OrderItem` we created in the first step.

3. Next, create a `PaymentInput.swift` file with the following content:

   ```
   import Vapor

   struct PaymentInput: Content {
       var orderId: Int
       var method: String
       var totalAmount: Int
   }
   ```

   Only three fields are needed here.

4. Lastly, we need an input that comes from the PMS. Create a `Product.swift` file, and enter the following code:

```swift
import Vapor

struct Product: Content {
    var id: Int
    var unitPrice: Int
}
```

The PMS is returning us more information than in this `struct`, but we only care about the price. We want to validate the amount the user will need to pay, so we need the price and the product id.

After creating the inputs, let's now work on the outputs.

Writing output models

Output models are the counterpart to input models; they define what the output of our service should look like.

A difference to the input models is that we don't need quite as many output models. We return information if we do the following:

- The order was successfully submitted.
- The payment was added.
- Orders are returned in a list.

The first point and the last one can be combined since they contain roughly the same information. So let's start with the following steps:

1. Open `Sources/App/Models/Output`.
2. Create `OrderItemResponse.swift` file and enter the following content:

```swift
import Vapor

struct OrderItemResponse: Content {
    var productId: Int
    var unitPrice: Int
    var quantity: Int
    var totalAmount: Int
}
```

Notice that this file is almost identical to the `OrderItemInput.swift` file. The difference is that we do not include the total amount since this amount will be calculated and does not need to be part of the input.

3. Create an `OrderResponse.swift` file, and enter the following content:

```
import Vapor

struct OrderResponse: Content {
    var id: Int
    var totalAmount: Int
    var paidAmount: Int
    var userId: Int
    var status: Int
    var createdAt: Date?
    var items:[OrderItemResponse]
}
```

Notice that this file also looks very similar to the `OrderInput.swift`. But we have added the order items here as well.

4. Enter the following function before the last } curly brace:

```
init(order: Order, items: [OrderItem]) {
        self.id = order.id!
        self.totalAmount = order.totalAmount
        self.paidAmount = order.paidAmount
        self.userId = order.userId
        self.status = order.status
        self.createdAt = order.createdAt
        self.items = []

        for item in items {
            let orderItemResponse = OrderItemResponse(productId:
            item.productId, unitPrice: item.unitPrice, quantity:
            item.quantity, totalAmount: item.totalAmount)
            self.items.append(orderItemResponse)
        }
    }
}
```

This allows us to create a full order output.

We have now created the database models and the input and the output models. Our service is only lacking logic to connect the different models to each other. So, let's work on the controllers, which will contain the logic for the service.

Creating our controllers

This service operates behind the scenes with user-provided input. To logically separate the two areas, we will create two controllers:

- `OrderController`: Manages everything related to real humans.
- `ProcessingController`: Manages everything behind the scenes, no human touch needed

Let's start with `OrderController`.

Writing the OrderController

This controller interacts with the user and will reference out inputs and outputs.

1. Start by creating an `OrderController.swift` file in `Sources/App/Controllers`, and enter the following code:

   ```
   import Fluent
   import Vapor

   final class OrderController {
   }
   ```

   This is just an empty controller, so let's add a few functions.

2. Add the functions from the preceding `routes.swift` file:

   ```
   func list(req: Request) throws -> EventLoopFuture<[Order]> {
   }
   func listMine(req: Request) throws -> EventLoopFuture<[Order]> {
   }
   func postPayment(req: Request) throws ->
    EventLoopFuture<AddedPaymentResponse> {
   }

   func post(req: Request) throws -> EventLoopFuture<OrderResponse> {
   }
   ```

3. Now we can fill in the code for the `list(req: Request)` function:

   ```
   return Order.query(on: req.db).all().map { orders in
         return orders.map { return OrderResponse(order: $0,
           items: $0.items) }
      }
   ```

4. The code for the `listMine(req: Request)` function looks very familiar:

```
return Order.query(on: req.db).all().map { orders in
        return orders.map { return OrderResponse(order: $0,
        items: $0.items) }
    }
```

Both functions return orders according to whether an admin or a consumer is asking. The next significant functions will save orders and payments.

5. Fill out the `post(req: Request)` function:

```
let orderInput = try req.content.decode(OrderInput.self)
    let order = Order(totalAmount: orderInput.totalAmount,
     firstname: orderInput.firstname,
     lastname: orderInput.lastname, street: orderInput.street,
     zip: orderInput.zip, city: orderInput.city)
    return order.save(on: req.db).flatMap {
        var saving:[EventLoopFuture<Void>] = []
        var items:[OrderItem] = []
        for inputItem in orderInput.items {
            let item = OrderItem(totalAmount:
             inputItem.unitPrice*inputItem.quantity,
             unitPrice: inputItem.unitPrice, quantity:
             inputItem.quantity, order: order)
            saving.append(item.save(on: req.db).map {
                items.append(item)
            })
        }
        return saving.flatten(on: req.make()).map {
            return OrderResponse(order: order, items: items)
        }
    }
```

While the function does a lot for the user, the code itself is simple and straightforward. We get the input for the order from the POST request. We then create the order based on that input. We save it in the database to get an ID, and then add the order items to the order. The order items are saved, and we return the order.

6. Fill out the `postPayment(req: Request)` function:

```
let paymentInput = try req.content.decode(PaymentInput.self)
    return Order.query(on: req.db).filter(\Order.$id ==
    paymentInput.orderId).all().flatMap { orders in
        if orders.count == 0 {
            return req.eventLoop.makeFailedFuture(
```

```
                    OrderError.orderNotFound)
        }
        let payment = OrderPayment(id: nil,
         totalAmount: paymentInput.totalAmount,
         method: paymentInput.method, order: orders.first!)
        return payment.save(on: req.db).transform(
         to: AddedPaymentResponse())
    }
```

This is taking in the payment input. The input is then saved to the order, and we return the `AddedPaymentResponse`.

And this takes care of everything we need for the user. Now let's look at our internal controller.

Writing the ProcessingController

The `ProcessingController` is an internal-only controller. It will be used for performing actions with orders that the user has no input into.

Follow these steps to create our controller:

1. Open `Sources/App/Controllers`, create a `ProcessingController.swift` file, and enter the following content into the file:

   ```
   import Fluent
   import Vapor

   final class ProcessingController {
   }
   ```

   This code is only the container for the class. We will need the following three functions:

   - `getOrders`: This returns a list of orders based on a status.
   - `processOrderInformation`: This checks the prices of an order according to the PMS.
   - `getProductInformation`: This returns the prices from the PMS.

2. Create the three function templates:

   ```
   func getOrders(status: Int = 0, on app: Application) throws ->
    EventLoopFuture<[Order]> {
   }
   ```

```
func processOrderInformation(_ order: Order, on app: Application)
->
 EventLoopFuture<Bool> {
}
func getProductInformation(productIds: [Int], client: Client) ->
 EventLoopFuture<[Product]> {
}
```

So far all these functions are not yet filled; we will work on that shortly. Notice that we are passing on `Application` to two of the functions. The reason is that when we are running the functions not from a user request, we typically don't have a request instance available. `Application` provides us what we need, though.

Next, we need to make sure we are getting the PSM URL so that we know where to get the prices from.

3. Enter the following just below the first { curly brace:

```
let productServiceUrl:String
init(_ productServiceUrl: String) {
    self.productServiceUrl = productServiceUrl
}
```

When initializing this controller, we are expecting the PSM URL. We will call this URL later to retrieve the product information.

Next, let's work on actually returning the information.

4. Fill out the `getProductInformation` function as follows:

```
func getProductInformation(productIds: [Int], client: Client) ->
EventLoopFuture<[Product]> {
    return client.get(URI(string: self.productServiceUrl),
    headers: ["Content-Type": "application/json"]).
    flatMapThrowing { (response:ClientResponse) in
        return try response.content.decode([Product].self)
    }
}
```

You can see that this part is surprisingly easy and doesn't need all that much additional logic. We request from a previously defined URL, and parse the information into our data model.

5. Use the just created function to process an order as follows:

```
func processOrderInformation(_ order: Order, on app: Application)
-> EventLoopFuture<Bool> {
        let productIds: [Int] = order.items.map { $0.productId }
        let expectedTotal = order.totalAmount
        return self.getProductInformation(productIds: productIds,
         client: app.make(Client.self)).flatMap {
          (products: [Product]) -> EventLoopFuture<Bool> in
            var total = 0
            for item in order.items {
                for product in products {
                    if product.id == item.productId {
                        total = total + product.unitPrice *
                         item.quantity
                    }
                }
            }
            if total != expectedTotal {
                return app.make(EventLoop.self).makeFailedFuture(
                 OrderError.totalsNotMatching)
            }
            order.totalAmount = total
            order.status = 1
            return order.save(on: app.databases.default()).
             transform(to: true)
        }
}
```

In the first line, we create an array of product ids for us (productIds). This array we can then pass onto the getProductInformation function. The result of that function is an EventLoopFuture that contains the products. We loop through the products to then calculate our own total price.

After the loop, we then compare to see if the total we calculated (total) matches the expected total (expectedTotal) from the user, if not we return a failed future. Otherwise, everything seems okay, and we assign a new status to the order and save it.

6. Now all that is left is to create our function to get orders:

```
func getOrders(status: Int = 0, on app: Application) throws ->
EventLoopFuture<[Order]> {
        return Order.query(on: app.databases.default()).
         filter(\Order.$status == status).all()
}
```

This code just returns all orders to us with a filter for the status. We leave the status as a parameter because we want to provide a way for us to use these functions in other scenarios as well.

Finally, we can now work on the part of the app that runs the controller. To schedule the task, we can use some functions from SwiftNIO.

 Using the functions from SwiftNIO here is excellent for what we are doing. Depending on what you need, you may want to use more sophisticated job queue systems that include recovery and retries.

7. Fill out the boot function in `boot.swift` like the following:

```
import Vapor
import NIO

private var verifyOrdersTask: RepeatedTask? = nil

public func boot(_ app: Application) throws {
    let url = Environment.get("PRODUCT_SERVICE_URL") ??
     "http://localhost:8080/v1/products"

    let processingController = ProcessingController(url)
    verifyOrdersTask = app.make(EventLoop.self).
     scheduleRepeatedAsyncTask(
        initialDelay: .seconds(0),
        delay: .seconds(60)
    ) { [weak app] task -> EventLoopFuture<Void> in
        let app = app!
        var returnFuture:EventLoopFuture<Void>
        do {
            returnFuture = try processingController.
             getOrders(status: 0, on: app).flatMap {
             orders -> EventLoopFuture<Void> in
                var processingFutures:[EventLoopFuture<Void>] = []
                for order in orders {
                    processingFutures.append(processingController.
                    processOrderInformation(order, on: app).
                    transform(to: ()))
                }
                return processingFutures.flatten(on: app.make(
                 EventLoop.self))
            }
        }
        catch let error {
            returnFuture = app.make(EventLoop.self).
```

```
                        makeFailedFuture(error)
                    }
                    return returnFuture
            }
        }
```

In this code, we create an instance of `ProcessingController` (the only one in the service), and then we use SwiftNIO to start a repeating task. In this task, we simply ask for all open orders and then process them. We do that by calling the corresponding functions of our controller.

Note how we are pulling the PSM URL from the environment. We then merely call the functions from our `ProcessingController`.

So, this is now finished. We have now written the controllers and models as well as a routine to process our orders as they come in. Let's next look at how to extend this service.

Extending the order management service

This service is, of course, oversimplified and does not fully work within the context of a real-life shopping platform. In this section, we will explore what you could do, though, to get it ready for production. You may have extensions in mind that are not listed here, and that's perfectly okay. This section is meant to show you examples of how to extend the service so you can apply your own extension.

Remember that each microservice is unique. If you are planning on using this microservice for multiple shops, copy it for every shop and customize it then. It's not meant to be one-size-fits-all.

We will look at the following sections:

- Adding taxes
- Adding payment methods
- Adding refunds and coupons

Let's start with taxes.

Adding taxes

Taxes are something a real-life shop needs to consider and implement. You notice that we have not implemented any taxes into this service. The taxes you add will depend on the legal framework. But let's assume you wanted to add a simple sales tax. You would extend `Product` with a tax percentage in the PSM. The changes for the order management service would then involve the following steps:

1. Edit the `Order.swift` file in `Models` as follows:

```
final class Order: Model, Content {
...
    @Field(key: "taxAmount")
    var taxAmount: Int
...
```

This would save the total tax amount in the order.

2. Edit the `OrderItem.swift` file in `Models` as follows:

```
final class OrderItem: Model, Content {
...
    @Field(key: "taxAmount")
    var taxAmount: Int
...
```

Here we are also adding the tax amount per item. Naturally, you will have to verify the tax amount as well. So you could edit the `processOrderInformation` function by adding the following code:

```
...
var total = 0
var totalTax = 0
            for item in order.items {
                for product in products {
                    if product.id == item.productId {
                        total = total + product.unitPrice *
                         item.quantity
                        totalTax = totalTax + (product.unitPrice *
                         product.tax * item.quantity)
                    }
                }
            }
            if total != expectedTotal {
                return app.make(EventLoop.self).makeFailedFuture(
                 OrderError.totalsNotMatching)
            }
```

```
order.totalTax = totalTax
order.totalAmount = total + totalTax
...
```

All we do is add the code for taxes and add it to the total.

 Note that we now need to add `totalTax` to `totalAmount`.

3. For that to work, you need to add a tax to `Product` so it can be fetched from the PSM:

```
...
    var tax: Decimal
...
```

And this would have added a tax field.

 To determine the actual tax, it is worth looking into a service like taxjar.com; depending on your country and regulation, it can take quite a lot of work to figure this out correctly.

This is only an example of what you could do to extend the service with this functionality. Let's look at adding payment methods next.

Adding payment methods

Adding payment methods is, generally speaking, no easy task. Each approach is unique and usually involves a few steps. For example, a credit-card provider has measures that might vary based on the used card provider. Then PayPal has its process, and so do other providers. Some payment methods generally require some pre-authorization. This is when your credit card is requested but not charged yet. For that to work in your service, you could add some status to `OrderPayment`, like the following:

```
final class OrderPayment: Model, Content {
...
    // 0 = initiated
    // 1 = authorized
    // 2 = rejected
    // 3 = charged
    @Field(key: "status")
```

```
        var status: Int
  ...
```

Of course, you will have to modify the system in other places as well for this to make sense.

 If you want to see a full-fledged implementation of an order system with payment methods, you should check out `https://github.com/SwiftCommerce/OrderSystem`.

Lastly, let's look at how coupons and refunds could be added.

Adding refunds and coupons

Just like the other two topics, there is no reliable way to implement this without more context. Coupons can be based on a percentage or a flat amount; they may also only apply to some products. Similar to how we added the tax, we could also add `couponAmount`.

Likewise, with refunds, creating another `refundAmount` field will enable you to record the amount of an order that is refunded. The transaction itself could then technically be registered as a negative transaction in the `OrderPayment.swift`.

As you can see, there is a lot that can be done to extend this service and make it more usable. This section should have given you an idea of how it can be done and what it should look like. Let's now summarize the entire chapter.

Summary

You did it! The order management service is now ready and can run. You set up your template and configured it for this framework. Then you specified the routes. After that, you created the models we needed, and created the public controller for the routes. The internal controller came after that and we discussed how to implement routines.

Finally, we looked at how you could extend the service to include some taxes, add additional payment methods, and how adding coupons and refunds might work.

You saw that the OMS is different from the other two services, but learned how to connect it to the PMS and how to implement an asynchronous price check.

Now that we have essentially finished the backend services, we will look at the best practices for Swift microservice development in the next chapter.

Questions

To enhance your understanding, work through the following exercises:

1. Can you write all the tests needed for this microservice?
2. Can you complete the tax setup from this chapter and test it with a 10% flat tax?
3. Can you implement a routine that cancels orders if they are not paid within 30 days?
4. Can you write a function that informs the user when the order is shipped?

12
Best Practices

This chapter will give an overview of what practices are helpful and recommended for microservices. So far, you have seen and learned how to write microservices in Swift with Vapor. In this chapter, we are going to check out some best practices that will help you write your own services.

We will look at how simplicity is the strength of microservices and how to achieve it. Then we will look at some Swift-specific perks that will go a long way for microservices. Often, code is either over-simplified or over-complicated; one section in this chapter aims to guide you through those decisions. Afterward, we will analyze how best to balance these two approaches with microservices. Finally, we will look into troubleshooting and debugging microservices. By the end of this chapter, you will be well equipped to write server-side Swift applications with efficient practices.

This chapter covers the following topics:

- Simplicity for maintainability and stability
- Embracing Swift language perks
- Using abstract and concrete implementations
- Combining microservices
- Troubleshooting and debugging microservices

Let's begin!

Technical requirements

This section covers what you will need to have running on your machine so that you can write this microservice. The following components need to be installed:

- Vapor toolbox
- Swift 5
- Xcode 11+
- macOS/Linux

We are also assuming that you have worked through the previous chapters and know how to write a Vapor microservice. All the code in this chapter will run the same on macOS and Linux.

The GitHub URL for this chapter: `https://github.com/PacktPublishing/Hands-On-Swift-5-Microservices-Development/tree/master/Chapter 12`.

Simplicity for maintainability and stability

Simplicity is great; every developer who has seen complex code knows this. Swift was designed to be simple and we need to take this further and also keep our microservices simple. What do we mean by maintainability and stability? For code to be maintainable and stable, it needs to be the following:

- Easily readable: The easier code is to read, the faster someone (including you) can read it later.
- Well structured: Includes the structure of files and the code within those files.
- As simple as possible and reasonable: Easy code is better than complicated code.

Let's look at the following topics:

- Simplicity through libraries: Using third-party libraries is a great way to reduce the complexity of your code.
- Using straightforward names makes it intuitive and easy to understand the intent.
- Separation of concerns: Keep things separated to avoid confusion.

We start with the first point.

Simplicity through libraries

Using third-party libraries is a great way to reduce complexity. You have probably used libraries in other projects. Using readily available libraries that fulfill the need that you have will, in many cases, be a smarter choice than rewriting it yourself. Common cases in which you will find a library include the following:

- Networking (for example, SwiftNIO): Libraries that take care of networking, requests, and API calls.
- Images and media (for example, MediaManager): These helpers manage common media files for you.
- Email providers (for example, SendGrid): With these packages, you have nice, clean APIs for your code.
- File-hosting and storage (for example, AWS S3): Libraries such as AWS S3 can help you store files well.
- Popular software (Stripe, Google Cloud, and so on): Most popular software offers a Swift package that can help you organize your code well.

Before you think you need to write something, it can be worthwhile to run a quick search to see whether someone has done it already. In some cases, you will also see that it might be worth switching from your previous solution if it means you can save time writing a library of your own. For example, you might be using Google Cloud for now, but discover that the S3 integration for Vapor works much better for you. In that case, you might want to switch from Google Cloud to AWS.

If the library you are looking for does not exist, you might want to write one yourself. If you do, you can (and should, in my opinion) open source it and make it available for others.

Even for your own project, you might want to write certain parts of your software as a library. The model structure is a good example. It could be a library that is used by the server as well as the client.

Now that you have learned how libraries can help, let's explore how name-giving plays a central role in simplicity.

Using straightforward names

Names can be both confusing and eye-opening. You want to avoid long and confusing names. An example would be this class name from a Java project:
`SimpleBeanFactoryAwareAspectInstanceFactory`.

Naturally, some names will be longer than others, but try not to chain too many words together. Also, try to name them so that the purpose becomes clear either by context or by name. `UserController` is a straightforward name; `UserManagementServiceController`, however, could be confusing.

Let's demonstrate the importance here. Take a look at this code:

```
class ControllerA {
    routeA() -> EventLoopFuture<A> {
        var f = "John"
        var l = "Cooper"
        // ...
        return b
    }
}
```

Now compare this to the following code:

```
class UserController {
 routeA() -> EventLoopFuture<UserUpdate> {
 var firstname = "John"
 var lastname = "Cooper"
 // ...
 return update
 }
}
```

Do you see that the second code is much easier to read and understand than the first? By giving our variables, functions, and classes meaningful names, the reader can know what is happening without having much context. Now, let's be real for a moment – all of us can be lazy at times and drop some formality, and, hear me, that is okay! I would simply encourage you to stick to the following guidelines:

- Whenever you are bug-fixing or intensely working on a feature, clean up before you commit to Git. Don't let messy code become part of your workspace longer than you need it to be in "lab mode."
- Certain variables *can* be shortened and no one will misunderstand them. For example, `result` can be `res`, `index` can be `i`, and so on. There is nothing wrong so long as it is intuitive to guess.

Alright, after looking at names, let's now explore the separation of concerns.

Separation of concerns

Names and libraries can make your application organized, but another very important principle is also the "separation of concerns." This means keeping things separated as much as possible. So, for example, your `UserController` should not be dealing with addresses; there should be an `AddressController`.

Using a microservice architecture at all is already a step in the right direction since you will naturally split up your application into different parts (the microservices). Each service is meant to only deal with a particular set of functions for the application. You should simply apply this concept within each service as well.

The same principle here also applies to other parts in your application, for example, the models, helpers, or utilities. Try to group them together in a way that makes sense but separates them enough. Let's take a look at an example application structure:

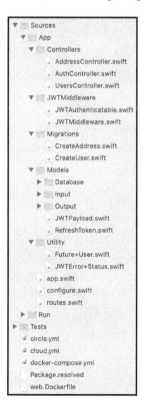

You can see how everything is neatly split up and makes sense.

 Sometimes you will find it helpful to group things together in the same file. For example, it might make more sense to have one `String-Extensions.swift` file instead of `String-Email.swift`, `String-Hash.swift`, and so on. It really comes down to how hard it will be for you to find the piece of code you are looking for.

Now that we have looked at separating concerns, you should be well prepared to write applications in a well-organized manner. Let's now look at the language perks specific to the Swift language.

Embracing Swift language perks

Swift itself has a lot of features to offer that make writing clean and understandable code easier. In this section, we will look at examples that demonstrate some of those features. Swift has remarkably many modern features in contrast to other languages, such as Go or Rust. By the end of this section, you should know how to use some of them well. Using them not only helps you write better code, but it also improves the performance of your application as you use Swift in the way that it was intended.

We will look into the following features:

- Using extensions to enhance objects with new functions
- Exploring protocols that allow you to define the interface for your code
- Understanding the difference between classes and structs

Let's take a look!

Using extensions

Extensions are a powerful yet easy way to decrease the complexity of your code. Instead of creating new classes or subclasses for your own logic, you can simply plug what you want into the existing class. For example, if we want a function that verifies that a string is a valid email, we could do so in the following way:

```
func isEmail(email: String) -> Bool {
    // ...
    return true
}
var testString = "test@test.com"
```

```
if checkEmail(email: testString) {
    print("yep")
}
```

Or, the cleaner way would be as follows:

```
extension String {
    func isEmail() -> Bool {
        // ...
        return true
    }
}
var testString = "test@test.com"
if testString.checkEmail() {
    print("yep")
}
```

Notice how the second code block makes more sense? By making the function an extension of `String`, the function is associated with the only parameter there is, which reduces the amount to write, but also keeps things where they belong. It keeps our logic nicely separated, which ties into the aspect of separation of concerns from before.

Exploring protocols

Protocols are a powerful way to ensure your application is consistent in structure. They enforce that a class or struct has specific variables and functions available. Your application logic can then rely on that, having the defined functions and variables available. Instead of requiring a class type, you can also require just the protocol and it will accept any applicable class.

Let's take a look at an example:

```
protocol HasEmail {
    var email: String { get set }
}
struct User: Model, HasEmail {
    var email: String
}
```

We have a `HasEmail` protocol, which is defining an `email` variable. Every type (`class`, `enum`, or `struct`) that is now implementing this protocol will need to define such a variable. You can see that `User` is doing that.

Within a controller, we could now do as follows:

```
func checkEmailFor(model: HasEmail) {
    if model.email == "" {
        return false
    } else {
        return true
    }
}
```

Instead of asking for `User`, we are now asking for `HasEmail`, which *could* be a user instance, but it could also be another type that is adopting `HasEmail`.

Protocols are very helpful, especially for data structures (such as models). You can combine this also with the previous point to write your own library. Having your own library that mainly consists of protocols will ensure your app code is clean and conforming to what you expect. Especially in projects with many models, this pays off.

Let's now look at a related topic, generic functions.

Using generic functions

A generic function is one that can take multiple types and work with them equally. Especially in server applications, where you deal with a lot of data, this becomes very handy. Instead of writing a function for each type of information, you can write it once and use it for every type.

Let's look at an example:

```
function saveModel<T:Model>(_ model: T, on app: Application) ->
EventLoopFuture<T> {
    return model.save(on: app).transform(to: model)
}
```

You can see that the function is using a generic type `T` that we call `model` in the signature of the function. We are also defining that this type has to implement `Model`.

Now, whenever we want to save a class that conforms to `Model`, we can do so as follows:

```
let user = User()
return self.saveModel(user, on: app)
```

See how such a function could be very useful when doing operations on a number of types that are all conforming to the same superclass or protocol?

In this simple example, we are not saving much, but in projects where you might want to perform a good number of transformations before saving a model, generic functions can be life-saving.

Now we have looked at the perks of the Swift language specifically. Extensions, protocols, and generic functions should now be part of your portfolio when writing server-side Swift applications! Let's now look at when to be abstract and when to be concrete in your implementations.

Using abstract and concrete implementations

When writing software, we are often faced with making decisions about how concrete our code is. For example, if you are tasked with writing a chat application, you need to have answers to the following questions:

- Is the chat between two people or can it be more than two?
- What kind of content is being exchanged? Text, image, video, audio, or a combination? Maybe all of it?
- How long of a chat history should be stored?

You can probably easily spot further questions that can come up. In a well-planned and thoroughly thought-through project, there would be an answer to all these questions. However, in almost all the projects that I have seen, many of these questions are overlooked, and well-intended projects still face these questions. Some of these questions are also too technical for the people who tasked you with this. However, let's pretend for a moment you have all the answers from your project manager. You sense, though, that, in the future, some updates will come your way. You are basically faced with the following two options:

- Option A: Write the app exactly matching the specifications.
- Option B: Write the app to be as generic and abstract as possible to allow for changes later on.

How do those two options differ? Take a look at what it could mean.

Option A:

- Only two people can chat.
- It is only text and images.
- Chat history is no longer than 3 days.

Option B:

- As many people as needed can communicate with each other.
- Every possible media format is supported.
- Chat history is limitless.

You can probably tell that option B requires a lot more work, testing, and overall effort. option A is what is requested. On a tight schedule and budget, the obvious choice would be A. It will do the job, but requires major restructuring when changes come down the line. In my experience, there is almost always some tension between what you, as the developer, envision it could be and what is requested.

As a general rule, try to stay as abstract as is reasonable without killing the timeline or budget. In the previous example, it makes no sense to go for the entirety of option B, but it probably does make sense to prepare the way for it. For example, you could implement it so that it would later be easier to have more than just two people chat with each other. You could also allow generic media, but only implement images at the moment. Especially with microservices, you *can* be abstract rather easily, so take advantage of it.

After looking at the tension between concrete versus abstract implementations, let's now look at how microservices can be combined.

Combining microservices

Off the back of the previous *Using abstract and concrete implementations* section, sometimes you may discover that you have been too generic and abstract. Adding microservices to your project does have a lot of benefits, but it also increases complexity and, depending on the dataflow, can introduce a lot of bugs. Especially when information is passed along from one service to another, a few things that can happen are as follows:

- Information is duplicated in each service.
- Each service verifies and validates inputs.
- Each service requires hosting resources (the servers the service runs on).
- Latency and overall slowness.

Let's take a look at the following example.

We have five microservices:

- User management service
- Address management service
- Payment information service
- Payment service
- Order service

When a user submits an order and wants to pay for it with their credit card, the following needs to happen:

1. The user management service needs to verify whether this user is still active and allowed to buy.
2. The address management service needs to return the correct address and send it to the payment service as well as the order service.
3. The payment information service needs to send the payment information to the payment service.
4. The payment service needs to send confirmation to the order service.
5. The order service needs to verify with each service and process the incoming data.
6. The order service sends an email through the user management service.

There are six steps and in all but the first step, microservices are talking to each other. This is quite messy to debug and maintain. Instead, imagine we combined the user and address management services into one, and we combined the payment information service, payment service, and order service into one service. Now we only have two services:

- User address management service
- Order service

Our steps now look like the following:

1. The user address management service can verify the user and provide the correct address for the order service.
2. The order service takes the information, loads internally the payment information, and processes the order.
3. The order service sends an email through the user management service.

That's only three steps now and only two services! This streamlines the dataflow. We also reduce the amount of data that needs to be exchanged between services, which reduces latency and makes things a bit faster.

Does this work every time? Of course not. In some cases, this is golden, in others, you want the opposite. In general, if more than two services need to talk to each other in a business logical step, you can probably reduce the dataflow. Not always by combining microservices, but that is a relatively easy way.

Alright, now that we have covered combining microservices, let's look at how to debug and troubleshoot microservices well.

Troubleshooting and debugging microservices

You should have a general idea of how to debug microservices now since we covered this well in Chapter 8, *Testing Microservices*. In this section, we are going to just look at a few core concepts that will tie this together with troubleshooting. The underlying question is usually: Why does it not do what I want it to do? In this section, you will learn how to find the answer.

Let's dive into the following topics:

- Using Xcode for debugging: Xcode offers some convenient tools for debugging.
- Using lldb for debugging: lldb is a great way to debug yourself in the command line.
- Staging and live systems: Separating your development from production is essential for every project.

We are beginning with debugging using Xcode.

Using Xcode for debugging

If you are a macOS user and you have been using Xcode in the past, you know well how easily Xcode allows debugging. Xcode, while flawed, allows debugging a lot more efficiently than some alternatives. Since Xcode 11, SPM is natively integrated into Xcode, which makes it much easier for us to write web services. If you run your service in Xcode and it crashes, Xcode will automatically try to tell you where exactly it crashed. It will show you the exact error and the trace of how it happened.

Check it out in the following example:

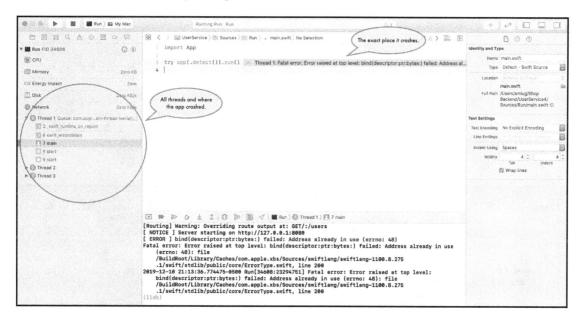

You can see that Xcode is helping us to find the problem. As a general rule of thumb, you should try to debug using Xcode; the alternatives require a good bit more work.

Xcode is using `lldb` to show us all this information.

Let's take a look at the most popular alternative to using Xcode: `lldb`.

Using lldb for debugging

If you do not want to use Xcode or you can't (because you may be on Linux), there is another way to achieve the same goal: using `lldb` to track down the problem. In fact, Xcode is using `lldb` to show us all the debug information we can see. To debug an app with `lldb` directly, do the following:

1. If your binary program is located at `.build/debug/Run` (which is typical for Vapor applications), type in the following:

   lldb ./.build/debug/Run

2. Your output should look like this:

```
amlug@amlug UserService4 % lldb ./.build/debug/Run
(lldb) target create "./.build/debug/Run"
Current executable set to './.build/debug/Run' (x86_64).
(lldb)
```

3. Now you simply need to enter `run` to start your program. The result will look like this:

```
(lldb) run
Process 34638 launched: '/Users/amlug/Shop Backend/UserService4/.build/debug/Run' (x86_64)
dyld: Library not loaded: /usr/local/opt/openssl/lib/libssl.1.0.0.dylib
  Referenced from: /Users/amlug/Shop Backend/UserService4/.build/debug/Run
  Reason: image not found
Process 34638 stopped
* thread #1, stop reason = signal SIGABRT
    frame #0: 0x0000000101a0f0de dyld`__abort_with_payload + 10
dyld`__abort_with_payload:
->  0x101a0f0de <+10>: jae     0x101a0f0e8               ; <+20>
    0x101a0f0e0 <+12>: movq    %rax, %rdi
    0x101a0f0e3 <+15>: jmp     0x101a0d601              ; cerror_nocancel
    0x101a0f0e8 <+20>: retq
Target 0: (Run) stopped.
```

You can see here the output is just as helpful as Xcode, though it is not sending you to the correct piece of code directly. However, it is still a powerful way to debug when you cannot use Xcode. Docker is a good example as well of when `lldb` can help you a lot.

Stage and live systems

Lastly, you should always run a stage and a live system if you can. The stage system should be as close to a copy of the live system as possible. Another term that is often used is "sandbox," and you may know that a lot of big companies follow this practice (PayPal, Stripe, and so on.). When you set up your routes, you can easily do something like the following:

For the live system, you would use:

```
https://api.domain.com/v1/users
```

For the stage system, you then could use a different term than v1, such as stage:

```
https://api.domain.com/stage/users
```

Alternatively, you could also use a different subdomain:

```
https://stage.api.domain.com/v1/users
```

Having such a system up and running can be a life-saver because it allows you to use it for local tests as well. If you want to test one individual service that depends on a few other services, you can utilize your stage system to test this individual service.

So, for example, say you run your user management service locally, but it uses the team management service from the stage system. In that case, you don't have to run the second service locally as well.

Alright, now you should have a good understanding of how to troubleshoot. Let's summarize this chapter.

Summary

You have explored how best to develop microservice applications using Swift. We have looked at general best practices, and then which practices we can use from the Swift language itself. You have looked at how libraries, names, and the separation of concerns can be essential tools. With Swift specifically, we have looked at how protocols, extensions, and generic functions are great for microservices. Then we looked at when it makes sense to combine microservices. We took a good look at how to debug, either with Xcode or without it. Lastly, we talked about the importance of having a staging system. You can use the knowledge you have acquired here to write well-organized and "Swifty" backend applications. Using the tools available is essential for writing apps that operate well, operate in the long term, and are easy to read years later as well.

Alright, you have a solid set of tools now to develop your own services. In the next chapter, we will talk about hosting microservices and what it takes for them to run.

Questions

To make sure your understanding is solid, answer the following questions:

1. Why would you want to develop a library for your application?
2. What is the advantage of protocols in Swift?
3. How can generic functions help you?
4. How do Xcode and `lldb` help you debug?

13
Hosting Microservices

Hosting microservices is not something most "normal" website hosts are familiar with. Traditional websites usually consist of HTML files, CSS, and JavaScript, and probably a scripting language such as PHP, Python, or Ruby. Very few providers would allow you to run native apps on a server unless you rent the entire server. Needless to say, this is a challenge when you want to host a Vapor application, let alone a group of them.

In this chapter, you will explore what it takes to host Swift and, specifically, Vapor applications. We will go through what is needed in general and then apply this knowledge so that you can actually host your API. We will set up Docker and learn how to configure environment variables. Step by step, you will learn how to host a Swift application on servers so that you know how to apply this to other applications. By the end of this chapter, you will know all you need to in order to run Vapor applications in production.

This chapter will cover the following topics:

- Setting up a microservice environment
- Exploring Swift on Linux
- Running Swift via Docker
- Using configuration and environment variables

Let's get started!

Technical requirements

This section covers what you will need to have running on your machine so that you can write the microservice for this chapter. The following components need to be installed:

- Vapor 4
- Swift 5
- XCode 11
- macOS/Linux

If you are planning on running multiple services on the same server, you should also be familiar with Nginx. We are also assuming that you have worked through the previous chapters and know how to write a Vapor microservice. All the code in this chapter will run alike on macOS and Linux.

The GitHub URL for this chapter is as follows: `https://github.com/PacktPublishing/Hands-On-Swift-5-Microservices-Development/tree/master/Chapter 13`.

Setting up a microservice environment

So far, you have been running your microservices locally on your computer. In this section, we'll talk about what a microservice environment should look like in ideal terms. A microservice environment consists of multiple servers that are running the microservices. Each of these servers can be treated independently since they may be physically separated. We'll start by looking at a single-server setup and progress toward a multi-server setup.

We'll explore the following topics:

- Starting with a simple service: We'll get a service up and running with just one server.
- Managing databases and microservices: We'll offload extra services to increase the performance of our application.
- Using the power of a load balancer: We'll bring multiple services together.
- Final setup: Most production apps have a similar setup to this.

Let's start with a simple setup.

Starting with a simple service

If we wanted to host the easiest microservice setup, it would consist of only one service. Some might argue that this would not be a microservice setup anymore since we are only dealing with one service, but let's assume that this is the easiest microservice setup we can start with. What do we need for that? A server, or computable entity. You might be wondering why we should differentiate between a "computable entity" and a "server". The answer is simple: in a world where clouds run servers, we are not always dealing with what you would classify as a "server" since the actual server might be doing a lot of different things and we are only using a small part of it. For simplicity purposes, let's assume that we are dealing with servers, even though you might find different terms for them, such as a Computing Unit.

So, we have a server; a single server that is running our Vapor app. How would we access the server, though? Servers are generally accessed through IP addresses, which are usually hidden behind a more human-friendly **Domain Name System** (**DNS**) name. So, for example, we have a domain called `http://api.myawesomeshop.com`.

The client would now resolve this to an IP address and try to load any data. It is important to note that, if no port is specified, the client will use port `80`. Why would this matter? Because a Vapor application is actually representing the entire server. Therefore, we need to listen to the correct port to answer requests correctly. You might have noticed that Vapor usually listens to port `8080`.

If we have an application running on our server now that is listening on port `8080`, an example request would actually look like this:

```
http://api.mywawesomeshop.com:8080/v1/products/categories
```

Now that we've specified the port, every client, including your browser, would be able to correctly access the API.

This is the easiest and most basic setup we could have: one server, running one Vapor app and a specific port and answering requests. Let's quickly discuss a few common issues that we came across here:

- **SSL is not activated by default**: Vapor *could* answer SSL requests. However, it is not preconfigured to and requires some intense setup and knowledge of how to do that. We will explore how to get around this problem later.

- **Once Vapor crashes, the server becomes unresponsive**: This is an issue across the board. The best prevention technique is to not let your app crash. However, if it does, there are ways to deal with that – we will look into that in a bit.
- **We want to serve the standard port** (80): In this case, running the app with "--port 80" would do the trick.

Now that we have looked into the most basic setup, let's talk about how to enhance it with databases and additional services.

Managing databases and microservices

You might want to use a database with your service. In fact, one or several of your services will probably need it. So, how would that work? In theory, there is no problem running a database application, such as MySQL or PostgreSQL, that can run on the same server as our application. As long as it is on a different port, which it is by default, multiple applications can run on the same server. Likewise, we can also run a second microservice on the same server, just on a different port. This is actually what you have been doing when developing as well: running multiple services on the same machine.

Generally speaking, there is nothing wrong with doing that. However, you do want to think about the following:

- Can your server manage the applications that are running? Do you have enough hardware resources?
- If one of your services spikes in CPU and RAM usage, how does that affect the other services?
- Has the server been correctly configured for each running application?

Each application has its own answers to those questions but as we progress to a more sophisticated setup, it makes sense to separate the services onto separate servers as well. This also applies to the previously introduced principle of separation of concerns in Chapter 12, *Best Practices*. The main benefits of why it is usually better to run services and databases on different servers are as follows:

- **Individual tuning for the server**: A database might need significant amounts of RAM, whereas the service mainly needs CPU. In fact, some processors operate better for storage than computing and vice versa on the hardware level. Do not underestimate this for production-ready apps.

- **Individual recovery and backups**: Some data is more important than others. You might need frequent backups and quick recovery for your database but don't care about it as much for your Vapor app since it doesn't store any data. Having multiple servers allows this to happen.

 You might be wondering if using Docker might solve most of these issues while allowing you to run on the same machine. The easy answer is that it does. You *could* run Docker on one machine with all your services and the database. The only problem is if your entire server crashes, including Docker. In a world where computing power and servers, through the cloud, are really affordable, it makes more sense to use different servers.

Now, you're probably wondering if using different ports is the most practical option. We call services like this:

```
http://api.myawesomeshop.com:8080/v1/products/categories
http://api.myawesomeshop.com:8081/v1/orders/history
```

In this case, we could reduce the URL's length because the port becomes part of uniquely identifying the service anyway. So, how can we solve this? The answer is simple: a load balancer.

We'll check this out in the next section.

Using the power of a load balancer

A load balancer is a server (of sorts) that does nothing but redirect traffic to the correct recipient, as well as balance traffic. Our preceding URLs could now look like this:

```
http://api.myawesomeshop.com/v1/products/categories
http://api.myawesomeshop.com/v1/orders/history
```

The load balancer listens to port `80` as this is the default port for the web. For example, from our previous example, if the URL matches "`/products/`", it would redirect to port `8080` and if it matches "`/orders/`", it would redirect to port `8081`. We could configure any port we want, really; the load balancer takes care of the conversion for us. Such a load balancer could be a simple server that takes care of the redirecting process, such as Nginx. If you have to run microservices on one server, using Nginx will help you keep a usual URL structure. Now, you might be claiming (and rightly so) that using a load balancer on the same machine is also violating the principle of separation of concerns.

In that case, you would offload the load balancer to another server. All cloud providers provide managed load balancers that completely take care of redirecting traffic for you. Whenever possible, I would recommend using those since they are affordable and reliable.

Introducing the load balancer brings us to the final setup stage: a production-ready setup.

Final setup

In this section, we'll describe the ideal and final microservice setup. Naturally, this can vary, depending on the application, but the overall principles will remain the same. The most important one is to keep the concerns separated. This means your database applications should not be on the same server as your Vapor applications.

The load balancer serves as a central point of access for all requests. It redirects the requests to each service, depending on the route. The services will try to avoid communication between themselves as much as possible. Each service is solely responsible for its own function and the load balancer but ties them together so that they're part of the same application.

The following diagram shows what this setup would look like:

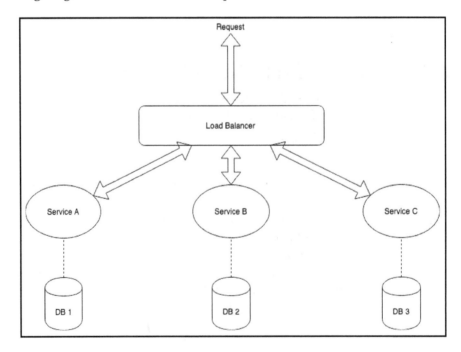

As you can see, the database servers are also separated. Ideally, you want to have each service operate completely independently, including their related services, such as the databases.

In some cases, you might decide to put a few of the services on the same server. In those cases, I would recommend that you put the databases together and the Vapor applications together. Most cloud hosting providers offer managed database servers, which are usually a safe choice for such groupings.

Now that we have looked at the general setup, let's take a look at how Swift runs on Linux.

Exploring Swift on Linux

Swift on Linux was a big surprise when Apple released Swift so that it was open source. However, running Swift on Linux is not quite the same as running it on macOS, iOS, iPadOS, or tvOS. Running Swift on Linux means essentially running it in an environment that is very different from Apple platforms. In this section, we will look at two specific aspects:

- The current state of Swift on Linux: Where are we at with Swift for Linux?
- Installing Linux on Ubuntu: We'll install Swift on an Ubuntu instance.

Let's start with the current state of Swift.

The current state of Swift on Linux

In the beginning, Swift had a hard time getting to use Linux well. While macOS is based on Unix (as is Linux), there are a lot of libraries that Apple did not decide to declare as open source or not open source all of it (such as Foundation). This is a problem in that a Swift application compiled for macOS may not behave exactly the same as for Linux. Now, if you have ever dealt with C or C++, you know this problem well. The good news is that Swift's evolution on the Linux platform has reduced this problem to a few minor edge cases. This has mainly happened because Apple itself provides a fair amount of libraries that are more than handy for Linux specifically (SwiftNIO, swift-metrics, and more).

Swift can run on many platforms at this point, including Android and Windows. However, it is important to keep in mind that we want our servers to run reliably. Therefore, I would only recommend using the officially supported platforms. For Linux, this currently only involves Ubuntu. However, Ubuntu is one of the most commonly used server distributions of Linux and is widely supported. Every server provider will be able to provide an Ubuntu server.

Now that you know where we stand, let's apply this knowledge and install Swift on Ubuntu.

Installing Linux on Ubuntu

Once we have a Ubuntu server, it is only a matter of installing the correct software packages. You may not have a free computer available that you can try this on. If you already have a cloud provider, you might want to start a cloud Ubuntu server to follow the instructions in this section.

 Typically, you don't install Swift on Linux manually for production systems. For debugging, however, it is more than useful to know how to install Swift by hand.

The instructions are very simple. To install Linux on Ubuntu, follow these steps:

1. Install a few tools, that is, `clang`, `curl`, and `python`, as well as the `dev` packages for all of them, like this:

   ```
   sudo apt-get install clang libcurl3 libpython2.7 libpython2.7-dev
   ```

2. Download Swift and unpack it, as follows:

   ```
   wget
   https://swift.org/builds/swift-5.0.1-release/ubuntu1804/swift-5.0.1
   -RELEASE/swift-5.0.1-RELEASE-ubuntu18.04.tar.gz
   tar xzf swift-5.0.1-RELEASE-ubuntu18.04.tar.gz
   ```

3. Move Swift to a better location and link its path:

   ```
   sudo mv swift-5.0.1-RELEASE-ubuntu18.04 /usr/share/swift
   echo "export PATH=/usr/share/swift/usr/bin:$PATH" >> ~/.bashrc
   source ~/.bashrc
   ```

4. Now, we can verify that Swift has been installed:

```
swift --version
```

This should output the installed version of Swift.

5. The `swift` program works the same on Linux as it does on macOS. So, to compile a Vapor app, we would to the following:

```
swift build && ./.build/debug/Run
```

This is all we need to do in order to run Swift on Linux. Now that we've learned how to run Swift on Linux, let's look at the practical side of running Swift servers.

Running Swift via Docker

If we were to set up each of our servers manually, just like we did previously, we would never finish deploying. Fortunately, a handy tool called Docker not only automates this step, but it also allows for intelligent memory management for servers. Docker is a tool that containerizes applications and gives them isolated environments while also saving their state as we need it to run. This means that if we were to put the preceding steps in a Dockerfile, we could spin this file up whenever we needed it.

Luckily for us, Apple has already done that. We can access official Docker images for Swift that give us all we need. Docker is best-explained by looking at a Dockerfile, so let's take a look at the standard Vapor Dockerfile. A Dockerfile is a text file that contains all the instructions for Docker to create images that we can then run as containers.

Check out the following `Dockerfile`:

```
# ===================================
# Build image
# ===================================
FROM vapor/swift:5.1 as build
WORKDIR /build

# Copy entire repo into container
COPY . .

# Install sqlite3
RUN apt-get update -y \
        && apt-get install -y libsqlite3-dev

# Compile with optimizations
```

```
RUN swift build \
        --enable-test-discovery \
        -c release

# ==================================
# Run image
# ==================================
FROM vapor/ubuntu:18.04
WORKDIR /run

# Copy build artifacts
COPY --from=build /build/.build/release /run
# Copy Swift runtime libraries
COPY --from=build /usr/lib/swift/ /usr/lib/swift/

ENTRYPOINT ["./Run", "serve", "--env", "production", "--hostname",
"0.0.0.0", "--port", "80"]
```

In line 4, you can see that we are stating `FROM vapor/swift:5.1 as build`. This means
we are starting a new image, using the Swift 5.1 version from the Vapor repository. We call
this image `build` because of the `as`. Further down, you can see that we are also
calling `FROM vapor/ubuntu:18.04`. In the second image, we don't need to give a name as
it is not referenced by other images. The build image is only compiling our application. It
uses the official Swift image from Vapor to get everything we need to compile Swift. Then,
it compiles our application. The run image uses just the regular Ubuntu image and then
copies the application over. The reason it does this is that our actual server does not need
any of the source files, nor the Swift environment. So, for one, we are not exposing the
source code but we are also keeping it minimal.

Note that we can specify the port in the Dockerfile directly. This allows us
to use different ports easily.

Now that we have looked at Docker and learned how to set up Swift on Linux, let's take a
look at how to provide credentials to your application.

Environment variables

You learned how to pass configuration variables to your Vapor app on macOS in `Chapter 3`, *Getting Started with the Vapor Framework*. By simply making environment variables available, the application knows of your configuration credentials. On macOS, this looks like this:

```
export DATABASE_USER="user"
```

The same also works on a server that is not macOS. Note that your server may expect the variables in a different format, depending on the specific Linux distribution. In general, you want to make sure you know how to provide the environment variables to your application at runtime. You do not want to expose them to your code as defaults or in the Docker image.

Your credentials could get exposed through having them in your image, which poses a security threat but also makes it harder for you to change them. Therefore, you want to keep them flexible and out of your code. All server environments offer you a way to expose variables to your application at runtime.

For Ubuntu, it is the same as it is for macOS. So, if you run a server directly by having Ubuntu installed, the export function will do what it needs to do. Docker containers get their environment variables from Docker, however. Depending on how you run Docker, this might require you to look up the specific documentation. For standard Docker, you can do this by adding the `-e` argument for the variables, like so:

```
docker run -e SENDGRID_API_KEY="SG.IoE" -p 8080:8080 myservice
```

`SENDGRID_API_KEY` is the example variable.

Now that we have looked at how to pass configuration to the server, let's summarize this chapter.

Summary

Here we go! In this chapter, we looked at the current state of Swift on the server. We started by looking at a generic microservice structure and went over what it looks like. In the process, we went from a single-server system to a multi-server system, including a load balancer.

Then, we looked at how we would run our Vapor apps on a Linux system. We went through the entire Swift installation process, followed by looking at how Docker can simplify the installation process. Finally, we took a look at how configuration should be passed to the server application and what that looks like on macOS, Linux, and Docker.

In this chapter, you learned where Swift on the server stands. You learned how to install Swift on Ubuntu and how to run it through Docker. With these skills, you can essentially run any Swift application on Linux servers.

Now that you've learned the foundations of running server applications with Swift, in the next chapter, we'll deploy our app to the cloud!

Questions

To make sure your understanding of this chapter is solid, answer the following questions:

1. Why is it not advisable to run the entire backend on only one server?
2. How does Docker simplify your installation process?
3. How should you store your credentials in your database?
4. What role does the load balancer play?

14
Docker and the Cloud

When it comes to deploying microservices, Docker is by far the most-common and most-used technology to help us launch. We introduced Docker in `Chapter 13`, *Hosting Microservices*, and in this chapter, we will dig a little deeper. First, we are going to get a solid understanding of Docker itself and how it runs. Then, we will get a better idea of what running Docker looks like on different cloud providers.

After working through this chapter, you will know exactly how Docker ties into server-side Swift and you will know how different cloud providers handle Docker.

In this chapter, we will cover the following topics:

- Exploring Docker Containers and Images: Getting to know the heart of Docker
- Running Docker with AWS: The most popular cloud provider
- Running Docker with Google Cloud: Another option to run scalable backends
- Running Docker with Digital Ocean: Getting your backend up with Digital Ocean
- Running Docker with Heroku: Using Heroku to run your backend
- Using Kubernetes: A way to manage Docker well

Let's start with the basics of Docker!

Technical requirements

This section covers what you will need to have running on your machine so that you can write the microservice for this chapter. The following components need to be installed:

- Vapor 4
- Swift 5
- XCode 11+
- Docker

- macOS/Linux
- AWS CLI
- Google Cloud CLI
- Docker Machine

We are also assuming that you have worked through the previous chapters and know how to write a Vapor microservice. All the code in this chapter will run alike under macOS and Linux.

For this chapter, you might want to register for a cloud provider of your choice. We will go through the most popular ones, but if you have an account already, then it will make it easier for you to follow along.

The GitHub repository for this chapter: `https://github.com/PacktPublishing/Hands-On-Swift-5-Microservices-Development/tree/master/Chapter 14`.

Exploring Docker Containers and Images

At this point, you should have Docker installed on your machine. If not, head over to `https://docs.docker.com/install/` and go through the instructions for your system. In this section, we will explore the heart of Docker to get a better understanding of how it operates. Docker has Images, which are compiled system states, and Containers, which are running system states. Both are the central units that Docker interacts with.

In this section, we will look at the following topics:

- Setting up Docker: We are going to make sure Docker has been installed correctly.
- Images, Repositories, and Containers: Understanding the difference and use of these.
- Starting Hello World: Hello from Docker.

Let's start with setting up Docker.

Setting up Docker

Let's make sure your system has Docker installed on it correctly and that you can work through the next few steps. If you haven't installed Docker yet, go to `https://docs.docker.com/install/` and install it on your machine.

Open a Terminal (or console) and run the following command:

```
% docker version
```

Your output should now display the version, like this:

```
Client: Docker Engine - Community
 Version:           19.03.5
 API version:       1.40
 Go version:        go1.12.12
 Git commit:        633a0ea
 Built:             Wed Nov 13 07:22:34 2019
 OS/Arch:           darwin/amd64
 Experimental:      false

Server: Docker Engine - Community
 Engine:
  Version:          19.03.5
  API version:      1.40 (minimum version 1.12)
  Go version:       go1.12.12
  Git commit:       633a0ea
  Built:            Wed Nov 13 07:29:19 2019
  OS/Arch:          linux/amd64
  Experimental:     false
 containerd:
  Version:          v1.2.10
  GitCommit:        b34a5c8af56e510852c35414db4c1f4fa6172339
 runc:
  Version:          1.0.0-rc8+dev
  GitCommit:        3e425f80a8c931f88e6d94a8c831b9d5aa481657
 docker-init:
  Version:          0.18.0
  GitCommit:        fec3683
```

Make sure you have Docker 19 or newer installed. When you run Docker, it's actually the client of Docker we are using. On macOS, the server is part of Docker Desktop, which is actually doing most of the work. Make sure Docker Desktop is up and running too. If it is, you should see a small icon in the top bar, like this:

Now, we are all set to use Docker, so let's start by looking at Images and Containers.

Images, Repositories, and Containers

We briefly talked about Images and Containers in Chapter 2, *Understanding Server-Side Swift*. In this section, we will discuss the three main elements of Docker:

- Repositories
- Images
- Containers

Let's start with repositories.

Repositories

You probably know what repositories are from using Git or other versioning tools. It is the same thing for Docker. A repository saves different versions of Docker images. When you build your Docker image, it is locally stored on the computer where it was built. Then, we can push it into a repository, where it is saved and versioned.

From that repository, we can then pull it again when we want to run it as a container.

The following diagram explains how images and repositories are connected:

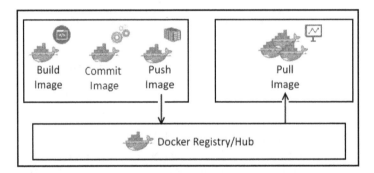

Now, let's take a look at images.

Images

Images are what you save in repositories. They consist of a "compiled" version of your Dockerfile, including all the files that need to be run. Dockerfiles are the files that describe what an image should be, similar to source code. A Dockerfile usually results in one or more images. Images can also depend on each other and be related.

Note, for example, what a Dockerfile for Swift looks like:

```
FROM swift:5.1.1
```

This means we are using another image to base our new image on. The preceding Swift image, whose version is 5.1.1., is actually using an Ubuntu image. Similar to how classes in programming can be related and based upon each other, Docker images can be based on each other too. The nice thing is that a new Docker image only contains the difference between the inherited image. This means our final image can be quite small.

Containers

Containers are images when they run on a host. So, when Docker launches our images, they become containers. In other words, containers are launched images. Whenever Docker is used to run a server application, it is classed as a container in which the application is run. So, the container resembles the operating system for the application.

An application that requires Debian Linux would have a container that resembles Debian Linux. An application that needs CentOS would have a CentOS environment. These, however, can run within an entirely different host system, such as macOS.

Starting Hello World

In this section, we will start an actual Docker image. By the end, you should have run a Docker container and seen what it looks like. Let's get Docker up and running. Open a Terminal and run the following command:

```
% docker run hello-world
```

If you receive the following output, you should make sure Docker Desktop has been started and is running:

```
docker: Cannot connect to the Docker daemon at unix:///var/run/docker.sock.
Is the docker daemon running?.
```

If everything is correct, you should see the following:

```
Unable to find image 'hello-world:latest' locally
latest: Pulling from library/hello-world
1b930d010525: Pull complete
Digest:
sha256:9572f7cdcee8591948c2963463447a53466950b3fc15a247fcad1917ca215a2f
Status: Downloaded newer image for hello-world:latest
```

```
Hello from Docker!
This message shows that your installation appears to be working correctly.
```

Notice how Docker is not finding the image, so it starts automatically pulling it? Docker is always checking the local cache, so make sure whether an image is already there or not. Remember that Docker images can be related to each other. When pulling the image, we really want Docker to load the related images. In this case, the `hello-world` image does not depend on a lot, but other Docker images, such as `swift`, depend on a few others. Managing images, however, is pretty shielded from us as developers, so we don't need to worry about it too much.

Now that we know how Docker operates and we have successfully started the "Hello World" application, let's get started with Docker on AWS.

Running Docker with AWS

Running Docker in AWS can be achieved in a few ways. **AWS** stands for **Amazon Web Services** and is the most popular and biggest cloud provider available. Countless websites are running on AWS, including Netflix, Airbnb, Amazon, and many more. In this section, we'll learn how to get Docker running on AWS.

The least convenient but most customizable way to do this is to install Docker ourselves on one of the cloud computers and then run our backends that way. Before we dive into how to run Docker in AWS, let's define a few things:

- **Amazon Elastic Compute Cloud (EC2):** This is where the virtual servers (`units/computing units`) are running. Whenever we say "server", this is often what we mean. These machines are often virtual and it is entirely up to us what we do with them. The operating system, settings, permissions, and so on are all up to us.
- **Fargate:** This a managed flavor of EC2 specifically meant for Docker. In this version, everything but Docker images are managed for us.
- **Amazon Elastic Container Services ECS:** ECS is an AWS service that allows us to run services in a managed fashion.
- **Task description:** A description and configuration for Docker containers. Services launched within ECS will use task descriptions to run those containers. A task can run more than one container, though often, one is all you need.

- **Elastic Container Registry** (**ECR**): AWS offers repositories that you can use to store the Docker images.
- **Load Balancer:** AWS provides a load balancer so that you can connect to the services.

In this section, we will explore the most AWS-native way to deploy Docker. AWS offers **Elastic Container Services** (**ECS**) as the most straightforward way to deploy Docker containers. The way ECS works can be seen in the following diagram:

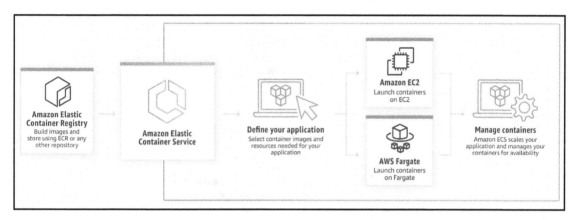

The flow starts with you pushing (uploading) your Docker images to ECR. A task definition of ECS will use that image to deploy a service. A service can have as many instances as desired. Each instance is essentially a Docker container running either on your own EC2 instances or on Fargate.

 Make sure you have the AWS CLI set up and running. If you need any help, go to `https://docs.aws.amazon.com/cli/latest/userguide/cli-chap-install.html`.

So, let's go through the following steps to get our service up and running:

1. Type in the following command to create a Docker repository:

   ```
   % aws ecr create-repository --repository-name examplevapor
   ```

   You should see the following output:

   ```
   {
       "repository": {
           "repositoryArn": "arn:aws:ecr:us-
               east-1:140099160703:repository/examplevapor",
   ```

```
            "registryId": "140099160703",
            "repositoryName": "examplevapor",
            "repositoryUri": "140099160703.dkr.ecr.us-
                east-1.amazonaws.com/examplevapor",
            "createdAt": 1580499621.0,
            "imageTagMutability": "MUTABLE",
            "imageScanningConfiguration": {
                "scanOnPush": false
            }
        }
    }
```

2. Now, we have to create a cluster in order to run our application:

```
% aws ecs create-cluster --cluster-name example-cluster
```

The output should look like this:

```
{
    "cluster": {
        "clusterArn": "arn:aws:ecs:us-
            east-1:140099160703:cluster/example-cluster",
        "clusterName": "example-cluster",
        "status": "ACTIVE",
        "registeredContainerInstancesCount": 0,
        "runningTasksCount": 0,
        "pendingTasksCount": 0,
        "activeServicesCount": 0,
        "statistics": [],
        "tags": [],
        "settings": [
            {
                "name": "containerInsights",
                "value": "disabled"
            }
        ]
    }
}
```

We are using an ECS cluster here. This is a good way to manage projects and services. This means you could put all the related services into one cluster.

Next, we need to create the task description. You can find it in the source code for this chapter, but here's its content in brief:

```
{
  "family": "vapor-example-app",
  "executionRoleArn":
"arn:aws:iam::140099160703:role/ecsTaskExecutionRole",
  "containerDefinitions": [
    {
      "name": "vapor-example-app",
      "portMappings": [
        {
          "hostPort": 8080,
          "protocol": "tcp",
          "containerPort": 8080
        }
      ],
      "essential": true,
      "environment": [
        {
          "name": "EXAMPLE_VAR",
          "value": "configValue"
        }
      ],
      "image": "140099160703.dkr.ecr.us-
        east-1.amazonaws.com/examplevapor:latest"
    }
  ],
  "memory": "512",
  "requiresCompatibilities": [
    "FARGATE"
  ],
  "networkMode": "awsvpc",
  "cpu": "256"
}
```

3. You need to replace the value of `image` with what you have in `repositoryUri`. You need to do this so that this task is referring to the repository we just created.

4. You also need to replace `executionRoleArn` with a role you need to create. In your browser, go to `https://console.aws.amazon.com/iam/home` and click on **Roles**.

5. Check if you already have a role named `ecsTaskExecutionRole`. If you do, copy the ARN of that role and paste it into the `taskdefinition.json` file.

6. If you don't, click on **Create Role**. Then, select **Elastic Container Service**:

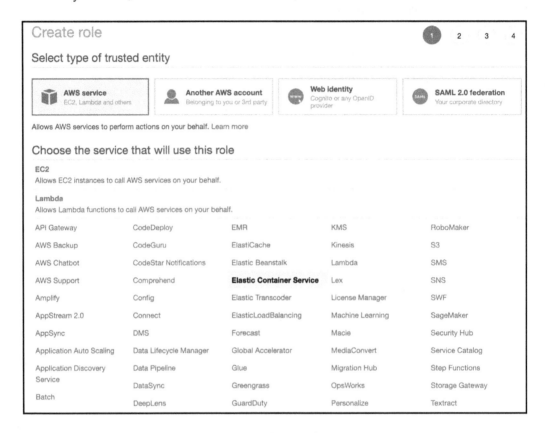

7. Next, select **Elastic Container Service Task**:

8. Click on **Next: Permissions** and select **AmazonECSTaskExecutionRolePolicy** as a policy. Then, click **Next**:

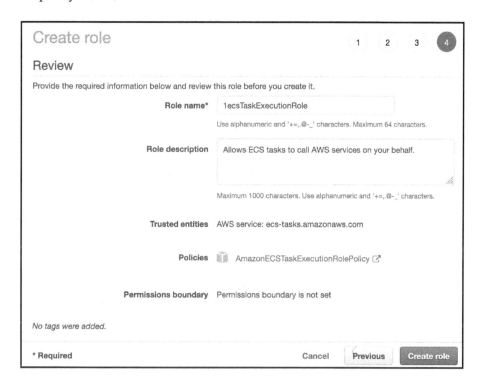

9. Give the role a name, for example, `ecsTaskExecutionRole` and click **Create role**.

10. Copy the ARN of this created role and paste it into the `taskdefinition.json` file.

11. Now, we can compile our Docker image. Type in the following to log in and authenticate Docker:

```
% $(aws ecr get-login --no-include-email --region us-east-1)
```

12. Next, we compile the actual Docker image:

```
% docker build -t examplevapor .
```

This should result in the following output (this may take a minute):

```
Successfully built 636a60295c3f
Successfully tagged examplevapor:latest
```

13. Now, we have to tag the image correctly so that AWS knows where to put it:

```
% docker tag examplevapor:latest 140099160703.dkr.ecr.us-
east-1.amazonaws.com/examplevapor:latest
```

14. Now, we can push the image, meaning we are uploading it into the repository:

```
% docker push 140099160703.dkr.ecr.us-
east-1.amazonaws.com/examplevapor:latest
```

The last two lines should look like this:

```
cc967c529ced: Pushed
latest: digest:
sha256:49c8a5bdf2d31c1d92804b1d31a812e4d394c57bc89d40f615dfd7f776b7
427a size: 1788
```

Now that we have the image in the repository, we can launch a service using that image.

15. Create a new task definition by using what we previously edited:

```
% aws ecs register-task-definition --cli-input-json
file://$HOME/Hands-On-Microservices-with-Swift-5/Chapter\
14/ExampleVaporApp/taskdefinition.json
```

16. List all the available task definitions:

```
% aws ecs list-task-definitions
```

The result should look like this:

```
{
    "taskDefinitionArns": [
        "arn:aws:ecs:us-east-1:140099160703:task-definition/vapor-
            example-app:1"
    ]
}
```

17. To launch a new service, we need to get the subnet ID, as well as the security group ID. Get the subnet ID by listing all our preconfigured subnets:

```
% aws ec2 describe-subnets
```

This should result in a list like this:

```
{
    "Subnets": [
        {
```

```
            "AvailabilityZone": "us-east-1c",
            "AvailabilityZoneId": "use1-az6",
            "AvailableIpAddressCount": 4091,
            "CidrBlock": "172.31.32.0/20",
            "DefaultForAz": true,
            "MapPublicIpOnLaunch": true,
            "State": "available",
            "SubnetId": "subnet-902638cc",
            "VpcId": "vpc-f497b98e",
            "OwnerId": "426628247310",
            "AssignIpv6AddressOnCreation": false,
            "Ipv6CidrBlockAssociationSet": [],
            "SubnetArn": "arn:aws:ec2:us-
              east-1:426628247310:subnet/subnet-902638cc"
        }
    ]
}
```

18. Now, let's grab our preexisting security group:

```
% aws ec2 describe-security-groups
```

The result should look like this:

```
{
    "SecurityGroups": [
        {
            "Description": "default VPC security group",
            "GroupName": "default",
            "IpPermissions": [
                {
                    "IpProtocol": "-1",
                    "IpRanges": [],
                    "Ipv6Ranges": [],
                    "PrefixListIds": [],
                    "UserIdGroupPairs": [
                        {
                            "GroupId": "sg-51339979",
                            "UserId": "426628247310"
                        }
                    ]
                }
            ],
            "OwnerId": "426628247310",
            "GroupId": "sg-51339979",
            "IpPermissionsEgress": [
                {
                    "IpProtocol": "-1",
```

```
                                "IpRanges": [
                                    {
                                        "CidrIp": "0.0.0.0/0"
                                    }
                                ],
                                "Ipv6Ranges": [],
                                "PrefixListIds": [],
                                "UserIdGroupPairs": []
                            }
                        ],
                        "VpcId": "vpc-f497b98e"
                }
            ]
        }
```

19. Now, we need to add a rule to allow traffic to port 8080:

```
% aws ec2 authorize-security-group-ingress --group-id sg-51339979 -
-protocol tcp --port 8080 --cidr 0.0.0.0/0
```

20. That's all we need to do for our service. Now, we can actually create the service
    with the parameters we used previously:

```
% aws ecs create-service --cluster example-cluster --service-name
vapor-example-service --task-definition vapor-example-app:1 --
desired-count 1 --launch-type "FARGATE" --network-configuration
"awsvpcConfiguration={subnets=[subnet-902638cc],securityGroups=[sg-
51339979],assignPublicIp=ENABLED}"
```

The result should look like this:

```
{
    "service": {
        "serviceArn": "arn:aws:ecs:us-
        east-1:140099160703:service/vapor-example-service",
        "serviceName": "vapor-example-service",
        "clusterArn": "arn:aws:ecs:us-
        east-1:140099160703:cluster/example-cluster",
        "loadBalancers": [],
        "serviceRegistries": [],
        "status": "ACTIVE",
        "desiredCount": 1,
        "runningCount": 0,
        "pendingCount": 0,
        "launchType": "FARGATE",
        "platformVersion": "LATEST",
        "taskDefinition": "arn:aws:ecs:us-east-1:140099160703:task-
        definition/vapor-example-app:3",
```

```
    "deploymentConfiguration": {
        "maximumPercent": 200,
        "minimumHealthyPercent": 100
    },
    "deployments": [
        {
            "id": "ecs-svc/8628131754895004324",
            "status": "PRIMARY",
            "taskDefinition": "arn:aws:ecs:us-
             east-1:140099160703:task-definition/vapor-example-
               app:3",
            "desiredCount": 1,
            "pendingCount": 0,
            "runningCount": 0,
            "createdAt": 1580503971.319,
            "updatedAt": 1580503971.319,
            "launchType": "FARGATE",
            "platformVersion": "1.3.0",
            "networkConfiguration": {
                "awsvpcConfiguration": {
                    "subnets": [
                        "subnet-470fc31b"
                    ],
                    "securityGroups": [
                        "sg-034e164b"
                    ],
                    "assignPublicIp": "ENABLED"
                }
            }
        }
    ],
    "roleArn": "arn:aws:iam::140099160703:role/aws-service-
     role/ecs.amazonaws.com/AWSServiceRoleForECS",
    "events": [],
    "createdAt": 1580503971.319,
    "placementConstraints": [],
    "placementStrategy": [],
    "networkConfiguration": {
        "awsvpcConfiguration": {
            "subnets": [
                "subnet-470fc31b"
            ],
            "securityGroups": [
                "sg-034e164b"
            ],
            "assignPublicIp": "DISABLED"
        }
    },
```

```
                    "schedulingStrategy": "REPLICA",
                    "enableECSManagedTags": false,
                    "propagateTags": "NONE"
            }
    }
```

Now, AWS ECS should be starting our service with the given instructions. This will take a moment, but after it's done, we can run the next command.

21. Run the following command to see all the tasks:

```
% aws ecs list-tasks --cluster example-cluster
```

The output should look like this:

```
{
    "taskArns": [
        "arn:aws:ecs:us-
east-1:426628247310:task/eba439a7-161d-458d-bfe7-30f9740c55bd"
    ]
}
```

22. We can use this ARN to get the specifics of the tasks:

```
% aws ecs describe-tasks --tasks arn:aws:ecs:us-
east-1:426628247310:task/eba439a7-161d-458d-bfe7-30f9740c55bd --
cluster example-cluster
```

This will return the following output:

```
{
    "tasks": [
        {
            "attachments": [
                {
                    "id": "83776154-c499-4523-8208-56b42d25bd50",
                    "type": "ElasticNetworkInterface",
                    "status": "ATTACHED",
                    "details": [
                        {
                            "name": "subnetId",
                            "value": "subnet-902638cc"
                        },
                        {
                            "name": "networkInterfaceId",
                            "value": "eni-0fa67334feeaeb953"
                        },
                        {
```

```
                        "name": "macAddress",
                        "value": "0e:be:55:3c:53:37"
                    },
                    {
                        "name": "privateIPv4Address",
                        "value": "172.31.42.196"
                    }
                ]
            }
        ],
        "availabilityZone": "us-east-1c",
        "clusterArn": "arn:aws:ecs:us-
         east-1:426628247310:cluster/example-cluster",
        "connectivity": "CONNECTED",
        "connectivityAt": 1580570455.494,
        "containers": [
            {
                "containerArn": "arn:aws:ecs:us-
                 east-1:426628247310:container/c6bc752f-
                 e8f6-4a0e-8afb-cb05405f8e7c",
                "taskArn": "arn:aws:ecs:us-
                 east-1:426628247310:task/eba439a7-161d-458d-
                 bfe7-30f9740c55bd",
                "name": "vapor-example-app",
                "image": "426628247310.dkr.ecr.us-
                 east-1.amazonaws.com/examplevapor",
                "imageDigest":
                "sha256:478fa5fc86c63b30b576974d93df0b0f0
                 baae48c0091e849520820b702a6529e",
                "runtimeId":
                "4dcabd86e65e6f8e33bd44d9698fd3b2df6e
                 00cfb34623b9cb23989f69ddc28e",
                "lastStatus": "RUNNING",
                "networkBindings": [],
                "networkInterfaces": [
                    {
                        "attachmentId": "83776154-
                         c499-4523-8208-56b42d25bd50",
                        "privateIpv4Address": "172.31.42.196"
                    }
                ],
                "healthStatus": "UNKNOWN",
                "cpu": "0"
            }
        ],
        "cpu": "256",
        "createdAt": 1580570451.531,
        "desiredStatus": "RUNNING",
```

```
            "group": "service:vapor-example-service",
            "healthStatus": "UNKNOWN",
            "lastStatus": "RUNNING",
            "launchType": "FARGATE",
            "memory": "512",
            "overrides": {
                "containerOverrides": [
                    {
                        "name": "vapor-example-app"
                    }
                ],
                "inferenceAcceleratorOverrides": []
            },
            "platformVersion": "1.3.0",
            "pullStartedAt": 1580570465.171,
            "pullStoppedAt": 1580570516.171,
            "startedAt": 1580570521.171,
            "startedBy": "ecs-svc/6023872132268435911",
            "tags": [],
            "taskArn": "arn:aws:ecs:us-east-1:426628247310:task
            /eba439a7-161d-458d-bfe7-30f9740c55bd",
            "taskDefinitionArn": "arn:aws:ecs:us-east-1:
            426628247310:task-definition/vapor-example-app:1",
            "version": 3
        }
    ],
    "failures": []
}
```

Grab the value for `networkInterfaceId`.

23. Use that value to get the public IP for that network interface:

```
% aws ec2 describe-network-interfaces --network-interface-ids
eni-0fa67334feeaeb953
```

The result looks like this:

```
{
    "NetworkInterfaces": [
        {
            "Association": {
                "IpOwnerId": "amazon",
                "PublicDnsName":
                "ec2-52-91-181-84.compute-1.amazonaws.com",
                "PublicIp": "52.91.181.84"
            },
            "Attachment": {
```

```
                    "AttachTime": "2020-02-01T15:20:57.000Z",
                    "AttachmentId": "eni-attach-08b8a63de74ff08eb",
                    "DeleteOnTermination": false,
                    "DeviceIndex": 1,
                    "InstanceOwnerId": "899097435024",
                    "Status": "attached"
                },
                "AvailabilityZone": "us-east-1c",
                "Description": "arn:aws:ecs:us-
                 east-1:426628247310:attachment/83776154-
                  c499-4523-8208-56b42d25bd50",
                "Groups": [
                    {
                        "GroupName": "default",
                        "GroupId": "sg-51339979"
                    }
                ],
                "InterfaceType": "interface",
                "Ipv6Addresses": [],
                "MacAddress": "0e:be:55:3c:53:37",
                "NetworkInterfaceId": "eni-0fa67334feeaeb953",
                "OwnerId": "426628247310",
                "PrivateDnsName": "ip-172-31-42-196.ec2.internal",
                "PrivateIpAddress": "172.31.42.196",
                "PrivateIpAddresses": [
                    {
                        "Association": {
                            "IpOwnerId": "amazon",
                            "PublicDnsName": "ec2-52-91-181-84
                              .compute-1.amazonaws.com",
                            "PublicIp": "52.91.181.84"
                        },
                        "Primary": true,
                        "PrivateDnsName":
                        "ip-172-31-42-196.ec2.internal",
                        "PrivateIpAddress": "172.31.42.196"
                    }
                ],
                "RequesterId": "578734482556",
                "RequesterManaged": true,
                "SourceDestCheck": true,
                "Status": "in-use",
                "SubnetId": "subnet-902638cc",
                "TagSet": [],
                "VpcId": "vpc-f497b98e"
        }
    ]
}
```

Now, this contains the `PublicIp`. Grab that and open your browser (or use curl):

`http://52.91.181.84:8080/`

Your browser should now return the following output:

`It works!`

And that's it – our Vapor app is now running with AWS!

That was quite a journey to get it up and running. Now, you should know why DevOps is a field that is increasing in demand. It is important for backend developers to know the basics, though, which is why we went through this journey here.

Awesome – we have successfully deployed our first app, which is the basis for everything else. In the next section, we will look at Google and how deploying works with Google Cloud.

Running Docker in Google Cloud

To run Docker in Google Cloud, we will use the App Engine. Google made it very easy to deploy Docker containers. Let's deploy our example app by going through the following steps:

1. Make sure you have Cloud SDK installed. If you don't, head over to `https://cloud.google.com/sdk/docs/quickstarts/` and install it.
2. Type the following command into the `ExampleVaporApp` folder for this chapter:

   ```
   % gcloud app deploy
   ```

   You should see the following output:

   ```
   Services to deploy:

   descriptor:      [/Users/amlug/projects/Hands-On-Microservices-
   with-Swift-5/Chapter 14/ExampleVaporApp/app.yaml]
   source:          [/Users/amlug/projects/Hands-On-Microservices-
   with-Swift-5/Chapter 14/ExampleVaporApp]
   target project:  [microservices-266818]
   target service:  [default]
   target version:  [20200131t132300]
   target url:      [https://microservices-266818.appspot.com]
   ```

```
Do you want to continue (Y/n)?

Enabling service [appengineflex.googleapis.com] on project
[microservices-266818]...
Operation "operations/acf.85a472ed-f7c4-430d-80f2-2b6de51995ed"
finished successfully.
Beginning deployment of service [default]...
Building and pushing image for service [default]
```

When this has finished executing, which could take up to 15 minutes, you should see the following:

```
Updating service [default] (this may take several minutes)...done.
Setting traffic split for service [default]...done.
Deployed service [default] to
[https://microservices-266818.appspot.com]

You can stream logs from the command line by running:
  $ gcloud app logs tail -s default

To view your application in the web browser run:
  $ gcloud app browse
```

Here, you can see that Google is using all you have learned about Docker. An image will be compiled and then pushed to a Google-managed registry. The image is then taken and deployed live.

3. To see the result, type in the following:

```
% gcloud app browse
```

Now, your browser should open and you should see the following:

```
It works!
```

You will notice that Google uses a domain such as `https://microservices-266818.appspot.com` for your service. Google automatically manages the underlying servers for us. If we wanted to deploy a second service, we can do so just as we did with this first one. To enable URL routing (/<version>/<servicename>), we need to create a `dispatch.yaml` file, like this:

```
dispatch:
  - url: "*/users/*"
    service: user-service

  - url: "*/products/*"
    service: products-service
```

This will take care of sending each request to the correct service.

 While Google is offering these nice shortcut commands, the underlying steps are identical to what we did previously with AWS. Notice how much simpler this is than AWS? Google hides almost all the steps we performed previously with AWS within those simple commands. The steps are, however, pretty much the same, whether we type them in or let a tool do everything for us.

That's it for Google. In this section, we learned how to deploy a simple application and how Google works with Docker behind the scenes. Now, let's take a look at Digital Ocean.

Running Docker with Digital Ocean

Digital Ocean is yet another cloud provider that offers easy and affordable hosting. Let's go through the following steps to set up a project:

1. Sign up for Digital Ocean by going `www.digitalocean.com`.
2. Click **API** from the navigation menu.
3. Click **Generate new Token** to create a new personal token that we can use to deploy.
4. Copy and paste that token.
5. Type `docker-machine` into your Terminal. If you get an error, run the following command to install it:

   ```
   % base=https://github.com/docker/machine/releases/download/v0.16.0
   &&curl -L $base/docker-machine-$(uname -s)-$(uname -m)
   >/usr/local/bin/docker-machine &&chmod +x /usr/local/bin/docker-
   machine
   ```

   See `https://docs.docker.com/machine/install-machine/` for more details on installing `docker-machine`.

6. Type in the following:

   ```
   % docker-machine create --digitalocean-size "s-2vcpu-4gb" --driver
   digitalocean --digitalocean-access-token PERSONAL_ACCESS_TOKEN
   example-prod-1
   ```

   The output should look like this:

   ```
   831a341ed6a53a1a3094c7cd6be0d815b9652080c83fecf2cdb example-prod-1
   Creating CA: /Users/amlug/.docker/machine/certs/ca.pem
   ```

```
Creating client certificate:
/Users/amlug/.docker/machine/certs/cert.pem
Running pre-create checks...
Creating machine...
(facebox-prod-1) Creating SSH key...
(facebox-prod-1) Creating Digital Ocean droplet...
(facebox-prod-1) Waiting for IP address to be assigned to the
Droplet...
Waiting for machine to be running, this may take a few minutes...
Detecting operating system of created instance...
Waiting for SSH to be available...
Detecting the provisioner...
Provisioning with ubuntu(systemd)...
Installing Docker...
Copying certs to the local machine directory...
Copying certs to the remote machine...
Setting Docker configuration on the remote daemon...
Checking connection to Docker...
Docker is up and running!
To see how to connect your Docker Client to the Docker Engine
running on this virtual machine, run: docker-machine env example-
prod-1
```

7. Verify that everything is up and running by typing the following:

```
% docker-machine ls
```

The output should be as follows:

```
NAME               ACTIVE    DRIVER         STATE    URL
SWARM DOCKER    ERRORS
example-prod-1     -          digitalocean   Running
tcp://174.138.49.157:2376    v19.03.5
```

8. Next, we need to connect to our machine with `docker-machine`:

```
% eval $(docker-machine env example-prod-1)
```

This will tell Docker what to do when we start it.

9. Now, we can build our Docker image:

```
% docker build -t examplevapor
```

The output is the same as it was for AWS.

10. Now, we can run it on our cloud service:

```
% docker run -d -p 80:8080 examplevapor
```

The output should look like this:

```
d5ad8e30b70b1fade7e6c865ce130c5950b2651d548f610146ff85da858ed408
```

11. After a minute, we can go to Digital Ocean for our public IP and open it in our browser:

```
http://174.138.49.157/
```

This should result in the following output:

```
It works!
```

That's it for Digital Ocean! Compared to Google and AWS, it is probably an in-between in terms of complexity.

Now that we've learned how to deploy to Digital Ocean, let's discuss Kubernetes, another important tool for deploying Docker containers.

Using Kubernetes

Kubernetes is a tool that was developed by Google and is now maintained by the Cloud Native Computing Foundation. It is used to manage Docker containers. When we were deploying to Google, it was actually using Kubernetes in the backend. Kubernetes is open source and freely available.

Kubernetes operates with the following main object types:

- **Pod**: One or more containers that are running on the same host. It is the basic unit that is used to deploy Docker containers.
- **Service:** A group of pods that work together. Each of your microservices would be a service within Kubernetes.
- **Volume:** Persistent storage that remains existent, even when a pod is restarted. The normal filesystem loses all its data after a restart in a pod.
- **ConfigMaps and Secrets:** These allow us to provide configuration and credentials to containers.

The main idea is that it helps us manage microservices, especially when it comes to deployment, scaling, and configuration. Google Cloud uses this naturally. AWS ECS is the same thing conceptually, just natively tied into AWS. Digital Ocean offers a managed version of Kubernetes, as does AWS with **Elastic Kubernetes Service (EKS)**.

Now that we have briefly talked about Kubernetes and what it can do to help us, we can finally summarize this chapter.

Summary

In this chapter, we learned about what it takes to deploy Vapor applications. We learned that this almost always happens through Docker. First, we looked at Docker and how it operates and how we can use it. We explored how the three introduced cloud providers all offer ways for us to deploy Docker containers.

Then, we looked at how to deploy to AWS and what it takes. In contrast to that, we did the same thing for Google Cloud. Finally, we also deployed to Digital Ocean. You may be wondering which one you should pick for your project. The truth is that they are all competitive and offer roughly the same features. Obviously, AWS and Google Cloud are offered by two companies that also run big projects themselves, but Digital Ocean has some noteworthy references too.

Now, we can tie what we've learned together and deploy our example shop backend in the next chapter.

Questions

Answer the following questions to make sure you understand the deployment of Vapor apps:

1. Why is Docker often used to deploy Vapor apps?
2. What is the difference between Docker images and Docker containers?
3. How is Kubernetes involved in deployments?

15
Deploying Microservices in the Cloud

Alright; the last few chapters have all lined up to get to this one. We want to finally deploy our developed backend application. We also want to set up an automatic **Continuous Deployment** (**CD**) so that everything will be updated just by the push of a button.

We are going to prepare an entire production-ready setup for our example app. This will be done using AWS—the same principles could be used with all other cloud providers as well.

In this chapter, we will go through the following points:

- Setting up **Amazon Web Services** (**AWS**) and a Docker repository: Let's get AWS and Docker set up to deploy applications.
- Setting up **Elastic Container Service** (**ECS**): ECS will run our containers, so we will set it up here.
- Using CodePipeline for CD: We want automatically deploy our services, so CodePipeline will help us here.

Let's get started!

Technical requirements

This section covers what you will need to have running on your machine so that you can write this microservice. The following components need to be installed:

- Vapor 4
- Swift 5
- Xcode 11+
- Docker

- macOS/Linux
- AWS **Command-Line Interface** (**CLI**)
- An AWS account

We are also assuming that you have worked through the previous chapters and know how to write a Vapor microservice. All the code in this chapter will run on macOS and Linux alike.

The GitHub URL for this chapter is `https://github.com/PacktPublishing/Hands-On-Swift-5-Microservices-Development/tree/master/Chapter 15`.

Setting up AWS and a Docker repository

In the last chapter, `Chapter 14`, *Docker and the Cloud*, we went through deploying our app mainly through the CLI; this time, we want to use the AWS Management Console a bit more as it provides us some convenience. The steps shown here assume that this AWS account just opened and has no pre-existing services. Go through the following steps to set up the account:

1. Log in to `console.aws.amazon.com`. You should see the following screen:

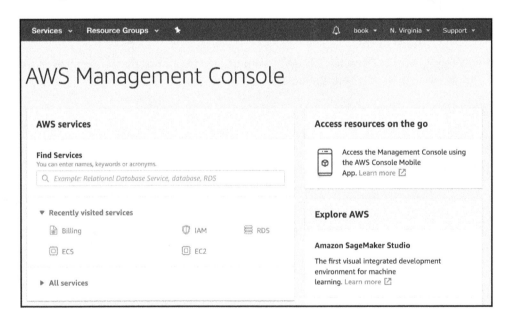

2. Type **ecs** in the **Find Services** field and go to the **ECS** page, as shown in the following screenshot:

3. Next, select **Repositories** right from **Amazon ECR**, as shown in the following screenshot:

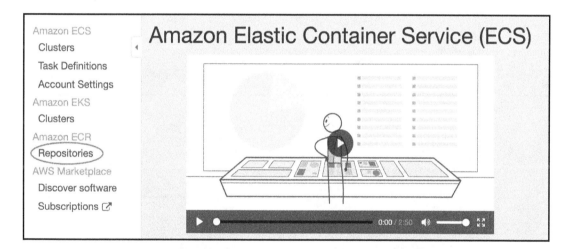

4. Then, create a new repository by clicking on **Create repository**, as shown in the following screenshot:

5. Fill out the text field with `users`, and proceed:

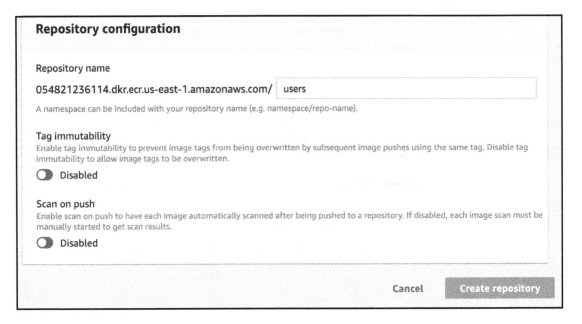

Now, we have created the first repository.

6. Repeat the step for `products` and `orders`. We should have three repositories now, as shown in the following screenshot:

In the previous chapter, `Chapter 14`, *Docker and the Cloud*, we have done the same thing, just through the command line.

7. Next, we need to set up the load balancer. Click on **Services** in the top bar, and then on **EC2**, as shown in the following screenshot:

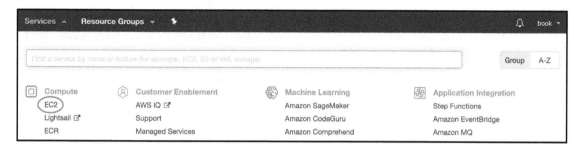

8. Select **Load Balancers** under **LOAD BALANCING**, as follows:

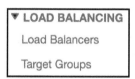

9. Click on **Application Load Balancer** and then on **Create**, as shown in the following screenshot:

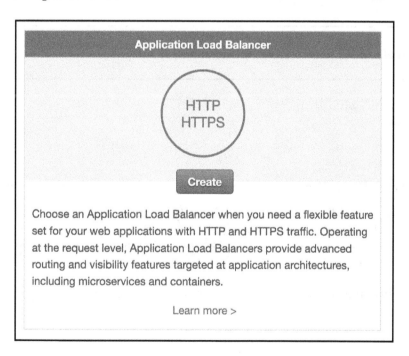

10. Type **ecommerce** into the **Name** field; leave the **Load Balancer Protocol** set to **HTTP,** and then select at least two listeners at the bottom of the screen, as shown in the following screenshot:

You also need to select availability zones, as follows:

The next step, **Step 2: Configure Security Settings**, will advise that we have not selected a secure listener. A secure listener requires a certificate, which is tied to a domain. We can leave this at port 80 now and adjust it later for a specific domain with a certificate.

11. Confirm this and go to **Step 3**, where we need to create a security group, as follows:

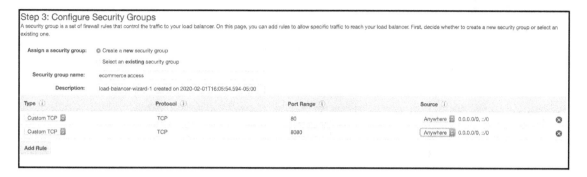

12. Call it `ecommerce access`, and then configure two ports, `80` and `8080`, as shown in the preceding screenshot.
13. Click on **Next: Configure Routing**, and adjust the settings as shown here:

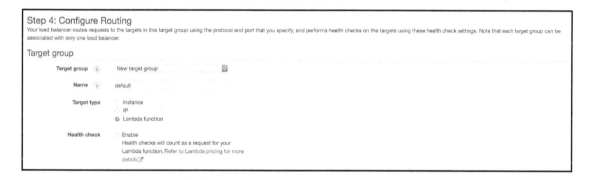

This is the default group that will receive all traffic that is not matching a routing group.

14. Click on **Next: Register Targets**.
15. Select **Add a function later** and click on **Next: Review**, as follows:

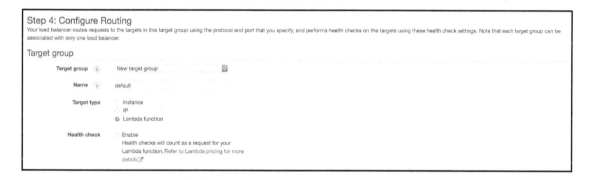

16. Click on **Review**, as follows:

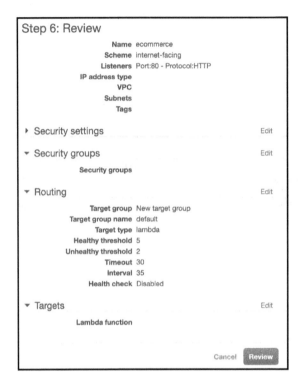

Now, the load balancer is being created. After a few seconds, you should see the following screen:

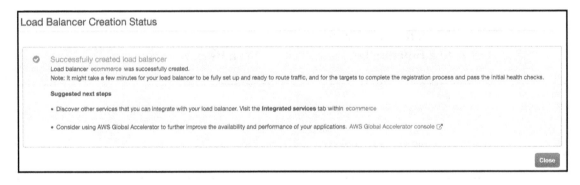

And that would be all for the load balancer at this point. We have now set up the repositories, as well as the load balancer. The load balancer will serve as the central point of access to redirect, as well as balance, traffic accordingly.

Now, we can go to the next section and set up ECS and the services.

Setting up ECS

We have the load balancer and the repositories already set up. Now, we need to set up the services. Proceed as follows:

1. Go to **ECS** and select **Clusters**.
2. Then, select **Create Cluster**, as shown in the following screenshot:

3. Select **Networking only**, as we will use AWS Fargate to deploy, as shown in the following screenshot:

4. Click **Next step**, and type `ecommerce` as the name of the cluster. Leave the rest blank, as shown in the following screenshot:

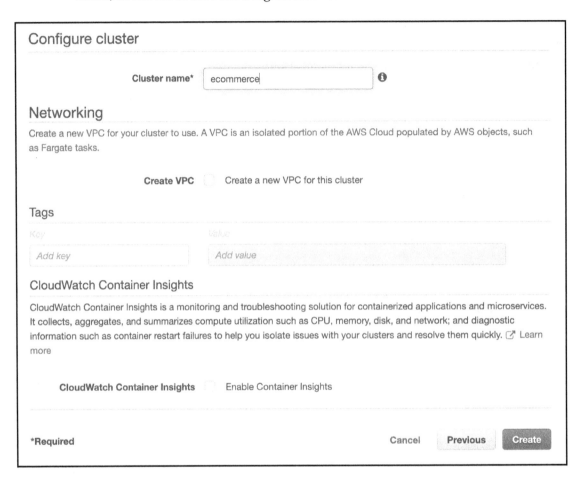

You should now see the following success message:

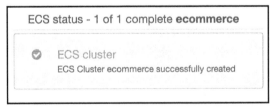

5. Next, we need to create the task definitions. Click on **Task Definitions** and select **Create new Task Definition**, as follows:

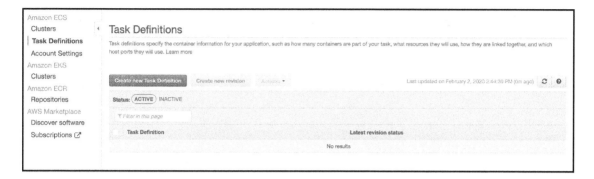

6. Select **FARGATE** as the type, and click **Next** as follows:

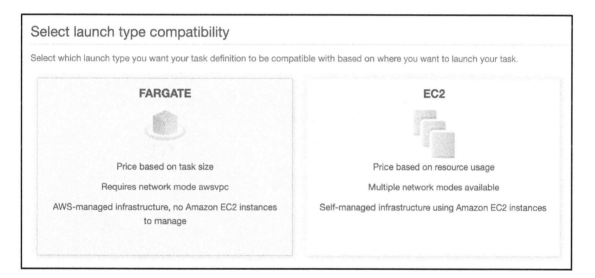

7. Now, type in `users` as the name, and leave the rest blank, as shown in the following screenshot:

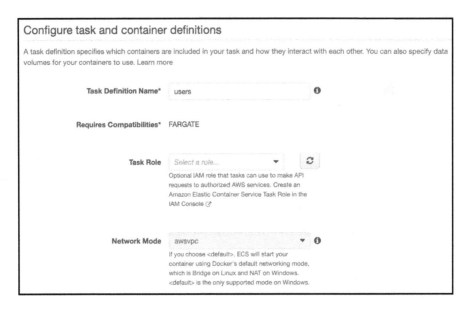

8. Scroll down and select **0.5GB** for RAM and **0.25 vCPU**. Then, click **Add container**, as shown in the following screenshot:

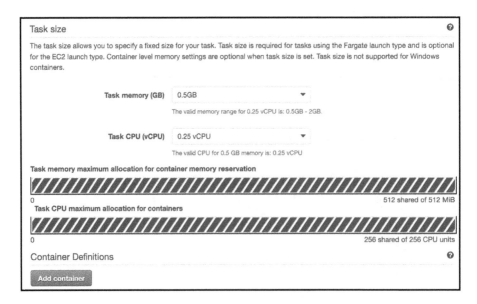

9. Now, you need to grab the **Uniform Resource Identifier** (**URI**) repository that we previously created for **users**. Enter it for **Image** and call the **Container name** just users. Set the **Container port** to 8080, as shown in the following screenshot:

10. Click **Add Container**, and then hit **Create Task Definition**, which results in the following screenshot:

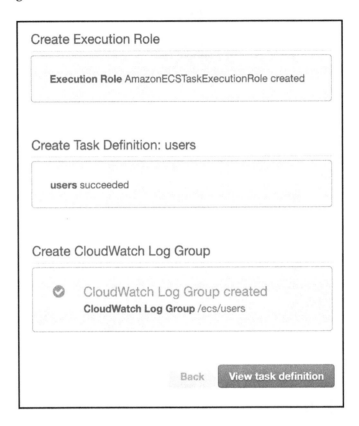

11. Now, click on **View task definition** and navigate back to the cluster.
12. Select the ecommerce cluster and click **Create** in the **Services** tab. Now, we are configuring our service.
13. Select launch type as **Fargate**, and select our previously created task definition users, revision 1.
14. Type in users for **Service name**, and leave the rest as it is.
15. Type in 1 for **Number of tasks**.
16. Leave the rest as it is, and click **Next Step**.
17. On the next screen, select the only **virtual private cloud** (**VPC**) we have, and at least two subnets. Select the security group we previously created and leave **Auto-assign public IP** as **ENABLED**, as shown in the following screenshot:

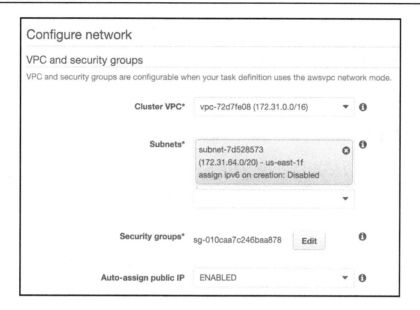

18. Select **Application Load Balancer** under **Load balancing,** as shown in the following screenshot:

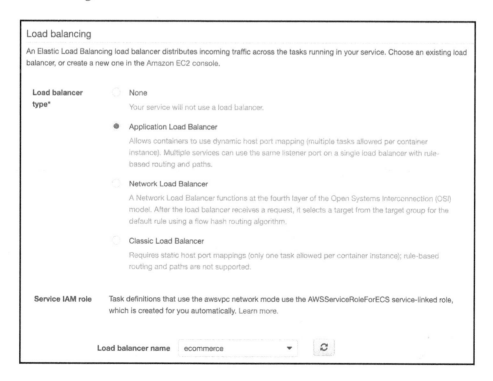

19. Select the only load balancer available, then select the single available listening port (80). Leave the rest as it is now, but write /v1/users* into the **Path pattern** and 1 in the **Evaluation order**, as shown in the following screenshot:

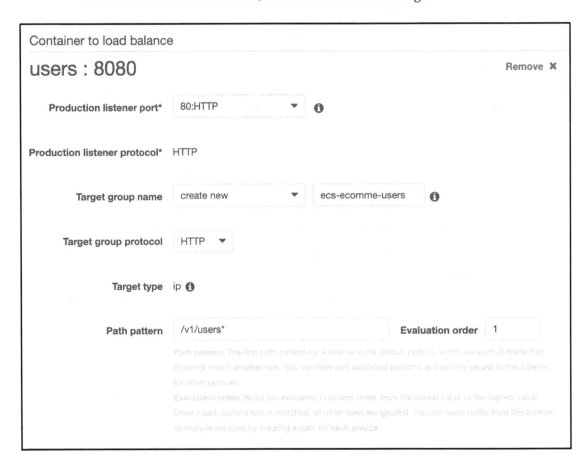

When you do this step again for the other services, you will need to write 2 for the second service, and 3 for the third. This signifies that the priority is a unique field, and while all our services have different tasks, the load balancer still expects a prioritized order.

20. Lastly, write /v1/users/health in **Health check path** and uncheck **Enable service discovery integration**, as we do not need it now. Then, click **Next step**.

21. Select **Do not adjust the service's desired count** at **Service Auto Scaling**, and click **Next Step** (we will cover this in the next chapter).

22. On the next screen, you will see a summary of this service. Click **Create Service**. The service is created now, as can be seen in the following screenshot:

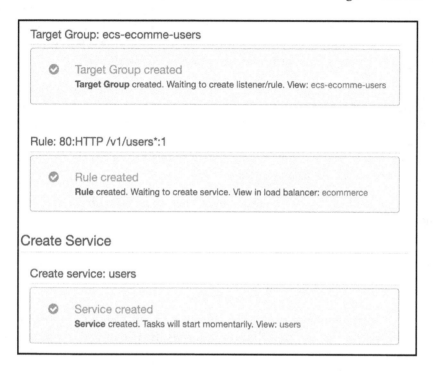

Now, you need to repeat the same steps for `orders` and `products` as well. Remember to use the names properly. Note that the services are attempting to start but will not succeed; we have not pushed a Docker image yet.

Now, we have gone through the entire process of setting up our services. You have learned how repositories, services, clusters, and tasks are set up in AWS. Now, we are going to look at how to automatically deploy using AWS CodePipeline, in the next section.

Using CodePipeline for CD

So, we have our three services set up, and they *would* be running once we upload a Docker image. You learned in the last chapter, Chapter 14, *Docker and the Cloud*, how to do that through your command line; however this time, we want to get AWS to do it from our source directly. The process to be automatically deployed is called CD.

Let's quickly talk about how CodePipeline operates. CodePipeline works in stages. At every stage, it is doing something with our code and sending it to the next stage (through the pipe). The stages, however, are often composed of other services such as CodeBuild. CodeBuild is a tool that essentially uses EC2 units to compile code for us. Both CodeBuild and CodePipeline are incredibly flexible and customizable. It is worth investing some time into learning more about how to use them.

To get started, you need to have three repositories set up in GitHub. They can be private or public; either will work fine. We need them for our three services, as follows:

- User Management Service
- Product Management Service
- Order Management Service

 In this particular case, GitHub should be used. Other Git repository hosts will also work, but this chapter assumes the use of GitHub as this is natively integrated into AWS.

Once you have your GitHub repositories ready, you can follow these steps:

1. Open the buildspec.json file that is in each folder and adjust the <REP_URL> to be the correct repository URL.
2. Open AWS CodePipeline under https://console.aws.amazon.com/codesuite/codepipeline/pipelines.
3. Click on **New Pipeline** and enter users under **Pipeline name**. Leave the rest as it is. Then, click **Next**, as shown in the following screenshot:

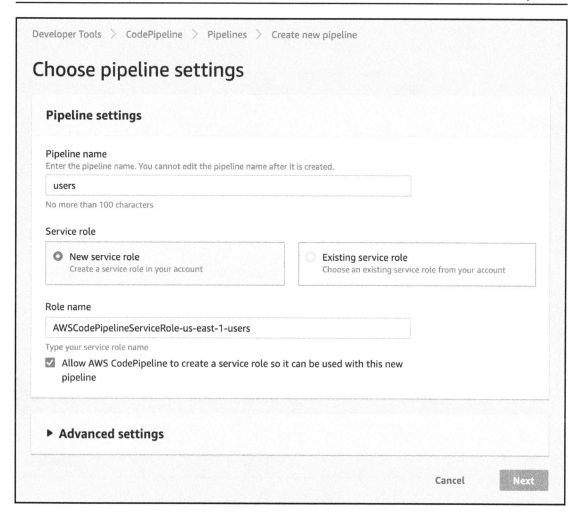

When you go through this again, make sure that you use the service role you have created in this step. Meaning it will say `New service role`, and that is okay here. You can then reuse that service role once you create the pipelines for orders and products.

4. On the next screen, select **GitHub** as the source. Then, click **Connect to GitHub**, as shown in the following screenshot:

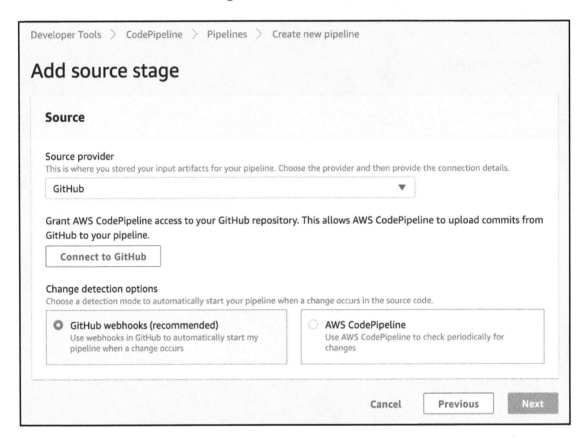

5. AWS will now guide you through a window that authorizes AWS to access your GitHub files. Allow AWS to do that, and once you're done, you can select the repository and the branch.

6. On the next screen, select **AWS CodeBuild** as the **Build provider**, and then click on **Create project**, as shown in the following screenshot:

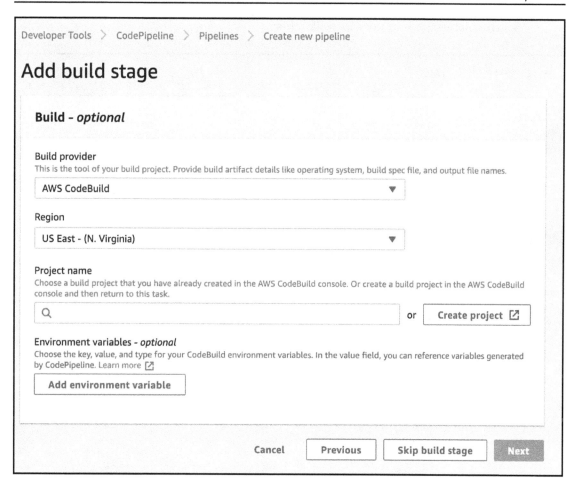

7. On the next screen, fill out the details, as follows:

- **Project name:** users
- **Environment image:** Managed Image
- **Operating system:** Amazon Linux 2
- **Runtime:** Standard
- **Image:** AWS/codebuild/amazonlinux2-x86_64-standard:2.0
- **Privileged:** Yes
- **Service Role:** New service role

8. Leave the rest as it is, and click **Continue to CodePipeline.**

9. Your screen should now look like this:

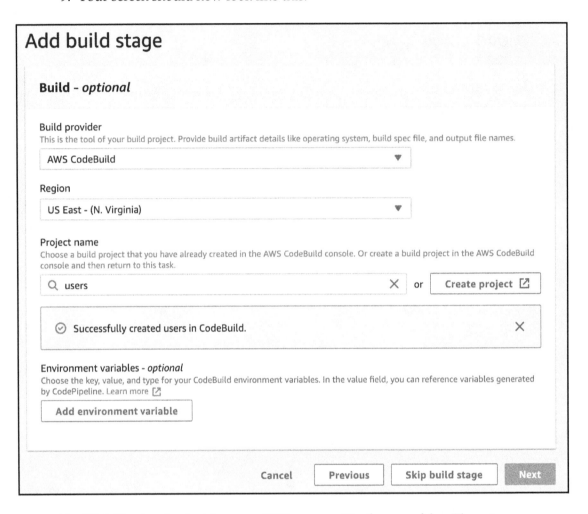

10. Click **Next** and select **Amazon ECS** as your **Deploy provider**. Then, type in `ecommerce` as the cluster and `users` as the service. Your screen should look like this:

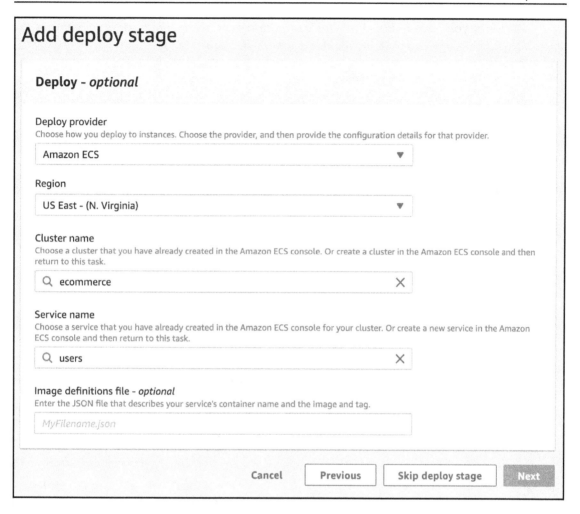

Add deploy stage

Deploy - *optional*

Deploy provider
Choose how you deploy to instances. Choose the provider, and then provide the configuration details for that provider.

| Amazon ECS ▼ |

Region

| US East - (N. Virginia) ▼ |

Cluster name
Choose a cluster that you have already created in the Amazon ECS console. Or create a cluster in the Amazon ECS console and then return to this task.

| 🔍 ecommerce ✕ |

Service name
Choose a service that you have already created in the Amazon ECS console for your cluster. Or create a new service in the Amazon ECS console and then return to this task.

| 🔍 users ✕ |

Image definitions file - *optional*
Enter the JSON file that describes your service's container name and the image and tag.

| *MyFilename.json* |

Cancel   Previous   Skip deploy stage   Next

11. Click **Next**, and then, on the review screen, click **Create Pipeline**.
12. You will now be redirected to the CodePipeline screen, which shows you all the steps your code is now going through.
13. You will notice that the process does not go beyond the CodeBuild stage, and there is an error. We need to adjust some roles. Go to **Identity and Access Management (IAM)** by clicking on **Services** and then selecting **IAM**. Then, select **Roles**, and select the newly created role. It should have **CodeBuild** in it and will look like **codebuild-users-service-role**. Select **Attach Policy**, and then search for **AmazonEC2ContainerRegistryFullAccess** and it to the role.

14. Once you have finished this for `users` and everything looks good, repeat this section for `products` and `orders`.

The final screen for a pipeline looks like this:

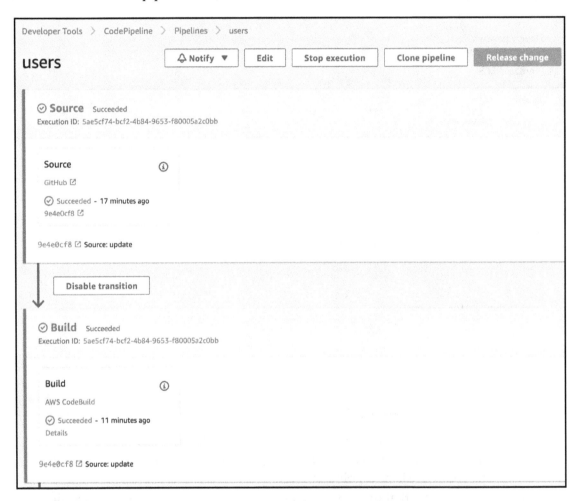

At the bottom, we have the **Deploy** section, which has succeeded now, as can be seen in the following screenshot:

Yay! We did it! Our services should have compiled and deployed now. Notice that you only need to commit and push to GitHub for it to automatically deploy to your system.

Summary

In this chapter, you have learned how to set up AWS to run Vapor applications as a microservice architecture. We went through the process of setting up a load balancer and creating a cluster that can run the services.

We then went through the process of setting up an automatic CD, and we connected it to a GitHub repository, which means that pushing code to that repository will result in the automatic deployment of our service to AWS. In the end, we have a fully functional API up and running.

It is worth noting here that I have personally talked to Amazon engineers to confirm that Amazon itself uses this exact approach to deploy their microservices. While this approach might be a little complicated, it has been tested and proven to be reliable by companies such as Amazon and others.

Questions

To make sure your understanding is correct, answer the following questions:

1. What are we using CodePipeline for?
2. What is the difference between CodePipeline and CodeBuild?
3. What are the advantages of Fargate here?

16
Scaling and Monitoring Microservices

Our app is now up and running. The real strength of microservice architecture is, however, that the services can be treated individually. This is particularly helpful when it comes to scaling quickly, according to need. In our example app, let's assume that we have a lot of users viewing the products, but only a few ones ordering. So, in that case, we would want the product's service to scale up while the order and user services remain the same. After reading this chapter, you should have a good understanding of how scaling and monitoring work, and how different cloud providers deal with the issue.

In this chapter, we will go through the following points:

- Scaling microservices and the importance of monitoring: Let's explore how scaling works generically.
- Scaling and monitoring using **Amazon Web Services** (**AWS**): Let's take a look at what AWS offers for scaling.
- Scaling and monitoring using Google Cloud: Google Cloud offers integrated scaling.
- Scaling and monitoring using DigitalOcean: Scaling with DigitalOcean.
- Additional cloud providers: Some other relevant cloud providers are explored here.

Let's get started!

Technical requirements

This section covers what you will need to have running on your machine so that you can write this microservice. The following components need to be installed:

- Vapor 4
- Swift 5
- Xcode 11+
- Docker
- macOS/Linux

We are also assuming that you have worked through the previous chapters and know how to write a Vapor microservice. All the code in this chapter will run under macOS and Linux alike.

The GitHub repository for this chapter: `https://github.com/PacktPublishing/Hands-On-Swift-5-Microservices-Development/tree/master/Chapter 16`

Scaling microservices and the importance of monitoring

Scaling is increasing or decreasing the resources available for a microservice. A big part of the appeal of microservices is that we can individually scale services up and down, just how we need them. When the traffic or workload of a microservice increases, the service should get more resources, either in CPU and RAM upgrades or additional servers.

We, of course, would like this to happen automatically, and without us doing anything. In this section, we want to take a look at how scaling and monitoring work with microservices in general.

Let's look into the following topics:

- Monitoring: This tells us when we need to scale.
- Scaling: Adding resources to our setup.

Scaling begins with monitoring, so let's take a closer look.

Monitoring

Monitoring always means we are checking what the current status of a service is. For us to know whether we need to scale up or down depends on the state of a service. If a service is under increased load or traffic, the available resources are increasingly used. We want to know at which point we need to get more resources, or if we can free some up because we have too many. There are several things we could look into to determine whether or not we need to upscale or downscale.

A list of things that are relevant for monitoring includes the following:

- CPU usage
- RAM usage
- Current requests per minute
- Active database connections

You can probably think of a few other indications that we *could* look at when monitoring our service. In reality, CPU usage has been one of the strongest and most reliable factors to check for, as everything else depends on it. If we get an increase in requests, the CPU has to do more than when we have fewer requests, meaning CPU usage goes up.

On the other hand, the CPU does not always give us the full picture either. The number of current requests per minute, for example, gives valuable insight into how many actual people are using a microservice. That could be a metric you want to use to increase resources, depending on the use case. Active database connections are also important when it comes to scaling the database. Active connections are not the same as current requests per minute or active users using our app, but you could use them to increase resources for your database.

Monitoring is also concerned with development over time. This means that it is less important for us if CPU usage is temporarily high; it is more important to us when it is consistently high.

Scaling

Scaling is the process of adding more resources or taking resources away from a service. Once monitoring is in place, we know what action needs to happen. But what does scaling look like?

If we talk about scaling outside of Docker, it almost always means we need to physically or virtually add servers to our service for us to have more resources available. Those servers need to be included in the load balancer's setup, as seen in the previous chapter, Chapter 15, *Deploying Microservices in the Cloud*, and they need to be correctly configured. If it means we are adding physical servers to the setup, those need to be installed, started, and set up as well—unless idle hardware is available. If we have the equipment available but it is just idle, undoubtedly we can use it right away. It still needs to be set up, however. Before Docker, scaling was a relatively slow and very manual process. A few projects I was involved in had to scale up, and it took days.

There are mostly two ways of scaling resources up and down:

- **Horizontal scaling**: We add more servers to the mix.
- **Vertical scaling**: We increase the resources of one server.

Both come with pros and cons. Generally speaking, however, it is easier to carry out horizontal scaling. Adding more servers to the mix can happen without taking our central server offline, while vertical scaling involves at least restarting the server. In the era of cloud computing, the differences are increasingly diminishing since virtual servers can be up- and downgraded much faster. The scaling we are looking at in this chapter, however, is horizontal, as this is common for microservices.

 Sometimes, you may need to vertically scale as well if you see that your servers are using a lot of RAM and CPU. Adding more servers can be pricier than increasing the resources of each server.

Nowadays, with clouds and server farms available on demand, things get significantly more comfortable. Even if we want to scale up individual servers in the cloud, it will take minutes, instead of days, to do so. It is better still if we can scale up with the correct configuration and are fully automized, which is where Docker plays a central role. Thanks to Docker images, we can easily start new instances, even on the same hardware, and provide more resources in a matter of seconds.

In this section, we have learned how scaling and monitoring are connected, and what each can entail. We have looked at how Docker allows this to be a lot easier. Now, examine what this looks like in reality.

Scaling and monitoring using AWS

In this section, we want to set up autoscaling and monitoring in AWS. You should have an **Elastic Container Services** (**ECS**) cluster set up and running, as described in Chapter 15, *Deploying Microservices in the Cloud*.

Go through the following steps to get started:

1. Go into your ECS cluster, which was created in Chapter 15, *Deploying Microservices in the Cloud*, and select the service for which you want to enable autoscaling. You should then see the following screen:

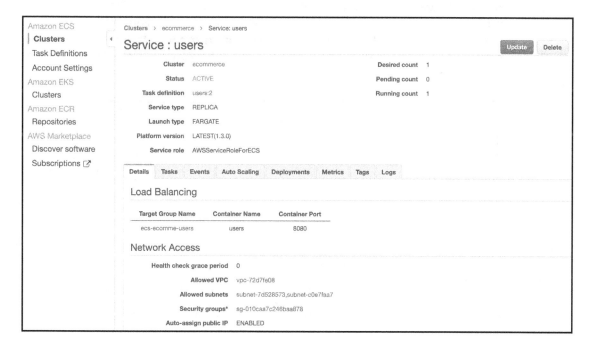

2. Click **Update**, and then click **Next step** until you get to the **Set Auto Scaling (optional)** screen, as shown in the following screenshot:

3. Now, click the second option, **Configure Service Auto Scaling to adjust your service's desired count**, and fill out the details. You can pick a **Minimum number of tasks** that you want to run, bigger or equal to 0. You need to specify the **Desired number of tasks** and the **Maximum number of tasks**. The **Desired number of tasks** is what will run by default. All this can be seen in the following screenshot:

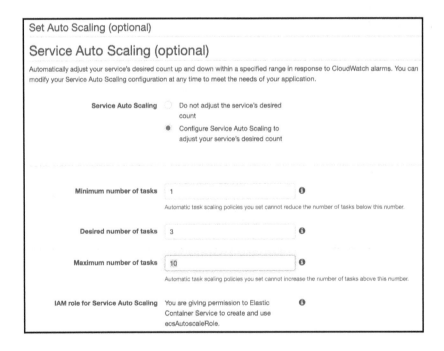

Always go higher than 0 on the minimum number.

4. Now, we need to add a scaling policy. Click **Add scaling policy** and fill out the details, similar to this:

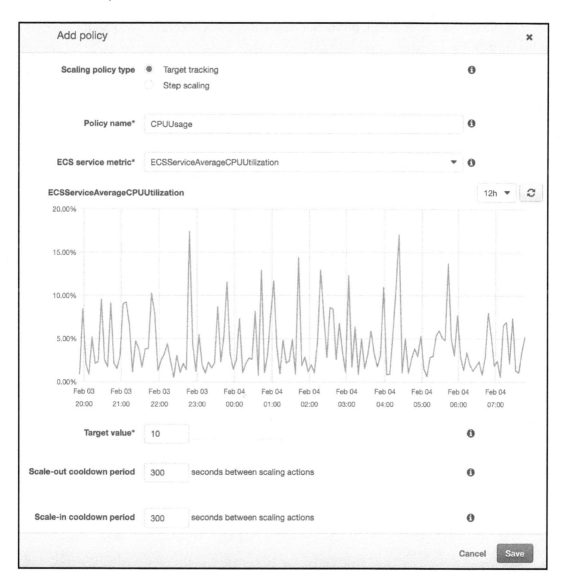

See how what we learned previously in the *Monitoring* and *Scaling* sections is now being picked up here by AWS? AWS is using the average CPU utilization to then scale up or down. Additionally, AWS offers a few values that can make the process smoother or faster. You can give cooldown periods, to scale up or down. This is useful when you know you need to scale up quickly but want to scale down slower when needed. You can be as creative and as complicated as you desire to set up your scaling policies.

5. Click **Save**, and then **Update Service**. After a few seconds, you should see these results:

6. Autoscaling is now set up. You can now use a tool such as `https://loader.io/` to stress test your service if you wanted to do so. For important projects and services, it makes sense to test scaling to get a feel for how it operates. Some fine-tuning regarding CPU and memory will probably be required, but your app can promptly respond to increasing traffic properly.

> When testing your servers, do not forget to also check and deal with your database server. In my experience, the database server is often more of a bottleneck than your frontend/API servers.

Now that we have successfully set up autoscaling for AWS, let's see what this would look like in Google Cloud.

Scaling and monitoring using Google Cloud

Scaling in Google Cloud is conceptually similar to AWS. You have a load balancer, instances, and policies that can scale your instances up or down. Google Cloud also, just like AWS, offers more than only one way to manage services and autoscaling: Kubernetes can be directly managed within Google Cloud (just like in the AWS **Elastic Kubernetes Service** (**EKS**); see `Chapter 14`, *Docker and the Cloud*, for details).

Let's assume, though, that we have set up our app through App Engine like we did in `Chapter 15`, *Deploying Microservices in the Cloud*. In that case, autoscaling is already enabled by default! There is nothing more we need to do. Google is automatically checking the CPU, RAM, and other metrics, and scales up and down depending on your needs.

If, however, you have a more sophisticated setup, in which you have set up a few instances of your own, you can have autoscaling set up when setting up managed instance groups.

The following screenshot shows the setup when setting up a new managed instance group. Notice how you can add autoscaling policies here—very similar to AWS, as shown previously:

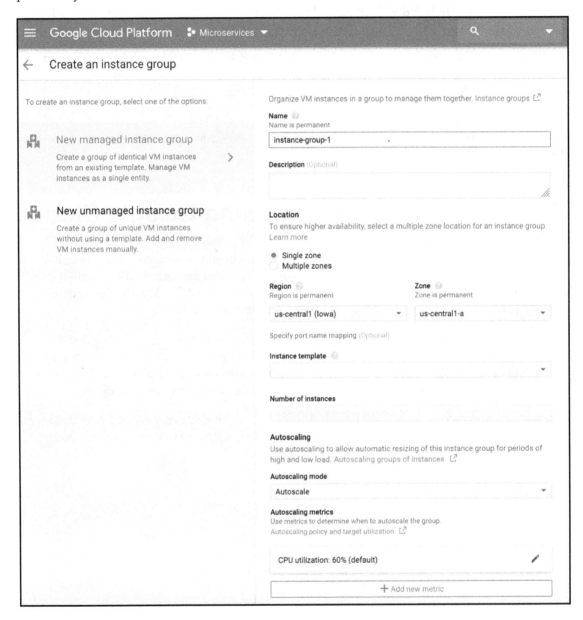

And that is it; App Engine is now doing the rest for you. Notice how the settings are, in principle, the same between Google Cloud and AWS? The reason is that scaling has become universally similar across different providers and solutions. Everyone is looking for the same things to scale up or down.

Now that we have had a brief look at Google Cloud, let's see how DigitalOcean does this in comparison.

Scaling and monitoring using DigitalOcean

When you are using DigitalOcean, you currently only have one option to autoscale: using their managed Kubernetes service. You will need to set up your application using Kubernetes first. The use and configuration of Kubernetes go beyond what this book covers, but if you do have a Kubernetes setup running on DigitalOcean, you can easily set up autoscaling via the **Nodes** tab, as shown in the following screenshot:

When you hit **Resize or Autoscale**, as seen in the previous screenshot, you can pick your options, as follows:

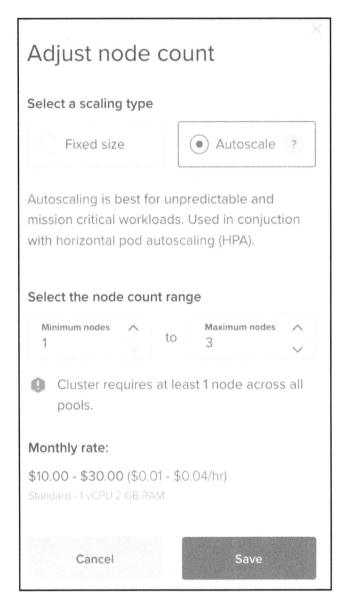

You can specify the number of pods (if you need a reminder of what pods are, check out Chapter 14, *Docker and the Cloud*, again) you want to have as a maximum and a minimum (at least one).

DigitalOcean is most upfront with costs and prices. Budget-conscious projects have a clear cost vision with DigitalOcean.

The scaling of the pods itself is done through the Kubernetes **Horizontal Pod Autoscaler (HAP)**. You can find all the details of how this works in the official documentation (`https:/ /kubernetes.io/docs/tasks/run-application/horizontal-pod-autoscale/`). The principles are the same as we talked about before.

DigitalOcean is conveniently hiding a lot of the configuration that typically goes with using Kubernetes, making it an easy choice if you just want to start using Kubernetes.

DigitalOcean has only recently started implementing *any* autoscaling features. It took until September 2019 before Kubernetes was an option.

We have now looked at DigitalOcean and how it has implemented autoscaling. Let's now briefly look at a few more cloud providers, in the next section.

Additional cloud providers

Besides AWS, Google Cloud, and DigitalOcean, there are a few more options available when it comes to cloud providers. Let's take a look at them here:

- Heroku
- IBM Cloud
- Microsoft Azure
- Oracle Cloud

Let's begin with Heroku.

Heroku

Heroku stands out from all the other providers mentioned because it does not provide its solution. All its services use the AWS **Elastic Compute Cloud (EC2)** platform.

It started as a service specifically for developers, to ease the burden of deployment and running applications. Heroku does not officially support Server-Side Swift yet; there are, however, a couple of ways to run Vapor on Heroku (see `https://grapeup.com/blog/read/ server-side-swift-with-vapor-end-to-end-application-with-heroku-cloud-46`).

When it comes to scaling, Heroku tries to be app-specific. It does not offer generic autoscaling, as AWS ECS would. As it initially started by supporting only Ruby projects, its tools and approaches are still heavily influenced by that. One of its recommendations for autoscaling involves using Rails Autoscale, which is only applicable to Ruby on Rails.

In conclusion, Heroku is a fair option for development purposes. Any production apps might run into issues, however, as autoscaling is not nearly as definable as it is with the other providers.

IBM Cloud

IBM Cloud is highly comparable to AWS and Google Cloud. It offers more or less the same features, at competitive prices. IBM is relatively new to the cloud business for smaller companies and individuals. It has run infrastructure for enterprise companies over decades, but just recently started to offer this to a broader audience. Its autoscaling services include Kubernetes, like the other providers as well, and a more custom service, which is provided mostly to enterprise customers (see `https://www.ibm.com/cloud/auto-scaling`).

Overall, IBM Cloud can certainly host your application and scale it up and down. It is, however, less documented and available than AWS or Google, mostly due to its enterprise focus.

Microsoft Azure

Microsoft Azure has been a popular newcomer to the cloud scene. Naturally, Azure is focused on Microsoft products such as .NET. It does, however, offer general computing resources as well. Since it provides Docker hosting, we can also host our Vapor applications there. Azure also provides autoscaling services, along with monitoring.

Just like AWS, Google, and DigitalOcean, it also offers a managed Kubernetes service, which can be used for autoscaling as well.

Oracle Cloud

Similar to IBM, Oracle had enterprise customers as it's focus. It offers Kubernetes and Docker hosting, just like the others, and so autoscaling and monitoring are mostly a matter of configuration.

All in all, almost every competitive cloud provider will offer autoscaling capabilities, as well as the related monitoring services. The choice of whom to choose comes mainly down to preference and budget. The prices vary, and you should consider the long-term effect. But overall, all providers are stable and reliable enough to host and scale your application.

Summary

In this chapter, we looked carefully at scaling and monitoring microservices. We started by looking at what monitoring and autoscaling are conceptually, and how they are generally implemented.

Then, we looked into how autoscaling is done with AWS, Google Cloud, and DigitalOcean. We then explored additional cloud providers. By now, you should have a solid understanding of how the different cloud providers operate, and what benefits they offer.

When you launch your next API using Vapor, you should be well equipped to have your services autoscale up and down according to traffic. Especially in projects where the demand is not foreseeable, this becomes invaluable.

Questions

To make sure you understand this chapter well, go through the following questions:

1. Which types of scaling are there?
2. How is autoscaling done in AWS ECS?
3. Why is Google Cloud's App Engine convenient when it comes to scaling?

Assessment Answers

Here, you can see the questions and answers to all chapters:

Chapter 1: Introduction to Microservices

Questions:

1. What is the definition of a microservice?
2. List three reasons why microservices can be helpful.
3. List three reasons not to choose microservices.
4. List four differences between a monolith and microservices.

Answers:

1. A microservice is a small business unit operating as independently as possible.
2. Three reasons:
    1. Independently scalable
    2. Independently maintainable
    3. Decreased complexity
3. Three reasons:
    1. Too small for a project (only one microservice).
    2. Not enough time or resources available to convert all legacy code.
    3. Increased initial work.
4. Four differences:
    1. A monolith has one code base; each microservice has its own.
    2. Monoliths usually operate with only one database; each microservice has its own database.
    3. Monoliths are hard to scale as the entire service must be scaled, while microservices can be scaled individually.
    4. Monoliths force you to use the same programming language for additions. Microservice additions can have different programming languages.

Chapter 2: Understanding Server-Side Swift

Questions:

1. Why is it helpful that Swift is a native language?
2. What is the preferred operating system for server-side Swift applications at the moment?
3. What is SwiftNIO?
4. How does Docker help?
5. Name three of the added benefits of Swift 5.

Answers:

1. Because it is faster, more secure, and easy to deploy.
2. Ubuntu.
3. A network and streaming library, written in and for Swift.
4. Docker provides flexibility when hosting Swift applications.
5. Three benefits:
    1. Extensions
    2. Generic functions
    3. Protocols

Chapter 3: Getting Started with the Vapor Framework

Questions:

1. Add a new route to your FirstApp application that interacts with a new controller.
2. Add a new model to your application and integrate it into your controllers.
3. Build a simple pagination app in which the requests can contain parameters such as `sortBy` and `offset`.

Answers:

1. See GitHub, `Chapter2/FirstAppExtended`.
2. See GitHub, `Chapter2/FirstAppExtended`.
3. See GitHub, `Chapter2/FirstAppExtended`.

Chapter 4: Planning an Online Store Application

Questions:

1. How do you verify that a user has access to a function of a microservice?
2. What is a good lifespan for an access token?
3. Why is JSON a good choice for the inputs and outputs of microservices?

Answers:

1. A **JSON Web Token (JWT)** middleware (`SimpleJWTMiddleware`) verifies that only permitted users can access a function of a microservice.
2. This depends on the case. Some cases warrant 60 seconds, while others can have a lifespan of multiple hours or even days.
3. Because it is universally readable and lots of libraries support it well in many programming languages and environments.

Chapter 5: Creating Your First Microservice

Questions:

1. Why have we included `SimpleJWTMiddleware`?
2. How would you most likely run your microservices, and what server environment would you use?
3. Should you define models for your services altogether, or individually per service?

Answers:

1. Because it provides us with a basic middleware that takes care of authentification.
2. In Docker, with Ubuntu.
3. To keep services as independent as possible, they should be defined individually. You might decide to share a common library, but that is not the case typically.

Chapter 6: Application Structure and Database Design

Questions:

1. Why is it essential to use different repositories for Git and Docker for each service?
2. How do your services receive credentials for the database and JWT?
3. How can you run multiple Vapor applications at once?
4. Advanced: Push your Docker image into your Docker repository.

Answers:

1. We need to ensure the integrity of our services. Combining repositories can be dangerous as it invites code to get mixed.
2. Through environment variables.
3. By defining different ports for each service.
4. See `Chapter 15`, *Deploying Microservices in the Cloud,* for an example.

Chapter 7: Writing the User Service

Questions:

1. Extend the user service so that new users need to confirm their email first.
2. Save the last login time to a user's model.
3. Complete the address model by adding attributes such as `Country`, `LAT`, `LNG`, `State`, and so on.
4. Advanced: Write admin functions to allow an admin user (you have to define what that is) to edit another user's addresses and profile.

Answers:

See GitHub for a full example.

Chapter 8: Testing Microservices

Questions:

1. What is the fundamental difference between unit tests and functional tests?
2. How can unit tests and functional tests work together?
3. Write Postman tests for all endpoints of the user service.
4. Write more sophisticated tests when verifying the responses (for example, check that the token contains the correct information).
5. Write unit tests verifying that the JWT functions in the user service are working correctly.

Answers:

1. Unit tests are for individual functions. Functional tests are undertaken to test the overall functionality of a service.
2. While unit tests ensure that foundational functions operate properly, functional tests will ensure that functions are working together as intended.
3. See GitHub.
4. See GitHub.
5. See GitHub.

Chapter 9: Product Management Service

Questions:

1. Why do we not need to sign JWT in this service?
2. Add a new filter that only returns a product within a given price range.
3. Advanced: Add a way for products to be connected to more than one category (this will drastically improve but also complicate this service).

Answers:

1. Because the service will operate as entirely public.
2. See GitHub.
3. See GitHub.

Chapter 10: Understanding Microservices Communication

Questions:

1. When should microservices communicate with each other?
2. What are the two main protocols with which microservices can communicate with each other?
3. How can Swift be helpful in facilitating communication between microservices?
4. Describe three scenarios in which your shop application has to implement communication between services.

Answers:

1. Whenever they absolutely have to, but no more than that.
2. WebSockets and REST.
3. It is fast and provides good asynchronous tools.
4. Three scenarios:
   - Order confirmation (price check)
   - Shipping (third-party vendor API)
   - Payment (third-party payment API)

Chapter 11: Order Management Service

Questions:

1. Write all the tests needed for this microservice.
2. Complete the tax setup from this chapter and test it with a 10% flat tax.
3. Implement a routine that cancels orders if they are not paid within 30 days.
4. Write a function that informs the user when the order is being shipped.

Answers:

See GitHub.

Chapter 12: Best Practices

Questions:

1. Why would you want to develop a library for your application?
2. What is the advantage of protocols in Swift?
3. How can generic functions help you?
4. How do Xcode and `lldb` help you debug?

Answers:

1. Because you might have classes that you want to share across microservices.
2. You can define what you want types to have and what they look like without dictating the type itself.
3. They can cover a number of types, and therefore reduce work.
4. They help you find the exact line in which errors occurred.

Chapter 13: Hosting Microservices

Questions:

1. Why is it not advisable to run the entire backend on only one server?
2. How does Docker simplify your installation process?
3. How should you store your credentials to your database?
4. What role does the load balancer play?

Answers:

1. Because if one server crashes or shuts down, the entire backend would be offline.
2. It has pre-compiled images that are quick to boot and already set up.
3. In environment variables that are passed to the instances at runtime.
4. A load balancer balances traffic and routes traffic to the appropriate service. It's helpful as we can rely on a load balancer to only send us the traffic we can handle.

Chapter 14: Docker and the Cloud

Questions:

1. Why is Docker often used to deploy Vapor apps?
2. What is the difference between Docker images and Docker containers?
3. How is Kubernetes involved in deployments?

Answers:

1. Because it provides a straightforward way of setting up an operating system for Vapor.
2. Docker images contain compiled images. Docker containers run images that are in use.
3. Kubernetes provides tools and infrastructure to deploy Docker containers and manage them.

Chapter 15: Deploying Microservices in the Cloud

Questions:

1. What are we using CodePipeline for?
2. What is the difference between CodePipeline and CodeBuild?
3. What are the advantages of Fargate here?

Answers:

1. CodePipeline is used to implement **Continuous Deployment (CD)** so that we can automatically update our services online.
2. CodePipeline uses CodeBuild to compile/build images. CodePipeline acts as the manager for CodeBuild and other services.
3. Fargate provides serverless hosting of Docker containers. We do not need to worry about servers when using Fargate.

Chapter 16: Scaling and Monitoring Microservices

Questions:

1. Which types of scaling are there?
2. How is autoscaling done in **Amazon Web Services' (AWS) Elastic Container Service (ECS)**?
3. Why is Google Cloud's App Engine convenient?

Answers:

1. We have:
   - Horizontal scaling: Adding more servers to the mix.
   - Vertical scaling: Adding more resources (RAM and CPU) to a server.
2. AWS ECS uses horizontal scaling.
3. It takes care of hosting, scaling, and monitoring all at once.

Other Books You May Enjoy

If you enjoyed this book, you may be interested in these other books by Packt:

Mastering Swift 5 - Fifth Edition
Jon Hoffman

ISBN: 978-1-78913-986-0

- Understand core Swift components, including operators, collections, control flows, and functions
- Learn how and when to use classes, structures, and enumerations
- Understand how to use protocol-oriented design with extensions to write easier-to-manage code
- Use design patterns with Swift, to solve commonly occurring design problems
- Implement copy-on-write for you custom value types to improve performance
- Add concurrency to your applications using Grand Central Dispatch and Operation Queues
- Implement generics to write flexible and reusable code

iOS 13 Programming for Beginners - Fourth Edition
Ahmad Sahar, Craig Clayton

ISBN: 978-1-83882-190-6

- Get to grips with the fundamentals of Xcode 11 and Swift 5, the building blocks of iOS development
- Understand how to prototype an app using storyboards
- Discover the Model-View-Controller design pattern, and how to implement the desired functionality within the app
- Implement the latest iOS features such as Dark Mode and Sign In with Apple
- Understand how to convert an existing iPad app into a Mac app
- Design, deploy, and test your iOS applications with industry patterns and practices

Leave a review - let other readers know what you think

Please share your thoughts on this book with others by leaving a review on the site that you bought it from. If you purchased the book from Amazon, please leave us an honest review on this book's Amazon page. This is vital so that other potential readers can see and use your unbiased opinion to make purchasing decisions, we can understand what our customers think about our products, and our authors can see your feedback on the title that they have worked with Packt to create. It will only take a few minutes of your time, but is valuable to other potential customers, our authors, and Packt. Thank you!

Index